Exponential Transformation

The ExO Sprint playbook to evolve your organization to navigate industry disruption and change the world for the better

Diversion Books
A Division of Diversion Publishing Corp
443 Park Avenue South, Suite 1004
New York, New York 10016
www.DiversionBooks.com

For more information, email info@diversionbooks.com

First Diversion Books edition September 2018
Print ISBN: 9781635765199
eBook ISBN: 9781635765205

I've been involved as a Coach in three ExO Sprints. I can tell you the methodology delivers.

Augusto Fazioli – Partner, Business Integration Partners

Exponential Organizations allowed what seemed like lofty goals to become realities by giving us a framework in which to define what changing an industry really meant.

Travis Penfield – CEO & Founder, 49 Financial /AXA

Exponential Organizations is the best thing I've read in the field of organizational design in 20 years.

Len Nanjad – Principal, Nanjad Advisory Services Inc.

ExO is the best, in fact the only, organization I've come across that's good at surfing between what is here and what's to come.

John Kelly – Director of Deliberative Process Design, Civic Makers

The ExO Sprint changed how we think and how we look at innovation. It's really very different from all the innovation we've done up until now, and we've done a lot. It has definitely yielded new opportunities.

Aviv Hassidov – ExO Sprint Participant, HP Inc.

I have always admired and been awed by people who have floated successful businesses and are well known for creativity and innovation. I thought that it was a gift or special talent—more so, a talent that I lacked. My experience with the ExO Sprint has taught me that innovation is not just about having great ideas but also knowing how to convert those ideas into viable, impactful business opportunities. It has made me aware of the unlimited intellectual resources available in the world that we can tap into to solve almost any problem.

Priya Narayanswamy – ExO Sprint Participant, Dubai Electricity & Water Authority

We wish to acknowledge the incredibly talented ExO community of practitioners for their indefatigable commitment to shaping a bright global future, one exponential step at a time!

– Francisco, Michelle and Salim

Exponential Transformation

The ExO Sprint playbook to evolve your organization to navigate industry disruption and change the world for the better

Written by:
Francisco Palao, Michelle Lapierre, Salim Ismail

Designed by:
Francisco Poyatos

Foreword by:
Peter H. Diamandis

Co-created by:
An awesome community of 200+ transformation practitioners around the world

Authors

Francisco Palao is an award-winning entrepreneur and innovator with deep experience helping corporations transform. After receiving his PhD in artificial intelligence, Francisco launched several disruptive startups that led him to understand the importance of applying the right innovation methodologies together with cutting-edge technologies. He designed the ExO Sprint methodology and has been dedicated to its continual improvement and accessibility.

Michelle Lapierre has made a career of supporting business leadership and senior management in responding to change. As a consultant and business advisor, she has facilitated full-scale transformation in the public and private sectors through leadership, coaching and implementation support. Her work today empowers organizations to decode industry disruption using the ExO Sprint model.

Salim Ismail is a leading technology strategist who launched the global ExO movement with his bestselling book *Exponential Organizations*. After studying ExOs for several years, he distilled their characteristics into the 11 attributes that comprise the ExO Sprint model. Salim provides a captivating framework for understanding how to recognize and adapt in this new age, as well as thrive within it.

Contents

📖

🏛

ExO Sprint 83

ExO Sprint Case Studies 363

Annexes 375

Foreword

Change has never been as intense and fast as is today. Through rapid advances in exponential technologies such as artificial intelligence, 3D printing, synthetic biology and nanotechnology, we are dematerializing, demonetizing and democratizing energy, food, healthcare and education to the point where each will soon be accessible to every man, women and child anywhere at near-zero cost. The concept is called abundance, and its ultimate impact on society cannot be underestimated.

The speed at which these changes are now happening is hard to fathom, yet we see the effects all around us as traditional companies falter and fail, replaced by a new and nimble generation of businesses. "Life Comes At You Fast," as the saying goes, and technology is making fast even faster. We need new rules in order to adapt, and that's never been so true for business.

Technology is that force that takes things that were once scarce and makes them abundant. What will you do with the abundance being unlocked by emerging technologies? How will you handle the disruption to all of the usual norms in your industry as scarce resources become abundant?

A new breed of company has emerged that knows exactly how to respond. Exponential Organizations (ExOs)—so named for their ability to grow 10 times (10x) as fast as established organizational structures—are not just built to survive the impact of accelerating technologies, they thrive *because* of them. ExOs succeed by harnessing and managing what traditional companies find chaotic.

I often speak about my 6Ds framework—a lens through which I contextualize all technological change and opportunities.

Exponential Transformation provides a roadmap for grasping these opportunities and guides you in leading your organization on a company-wide transformation essential for both survival and success.

If you are ready to embark on a journey of creating a new ExO or transforming your existing organization into an ExO, I recommend following the blueprint expertly presented in this book. It offers proven strategies and tactics for changing your organization into an ExO through an intensive 10-week process called the ExO Sprint. You'll be in good company. Some of the world's most admired brands have taken this journey: Visa, Stanley Black & Decker, and Proctor & Gamble have all conducted ExO Sprints to create new companies or dramatically transform existing lines of business.

Transforming an existing organization or creating a new ExO requires knowing two things: what ingredients are needed and how to combine those ingredients successfully. The ExO attributes described in this book are your ingredients and the ExO Sprint is your recipe. What you do with them is up to you!

Exponential Transformation was written by amazing doers who have been commited for decades to working with companies to make a positive difference. Their strategies and tactics have been perfected building innovation labs and running world-class acceleration programs.

Francisco and Salim co-founded ExO Works to test and improve the ExO Sprint methodology. As COO of ExO Works, Michelle oversaw the ExO Sprint in practice with early adopters to find out what was working well and what needed to be better.

Waiting to "get it right"—the right timing or the right offering—won't work. Today, threats are often not perceived until it is too late to act. In exponential times, acting early, experimenting, becoming a data-driven organization that is getting feedback from your customers and then iterating rapidly is the new mechanism for success.

In writing this book, Francisco, Michelle and Salim have open-sourced the ExO Sprint methodology to anyone interested in making radical organizational changes that unlock massive potential. It's an extrodinary gesture, governed by the belief that having the best technology is simply not enough if you're not also bringing value to society.

These are the most extraordinary of times, offering the most extraordinary of opportunties. We will create more wealth in the next decade than we have the past century. A total restructuring of the institutions and processes under which we've previously operated is needed. With your commitment to lead your organization through to positive change, the future is even more exciting than the present.

Peter H. Diamandis, MD
Founder, Chairman & CEO, XPRIZE Foundation
Executive Founder, Singularity University
New York Times Bestselling Author of *Abundance* and *Bold*

Collaborators

+200 people from +30 countries on all continents

Aanshi Desai (India)

Akshay Caleb Cherian (India)

Alexandre Janssen (Netherlands)

Alexis G. Herrera (Mexico)

Alfredo Rivela (Spain)

Almira Radjab (Canada)

Alonso Daniel Santiago Tinajero (Mexico)

Amy Dolin Oliver (United States)

Ana Victoria Vera Martinez (Spain)

Andrea Castelli (Italy)

Andreas Konrads (Germany)

Andreina Salamanca Carmona (Venezuela)

Angela Morente Cheng (United States)

Angel Gutiérrez Borjabad (Spain)

Angie Benamati (United States)

Anitha Vadavatha (United States)

Anna Malet (Spain)

Ann Ralston (United States)

Anthony Onesto (United States)

Armando Abraham Halbinger Pérez (Mexico)

Asher Hasan (Pakistan)

Augusto Fazioli (Italy)

Aviv Hassidov (Spain)

Barry Phillip (Trinidad and Tobago)

Bill Johnston (United States)

Borja Nicolau (Spain)

Brad Humphries (United States)

Brad Konkle (United States)

Brinkley Warren (United States)

Bruce Yorga (Canada)

Bruno Barros (Brazil)

Bryan E. Johnson (United States)

Camilo Aristizabal (Colombia)

Carla Bereilh (Spain)

Carlos Lopez Macario (Mexico)

Carlos Renato Belo Azevedo (Brazil)

Carlo van de Weijer (Netherlands)

Carmen Pardo Noguera (Spain)

Cesar Castro (United States)

Charlotte Serres (France)

Che Fehrenbach (Canada)

Chelu Martín (Spain)

Christian Andrés Diaz León (Colombia)

Christian Miranda Estepa (Spain)

Christian von Stengel (Germany)

Christophe Jurczak (France)

Cira Roses Rebollar (Spain)

Dr. Clarence Tan (Australia)

Claudio Platto (Italy)

Corina Almagro (United States)

Courtney Blair (United States)

Cristina Estavillo (Spain)

Dale S. Ironson PhD (United States)

Daleyne Guay (Canada)

Daniel Marcos (Mexico)

Daniel Robledo Quijano (Colombia)

David Orban (Italy)

David Roberts (United States)

David Villeda Paz (Mexico)

Deniz Noyan (United Kingdom)

Derek McLean (United Kingdom)

Diego Gosselin Ruiz Maza (Mexico)

Diego Soroa (Spain)

Edmund Komar (Germany)

Edson Carillo (Brazil)

Eduardo Labarca Fuentes (Chile)

Eduardo V. C. Neves (Brazil)

Edwin Moreno (Mexico)

Emilie Sydney-Smith (United States)

Emili Serra (Spain)

Erick W. Contag (United States)

Eric Parkin (United States)

Eugenio Marin Fernandez (Spain)

Eva María Hidalgo Ruiz (Spain)

Evo Heyning (United States)

Fabrice Testa (Luxembourg)

Farnaz Ghadaki (Canada)

Fernando Cruz (Canada)

Floor Scheffer (Netherlands)

Francisco Jurado Pôvedano (Spain)

Francisco Milagres (Brazil)

Gary Ralston (United States)

German Montoya (United States)

Giang Nguyen (Vietnam)

Gina Mitchell (United States)

Ginés Haro Pastor (Spain)

Ginger Hildebrand (United States)

Gordon Vala-Webb (Canada)

Guayente SanMartin (Spain)

Guilherme Soarez (Brazil)

Harold Schultz Neto (Brazil)

Heather Rutherford (Australia)

Henrik Bo Larsen (Denmark)

Hugo Espejo (Mexico)

Ignacio J. Lizarralde (Argentina)

Irmin Juarico (Mexico)

Ivan Bofarull (Spain)

Ivan M. Ibañez (Mexico)

Ivan Ortenzi (Italy)

Jabeen Quadir (Canada)

Jackelyn Perea Velasquez (Perú)

Jack Sim (Singapore)

Jacques Malan (South Africa)

Jaime Ramirez (United States)

Jakob Damsbo (Denmark)

Jared East (United States)

Jaroslav Dokoupil (United Kingdom)

Jason Yotopoulos (United States)

Javier Megias (Spain)

Javier Rincón (Mexico)

Jay Elshaug (United States)

Jennifer van der Meer (United States)

Jerry Michalski (United States)

Jesús Candón (Spain)

Jhon M. Mantilla (Ecuador)

Jm Ibáñez (Spain)

Jo Ann Gainor (Canada)

João Rocha (Brazil)

Joaquin Serra (Spain)

Joel Dietz (United States)

John Hart (United States)

John N. Kelly (United States)

Jon Kruger (United States)

Jordi Wiegerinck (Brazil)

Jordy Egging (Netherlands)
Jorus Everaerd (Netherlands)
José Antonio de Miguel (Spain)
Jose Luis Cordeiro (Venezuela)
Josué Gomes de Alencar (Brazil)
Juan José Peláez Llaca (Mexico)
Juan Miguel Mora (United States)
Juan Ramón Ortiz Herrera (Mexico)
Kaila Colbin (New Zealand)
Karina Besprosvan (United States)
Kashif Hasnie (United States)
Katrina Kent (United States)
Kazunori Saito (Japan)
Kelsey Driscoll (United States)
Kent Langley (United States)
Kerin Morrison (United States)
Kevin Jasmin (United States)
Kevin John Noble (United States)
Kiriakos "Kirk" Evangeliou (United States)
KristinaMaría Troiano-Gutierrez (United States)
Kunitake Saso (Japan)
Lâle Başarır (Turkey)
Lara Kudryk Traska (United States)
Lars Heidemann (Germany)
Lars Lin Villebaek (Denmark)
Laurent Boinot (Canada)
Lawrence Pensack (United States)
Leila Entezam (United States)
Len Koerts (Spain)
Len Nanjad (Canada)
Lily Safrani (Canada)

Luciana Soledad Ledesma (United Kingdom)
Luis Francisco Palma Alvarez (Mexico)
Luis Gonzalez-Blanch (Spain)
Luis Marriott Chávez (Ecuador)
Luis Matias Rodriguez (South Africa)
Marc Bonavia (Spain)
Marcio Chaer (Brazil)
Marc Morros Camps (Spain)
Marconi Pereira (Brazil)
Marcus Shingles (United States)
Maria Elizabeth Zapata (Spain)
Maria Mujica (Argentina)
Mario López de Ávila Muñoz (Spain)
Marta De las Casas (Spain)
Martin S. Garcia Wilhelm (Mexico)
Mary Bennett (United States)
Matias Guerra (Spain)
Matt Brodman (United States)
Matthias Gotz (Germany)
Michael Leadbetter (United States)
Michal Monit PhD (Poland)
Miguel Almena (United States)
Mike Lingle (United States)
Mila Vukojevic (Canada)
Nabyl Charania (United States)
Nadeem Bukhari (United Kingdom)
Nell Watson (Belgium)
Novel Tjahyadi (United Arab Emirates)
Oliver Heesch (United Kingdom)
Oscar A. Martinez Valero (Mexico)
Oscar Schmitz (Argentina)

Pablo Angel Restrepo (Colombia)
Paco Ramos (Spain)
Patrick Bertrand (Canada)
Patrik Sandin (China)
Paul Epping (Netherlands)
Paul J. Prusa (United States)
Paul Niel (Hong Kong)
Pedro Gabay Villafaña (Mexico)
Pedro López Sela (Mexico)
Pedro Pinho (United States)
Peter Bjorn Eriksen (Denmark)
Peter Kristof PhD (Hungary)
Peter Maarten Westerhout (Netherlands)
Rachel Bradford (United States)
Ralf Bamert (Switzerland)
Ramon Vega Ainsa (Spain)
Raquel Martinez Jimenez (Spain)
Raúl Raya (Spain)
Renato Xavier de Lima (Brazil)
René de Paula Jr. (Brazil)
Riaan Singh (South Africa)
Ricardo Barros Villaça (Brazil)
Richard de Jeu (Netherlands)
Rob Blaauboer (Netherlands)
Robert Coop PhD (United States)
Roberto Nogueira (Brazil)
Rob Gonda (United States)
Rodrigo G. Castro (Costa Rica)
Roger Romance Hernandez (Spain)
Rolf Ask Clausen (Denmark)
Ross Thornley (United Kingdom)

Samantha McMahon (Canada)
Santiago Campos Cervera (Paraguay)
Sasha Grujicic (Canada)
Satomi Yoshida (Japan)
Shawn Cruz (United States)
Simone Bhan Ahuja (United States)
Soledad Llorente Cancho (Spain)
Soul Patel (United Kingdom)
Soushiant Zanganehpour (Canada)
Stanley S. Byers (United States)
Stephen Lang (United States)
Steve Shirmang (United States)
Sunil Malhotra (India)
Susan Moller (United States)
Tai Cheng (United States)
Teodor V. Panayotov (Bulgaria)
Thomas Fiumara (Italy)
Todd Porter (Japan)
Tom Anderson (United States)
Tommaso Canonici (Italy)
Tony Manley (United Kingdom)
Tony Saldanha (United States)
Trae Ashlie-Garen (Canada)
Tristan Kromer (United States)
Tunc Noyan (United Kingdom)
Vanessa Belmonte (United States)
Vincent Daranyi (United Kingdom)
Vivian Lan (Mexico)
Wayne Jin (United States)
Wolfgang Merkt (United Kingdom)
Xavier Bruch (Spain)
Xavier Olivella (Spain, EMEA)
Yan-Erik Decorde (France)

17

Introduction

Introduction

Welcome to the most transformative period in human history! We live today in a world of exponential technologies and accelerating breakthroughs, all of which present boundless opportunity. Accessing that opportunity, however, requires organizational evolution. No enterprise will be able to stay alive —much less thrive—without adapting to the exponential rate of change that accelerating technologies deliver.

This book serves as a roadmap in leading your organization through that transformation process.

In keeping with Moore's Law—which predicted that the processing power of computers would double every two years on average—the performance of anything powered by information technologies is also doubling every two years. Anything digitized realizes the same increasingly rapid, or exponential, growth rate seen in computing.

As exponential technologies converge and build upon one another—giving rise to the Fourth Industrial Revolution—they are bringing abundance to every industry and, simultaneously, disrupting them all in one way or another. While traditional business models work just fine in a scarcity-based environment, they are not designed to operate in the fast-approaching world of abundance.

Thousands of hours of real-life implementation of Exponential Organization (ExO) principles have gone into bringing you this new work. The first book to address ExO principles—Salim Ismail's *Exponential Organizations*—explained why the time was ripe for such organizations and described in detail what makes

them tick. Since then, we have established a process for how enterprises of all kinds can use ExO principles to succeed in this new world.

The ExO Sprint is a tested and proven 10-week process that allows any organization to implement the ExO model to address industry disruption and overcome internal resistance to change.

This book will outline the step-by-step process required to run an ExO Sprint and, ultimately, to become an Exponential Organization—to achieve company-wide transformation in terms of mindset, behavior and culture.

Whether you are an entrepreneur or an intrapreneur, a leader of a large enterprise or a small one, or simply a champion for change, this playbook will help you run an ExO Sprint that is adapted to your goals. You will gain a new understanding of the world around you and be equipped with the processes, tools and techniques required for your organization to keep pace.

You will also discover that you (as well as those you enlist to accompany you on this journey) will achieve personal and professional transformation. Organizational transformation, in fact, is primarily a matter of personal transformation. Herein lies the secret.

The transformation achieved in running an ExO Sprint will enable you to create an exponential impact that will accelerate your business and change the world for the better.

Welcome to your very own Exponential Transformation. Let's get started!

The Fourth Industrial Revolution

Our technology, our machines, are part of our humanity. We created them to extend ourselves, and that is what is unique about human beings.

– Ray Kurzweil

We are in the early days of the Fourth Industrial Revolution, which is bringing much more than just digital transformation. The Fourth Industrial Revolution represents a convergence of technological capability, intelligence and connectivity. It is a merging of new technologies that blur the lines between what's physical, digital and biological.

The result: a wholesale overhaul of industries the world over.

Previous industrial revolutions massively impacted society, with innovations influencing almost every aspect of daily life in some way or another. However, as Klaus Schwab, founder and executive chairman of the World Economic Forum, describes in his book *The Fourth Industrial Revolution*, this one is unprecedented in its scale, scope and complexity.

The exponential rate of development of emerging technologies has created a pace and scale of change that is unlike anything humanity has seen before. This is, in part, because so many technological advancements are happening simultaneously, while also building upon one another. Across every industry, accelerating technologies are intersecting and dramatically changing the way we live, work and interact.

These shifts naturally impact how we create and manage companies. It is not just a matter of doing what we already do better, faster or cheaper. Instead, it is the technology itself that is giving us the ability to build fundamentally different businesses.

INDUSTRY 1.0

Water and steam power enable mechanization

INDUSTRY 2.0

Electricity enables mass production

INDUSTRY 3.0

Computers and the internet enable automation

ROBOTICS

BIOTECH

BLOCKCHAIN

VIRTUAL REALITY | AUGMENTED REALITY

SOLAR ENERGY

3D PRINTING

ARTIFICIAL INTELLIGENCE

INDUSTRY 4.0
NOW

Shift to Abundance

Abundance is not something we acquire. It is something we tune into.

– Wayne Dyer

Traditional business models are based on scarcity, where value comes from selling a product or service that is limited in supply. Exponential technologies, however, generate an abundance of everything.

Peter Diamandis, the cofounder and executive chairman of Singularity University, refers to what he calls the 6Ds to describe a chain reaction of technological progress that leads to both upheaval and opportunity.

Once something is digitized, more people have access to it. Everyone has access to powerful technologies, giving individuals and entities the opportunity to create the next big breakthrough.

Entire industries are being impacted as problem spaces shift to new models based on an economy of abundance. When products or services become available through digital means and shed their physical restrictions, they can be produced and distributed at scale to become abundant at zero marginal cost.

Kodak's bankruptcy is an oft-cited example of disruption resulting from digitization as photos moved from the physical format to digital. But consider the specific implication this shift had on the actual business model. The industry moved from a scarcity-based model—just 12, 24 or 36 exposures per roll of film with associated costs for both the film and development—to an abundance-based model in which everyone has access to an unlimited number of pictures at virtually no cost. The problem space changed from an issue of how many pictures to take, to how to share photos, with cost no longer a part of the equation. This shift from scarcity to abundance enabled Instagram, which was acquired by Facebook for $1 billion just as Kodak was shuttering its doors, to achieve success with just 13 employees.

In addition to photography, consider just how thoroughly the old business models for music, movies, accommodation and transportation have been disrupted. Look at the shifts underway in healthcare, insurance, manufacturing, banking and energy. In the end, no industry is likely to escape disruption. What's also important to realize is that most of the disruption will come from outside the industries themselves, meaning that those unprepared for the inevitability and pace of change will be taken by surprise.

The biggest challenge faced by all industries is finding new types of business models that work in this new environment. Businesses must adapt when—and in anticipation of when—assets, users or opportunities shift from a scarcity-based model (limited by how many you have) to an abundance-based model (how to manage a limitless supply).

Most ExOs are already building business models based on abundance. For example, Waze taps into an abundance of GPS on our phones, Airbnb taps into an abundance of available rooms and 99designs taps into an abundance of designers.

While new businesses debut business models designed to eat everyone else's lunch, traditional business models continue to focus on selling a scarce product or service. In fact, most management thinking and organizational dynamics are still set up for a linear, predictable age.

It takes experimentation to find a brand new business model that leverages abundance and employs service-based thinking. Accessing abundance creates a need for new tools and new practices to manage that abundance. And these new tools and practices are exactly what Exponential Organizations have mastered.

Digitized

Anything that becomes digitized—representable by ones and zeros—can be accessed, shared and distributed by computer. It takes on the same exponential growth seen in computing.

Deceptive

Exponential trends aren't easily spotted in the early days. Growth is deceptively slow until it begins to be measured in whole numbers.

Disruptive

Digital technologies outperform previous non-digital models in both effectiveness and cost, disrupting existing markets for a product or service.

Demonetized

As technology becomes cheaper, sometimes to the point of being free, money is increasingly removed from the equation.

Dematerialized

The need for bulky or expensive single-use physical products—radio, camera, GPS, video, phones, maps—disappears as these items are incorporated into smartphones.

Democratized

Once something is digitized, more people can have access to it. Everyone has access to powerful technologies, giving individuals and entities the opportunity to create the next big breakthrough.

What is an Exponential Organization?

Any company designed for success in the 20th century is doomed to failure in the 21st.

– David Rose

A new breed of business proven to be capable of unlocking the abundance provided by emerging technologies and readily adaptable to a rapidly changing business environment has emerged. These companies have been coined Exponential Organizations for their ability to grow 10 times (10x) as fast as traditional organizations.

Salim Ismail's best-selling *Exponential Organizations* launched the global ExO movement. In it, he offers the following definition:

An Exponential Organization (ExO) is one whose impact (or output) is disproportionately large—at least 10x larger—compared to its peers because of the use of new organization techniques that leverage accelerating technologies.

After studying ExOs for several years, Ismail distilled their characteristics into 11 components, which today comprise the ExO model. This model provides a structure for understanding how to recognize and adapt to the ExO age and ultimately become a leader in it.

What does an Exponential Organization look like? Classic examples include Amazon, Google, Airbnb, Uber, Facebook and Skype. ExOs are transforming industries across the board, from manufacturing to retail to services—even philanthropy.

The ExO model allows organizations to adapt to the changes brought about by the Fourth Industrial Revolution, since ExOs are built to capitalize on accelerating technologies. Exponential technologies enable abundance, and ExOs are built to take advantage of that abundance.

The ExO model builds upon an iconic line of innovation tools and frameworks.

- *Blue Ocean Strategy: How to Create Uncontested Market Space and Make Competition Irrelevant*, by Renée Mauborgne and W. Chan Kim, focuses on product innovation and creating uncontested markets.

- Steve Blank's *The Startup Owner's Manual: The Step-by-Step Guide for Building a Great Company* introduces the Customer Development process and advocates "getting out of the building" to accelerate learning.

- With *The Lean Startup: How Today's Entrepreneurs Use Continuous Innovation to Create Radically Successful Businesses*, Eric Ries launched an influential movement for continuous innovation through rapid experimentation.

- Alexander Osterwalder's *Business Model Generation: A Handbook for Visionaries, Game Changers, and Challengers* provides a shared language and process for defining and shaping business models.

The ExO model wasn't created as a new concept to try out. It was created to provide a framework for what is already being done—and working supremely well—in the world today. It's the right approach for the Fourth Industrial Revolution, as it builds on the best of previous methodologies and adds elements to address exponential technologies and their 6D implications. The ExO framework is the basis of this book and the methodology it presents.

We are experiencing an exponential rate of change in every facet of our organizations today, far beyond any digital transformation of years past. Our answer to the rush of change is to harness the power of change itself. To do so, you must transform your linear organization into an Exponential Organization.

Where do you start? This is the purpose of *Exponential Transformation*: to provide a series of assignments, direction, support and guidance for organizational transformation that will deliver exponential results.

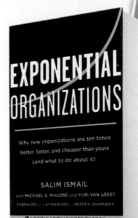

Industry
Transformation

Business Model
Innovation

Product
Innovation

Challenges of Transformation

They say I'm old-fashioned, and live in the past,
but sometimes I think progress progresses too fast!

– Dr. Seuss

28

The information in this book opens a path to the massive leverage that technology offers. But the path isn't always an easy one to follow. Pushing boundaries further and faster than ever before can be uncomfortable. Rest assured, however: groundbreaking innovation is most likely to emerge from the most uncomfortable of spaces.

One of the greatest challenges you will face on your ExO journey is the **organizational immune system**, which will almost certainly rally its defenses to try to halt your progress and squelch any attempt at transformation. Every organization has an immune system response, and its primary objective is to preserve the status quo. (You might even be surprised to discover that you yourself are part of the immune system!)

In addition to battling the corporate immune response, organizations face additional challenges when they attempt transformation.

- How to find the right business model that connects to an economy of abundance rather than scarcity

- How to shift the mindset within the organization from efficiency-based thinking to a focus on innovation

- How to build and retain innovation capacity within the organization

- How to access knowledge from outside the organization

- How to overcome lack of speed and engagement within the organization

The ExO Sprint cracks the code on how to overcome these challenges and suppress a company's immune system long enough for the enterprise to break through and become an Exponential Organization.

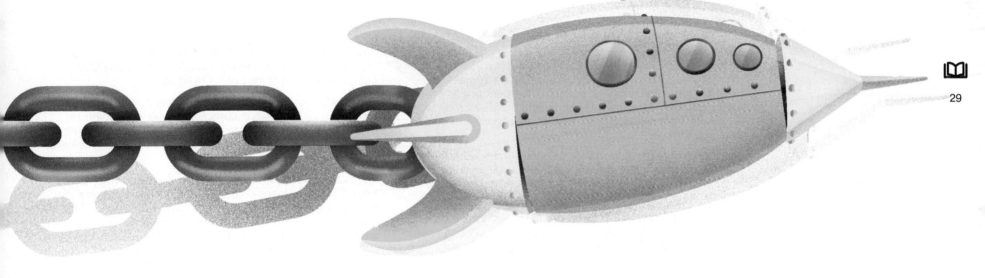

The ExO Sprint

This book teaches you how to run an ExO Sprint. It explains how the ExO Sprint makes use of specific tools such as the Business Model Canvas and our own ExO Canvas. It also details how the transformation your organization will experience as a result of the ExO Sprint begins with people and progresses to the application of advanced processes and technology throughout the organization.

Acceleration will happen in your organization because the people who engage in the ExO Sprint will also transform. It is their change that will seed the organizational transformation you're after.

Depending on the size of your company, transformation may happen all at once, division by division, or even, as in the case of Tesla's origins, from a small tent in the corner of a large warehouse.

In the next sections, you will learn how the ExO Sprint is structured and executed, as well as what preparations are necessary in advance of launching the ExO Sprint. You will also learn how to select the best people to run your Sprint so that it has the highest probability of success.

The ExO Sprint has been successfully run in large, medium and small organizations around the world. We have used these tools in powerful organizations across multiple industries including

Procter & Gamble (P&G), Stanley Black & Decker, HP Inc. and Visa. Some of their stories are included in the Case Studies section at the end of the book. Pg 363

The ExO Sprints we have run have proven that the model works. More than 200 innovation consultants have participated in delivering ExO Sprints. Their feedback and refinements along the way have led to the version of the ExO Sprint methodology presented here.

The ExO Sprint includes two streams of activity. The first, the Edge Stream, focuses on developing initiatives **outside** the existing organization and business lines. The second, the Core Stream, emphasizes developing initiatives to be implemented **within** the current organization. We will discuss later why this distinction is important, as well as the value of each. Choosing which stream to use—or whether to use both—depends on your goals and the needs of your company.

The ExO Sprint provides a learn-by-doing approach to finding a business model that connects with abundance, overcomes the challenges organizations typically encounter when attempting transformation and builds innovation capability into your teams. ExO Sprints result in actionable ExO projects that, once completed, transform an existing business into an Exponential Organization—or even a set of them.

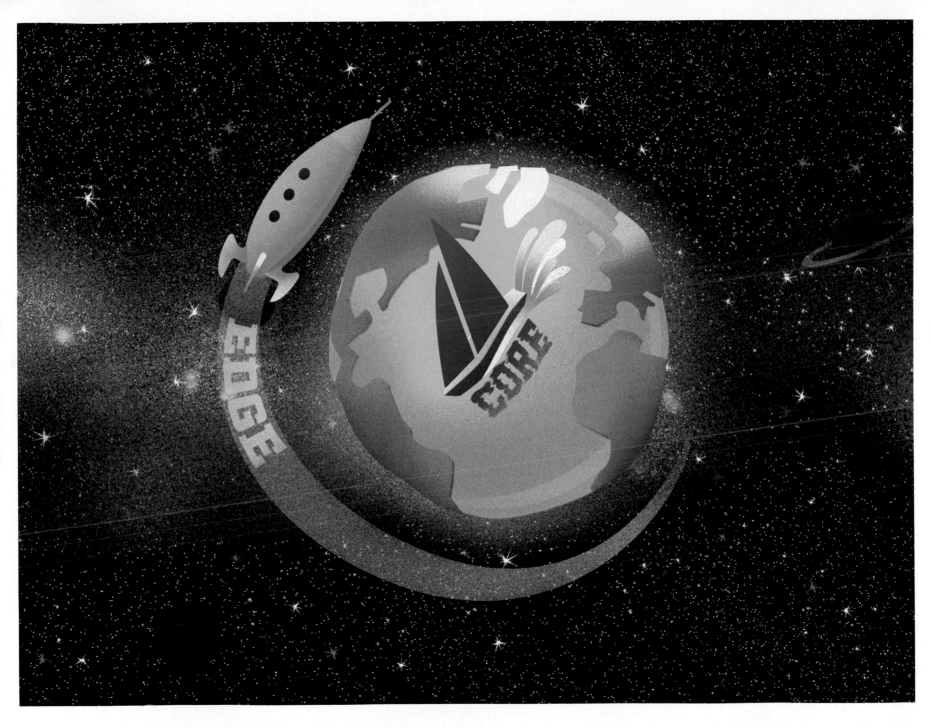

Who Should Read This Book?

Never doubt that a small group of thoughtful, committed citizens can change the world; indeed, it's the only thing that ever has.

– Margaret Meade

Regardless of whether your current organization is an industry leader or a smaller player, it must transform if it is to thrive in the face of industry disruption from unexpected external sources. (New players should build agility in from the start.) This book, and the process it guides you through, is designed to be applicable to organizations of all shapes and sizes.

Whether you are an entrepreneur or an intrapreneur, a leader of a large enterprise or a small one, or simply a champion for change, the underlying ExO principles are the same.

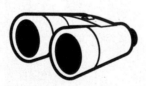

Are you an entrepreneur or part of a startup team looking to disrupt an industry by creating a new Exponential Organization from the ground up? If so, you are in the fortunate position of being able to start with a blank slate. As such, you'll follow the Edge Stream.

Are you an innovation-oriented leader looking to keep your company safe by adapting it to external industry disruption? If so, you will apply the Core Stream to focus within your existing business.

Are you a disruption-oriented leader looking not only to transform your own business but also the industry within which it operates? Or perhaps even create a new one? Apply both the Edge and Core streams to meet these goals.

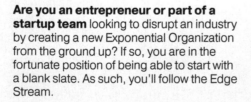

To ensure you are on the right path, ask yourself the following
questions before embarking on an ExO Sprint:

*Does our organization suffer from an immune system response
when attempting anything disruptive?*

Do we want to lead—or at least stay ahead of—industry disruption?

Do we want to grow our business by 10x?

*Do we want to accelerate the metabolism of our organization to
respond more nimbly to changes in the external world?*

Are we ready to experiment with new approaches?

*Are we ready to learn from inexpensive failures and use those insights
to evolve faster and further?*

Do we want to achieve positive change in the world?

If you have answered "Yes" to any of these questions,
congratulations! You are already on your way. This book will guide
you on the remainder of your journey by outlining the components of
a model for change and showing you step by step how to apply them.

How to Use This Book

Great dreams aren't just visions. They're visions coupled to strategies for making them real.

– Astro Teller

If the topics touched on in the previous sections are new to you, take the time to research them further. A solid understanding of why and how every industry is being disrupted will set the imperative for your business transformation. To get you started, we've provided a list of resources that lay much of this groundwork (see the Recommended Reading section at the end of the book).
➡ Pg 388

Perhaps you're well acquainted with the imperative for transforming or building your business to leverage the benefits of accelerating technologies but are new to how to approach the challenge. In this case, clearly understanding the building blocks for creating your new Exponential Organization is the next step. Look to the 11 ExO attributes described in the next section of the book, along with the ExO Canvas you will use to implement them.

If you're ready to get to work—you're already clear on the need to transform your business and you understand the components of the ExO model—go straight to the ExO Sprint sections of the book to get underway.

Once you've completed your first ExO Sprint, you will have amassed an invaluable base of knowledge within your organization. Experienced ExO Sprint team members will be able to carry exponential thinking and techniques forward into their daily work and can use this book to run additional ExO Sprint projects on their own.

Use *Exponential Transformation* as a coach, companion and guide as you conduct your ExO Sprints. Each section, including the Core and Edge stream assignments, is written to stand alone and be referenced as needed.

Are you ready for an unusual, exciting and rewarding journey? Ready, set, transform!

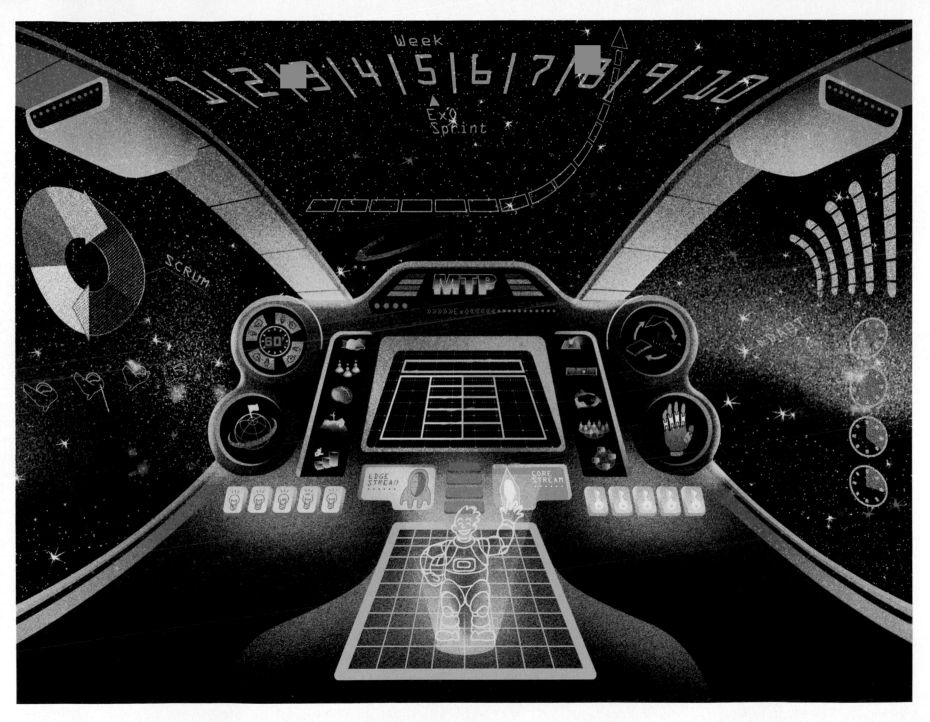

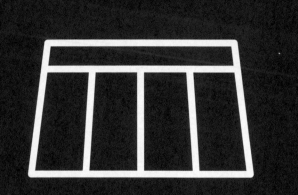

ExO
Model

ExO Model

Understanding the ExO model is the first step in becoming an Exponential Organization. Prepare to join the ranks of those organizations having greater than 10x the impact of their peers by applying practices that leverage accelerating technologies. This chapter describes each component of the ExO model in preparation for running your ExO Sprint.

The ExO model is comprised of 11 components, or attributes. ExO attributes are the building blocks that allow you to create an Exponential Organization with global reach and impact. They leverage existing and emerging technologies that enable an organization to access and manage abundance in the form of available resources, potential clients or useful information. In short, they are the practices that set industry leaders apart.

An overarching Massive Transformative Purpose (MTP) defines the goal that the organization strives to achieve.

Five externally focused ExO attributes allow organizations to **access** global abundance.

- STAFF ON DEMAND
- COMMUNITY & CROWD
- ALGORITHMS
- LEVERAGED ASSETS
- ENGAGEMENT

STAFF ON DEMAND   COMMUNITY & CROWD   ALGORITHMS   LEVERAGED ASSETS   ENGAGEMENT

Five internally focused ExO attributes enable organizations to **manage** abundance and drive culture, enabling them to grow exponentially.

- **INTERFACES**
- **DASHBOARDS**
- **EXPERIMENTATION**
- **AUTONOMY**
- **SOCIAL TECHNOLOGIES**

Each ExO attribute offers the opportunity to shift from a traditional mindset of managing scarce resources to one of abundance—and all the opportunity that abundance presents.

The ExO Canvas presented at the end of this section is an easy tool to help you design Exponential Organizations. ➡ Pg 76

As you read through the attributes, research any unfamiliar terms. Internet searches on a particular term or topic will open your awareness of the many ways it is currently used.

Take time to research how ExO attributes are being applied in the world today. Exploring actual examples will help the concepts come alive and inspire your thinking.

INTERFACES

DASHBOARDS

EXPERIMENTATION

AUTONOMY

SOCIAL TECHNOLOGIES

Massive Transformative Purpose

Next-generation organizations are not simply focused on delivering products or services for profit, but also have an underlying purpose to positively impact the world. In fact, the greatest business opportunities today can be found in seeking ways to solve the greatest global grand challenges.

The Massive Transformative Purpose (MTP) reflects an organization's aspiration—the core purpose of its existence. It describes the change in the world that you want to achieve, while recognizing that it will not be accomplished in the short term. An MTP is something that inspires action, expresses your passions and creates an emotional connection that drives you and others toward meaningful, positive change.

The MTP is a means of "going higher"—beyond traditional vision statements, which are specific to an organization, or mission statements, which describe how an organization expects to achieve its goals. Instead, your MTP articulates a purpose that you are striving to achieve.

The MTP is meant to be a North Star for the organization, providing direction when key choices are required. With increasingly autonomous and distributed workforces, it provides a frame of reference for keeping activities focused. Since an MTP does not address how the purpose will be achieved, it allows the organization to modify its approach—and even pivot—over time.

Significantly, the MTP is also the foundation upon which many of the ExO attributes are built. Any organization that wants to become an ExO must begin by defining its MTP. Once established, an MTP aligns your organization, creates a sense of shared direction and attracts the people you need to achieve your purpose.

Exponential technologies enable abundance, and ExOs are built to connect with abundance. The focus in every industry today is shifting from scarcity to abundance, a shift that sets the stage for ExOs to thrive. Framing your MTP offers an opportunity to think about how your organization relates to a particular area of abundance—whether it's an abundance of resources or the opportunity to have abundant impact.

For example, Google's MTP—"Organize the world's information"—relates to managing a growing abundance of information. "Health For Everyone" (the company name as well as its MTP) relates to abundance in the sense that it's a bold statement about solving a problem in an abundant way.

MTP

"If the dreams of your company don't scare you, they are too small."

– Richard Branson. founder, Virgin Group

AN MTP IS...

Purposeful

What do you want to achieve?

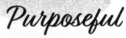

Descriptive of the World

What would the world look like once the MTP has been achieved?

Succinct

Is it short, simple and clear, and doesn't need explanation?

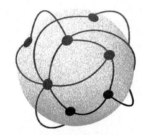

Massive

Is it global in scope, or does it have the potential to be?

Inspiring

If you shared your MTP with a stranger, would it inspire him or her to get involved?

Highly Aspirational

Is the MTP grand and bold? Does it lie just beyond what seems possible to achieve?

Positive

How does everyone win?

Connected to Abundance

How is a new abundance created or an existing abundance drawn upon?

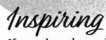

Transformative

How would the world be changed for the better if the MTP were achieved?

Passionate

Does the MTP convey your passion?

MTP Checklist

Is it simple, clear and easy to understand? ☐

Is it strong, bold and challenging? ☐

Does it reflect an important and meaningful purpose? ☐

Will it change the world for the better? ☐

Is it unique? ☐

Does it define why our organization exists? ☐

Does it reflect the passions of our company's leadership? ☐

Is it well communicated and understood throughout our organization? ☐

Does it draw a community and give it something to rally around? ☐

Does it seem almost impossible to fully achieve, yet imperative enough that we want to try? ☐

A Quick Check

Test a proposed MTP against the letters themselves.

Is it Massive? ☐

Is it Transformative? ☐

Is it a true Purpose? ☐

MTP EXAMPLES

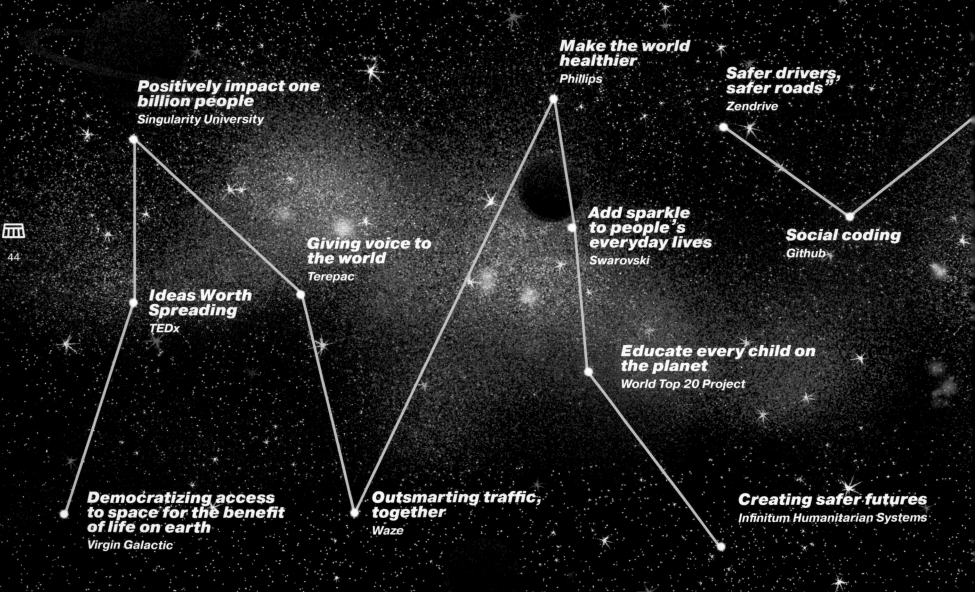

Positively impact one billion people
Singularity University

Make the world healthier
Phillips

Safer drivers, safer roads"
Zendrive

Giving voice to the world
Terepac

Add sparkle to people's everyday lives
Swarovski

Social coding
Github

Ideas Worth Spreading
TEDx

Educate every child on the planet
World Top 20 Project

Democratizing access to space for the benefit of life on earth
Virgin Galactic

Outsmarting traffic, together
Waze

Creating safer futures
Infinitum Humanitarian Systems

Changing business for good
Virgin Group

Accelerate the world's transition to sustainable energy
Tesla

Create a better everyday life for people
IKEA

Organize the world's information
Google

Food With Integrity
Chipotle

Help the next generation of women realize their full potential
Dove

Radical breakthroughs for the benefit of humanity
XPRIZE

Music for everyone
Spotify

Inspire and nurture the human spirit
Starbucks

Help individuals and businesses realize their full potential
Microsoft

Bring inspiration and innovation to every athlete in the world
Nike

Make sustainable living commonplace
Unilever

45

AN MTP IS NOT...

These examples of vision statements—not MTPs—describe what the companies want to become rather than the change they want to achieve.

A vision statement about **what the organization is or will become** in the future

A mission statement about **how the organization meets its purpose**

A **marketing slogan** promoting a product or service

Geared to the customer (statements often include "you")

Geared to the company (statements often include "us" or "we")

A statement that **restricts a company's ability to pivot** the business in the future

Be the world's most successful and important information technology company

IBM

These examples of mission statements—again, not MTPs—describe how the companies will achieve their vision/purpose.

Be Earth's most customer-centric company, where customers can find and discover anything they might want to buy online
Amazon

Be the world's most respected service brand
American Express

We strive to offer our customers the lowest possible prices, the best available selection and the utmost convenience
Amazon

We meet everyday needs for nutrition, hygiene and personal care with brands that help people feel good, look good and get more out of life
Unilever

To provide the best customer service possible
Zappos

HOW TO CRAFT AN MTP

Crafting an MTP can be challenging. In the early stages of forming your MTP, try separating the intent—what you want to achieve—from the actual wording. It is easy to get sidetracked by the phrasing when you're still in the phase of pinpointing the actual purpose.

A startup focused on defining an MTP can begin with a blank slate. An existing organization, on the other hand, is constrained by its need to consider how to elevate its current offering and strengths for a broader purpose.

Allow time to test and refine your draft MTP. An MTP often starts as a "crazy idea" before it becomes fuel for pulling people together. Talk about it with early adopters—those who share your passion—to see how well it stands up once it's off the page. Is it meaningful to them? Is it easy to understand without explanation or context? Did it generate interest? Excitement? Motivation?

Keep all versions of your MTP drafts. You may find value in returning to earlier versions or using elements of those versions as the MTP evolves.

Your ultimate objective is to determine if the MTP can draw a new community or be taken up by an existing community. To do so, it must be easy to communicate and reflect a value that resonates with others. Test potential MTPs on small groups and consider their feedback before making anything official.

CRAFTING AN MTP

A
WHY
HOW
WHAT
Approach

Try a WHY/HOW/WHAT approach to defining an MTP by asking the following three questions:

WHY
DOES THE ORGANIZATION EXIST?

Define the problem space

HOW
WILL THE ORGANIZATION ADDRESS THE NEED OR OPPORTUNITY?

Imagine the transformation

WHAT
WILL THE ORGANIZATION DELIVER?

Brainstorm ideas

Framing your thinking according to these three categories helps to separate your MTP from your execution. Your MTP will be found in the answer to the WHY question.

CRAFTING AN MTP

A "5 WHYS" Approach

The "5 Whys" offer a brainstorming technique to uncover your purpose. Invite individuals from across the organization to participate, making sure to cross hierarchies and functions. Key clients or partners can also offer valuable perspective.

Begin by asking

"WHY DOES THE ORGANIZATION EXIST?"

Allow 90 seconds for each individual to write down thoughts on sticky notes (one answer per note) and have everyone read their answers aloud. Listen to everybody's input and then, as a group, choose one of the answers for further development.

For the item chosen for further exploration, you'll then ask,

"WHY ARE WE DOING THIS?"

and repeat the first process.

Do this three more times. Use a different sticky note pad color for each round, and after each round, put all the sticky notes up on the wall, organized by color.

Eventually, the group answer will be something along the lines of, "To save the world." Once that

"TO SAVE THE WORLD"

happens, back up one step to the previous round of answers, where you will likely find some version of what the group perceives as the company's MTP.

Take time to reflect on the results. Group similar ideas and identify common themes in order to ultimately determine what's most important to the organization.

CRAFTING AN MTP

An **Open** **Discussion** Approach

To launch an authentic conversation about the passion underlying your MTP, have each member of a discussion group take a few moments to journal responses to these questions.

WHAT IS THE CHANGE YOU WANT TO SEE IN THE WORLD?

HOW WILL THIS CHANGE POSITIVELY IMPACT SOCIETY?

WHAT GETS YOU OUT OF BED EVERY MORNING?

FOR WHAT GREATER CAUSE WOULD YOU GLADLY VOLUNTEER TIME?

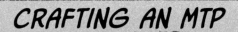

CRAFTING AN MTP

A **Storytelling** Approach

A storytelling approach can be an effective way to arrive at an MTP. What is the narrative behind what inspires your organization? Consider this example from Wellness, a regional training gym in southern Brazil.

> We believe in superpowers.
>
> We are born with superpowers; every kid is. When we are kids, we are ninjas, super-heroes, soccer stars or athletes of all kinds. Time goes by and at some point, things get too serious for superheroes...You need to produce, grow up, become an adult, and suddenly we are stuck. Why do we lose the magic of unlimited capability we had when we were kids?
>
> We at Wellness believe that this magic is not dead, only dormant. Sport allows us to spark the flame of self-confidence and overcome barriers. Physical exercise is a one-way trip to self-knowledge, and when you know yourself, you realize that you are capable of extraordinary feats.
>
> We believe that everyone has unlimited capacity and that through physical exercise, we can make the world a more active and conscious place. How? By awakening the superhero in each of you.

In the end, this organization chose "Awakening the superheroes" as its MTP.

SCALE

SCALE is the acronym for the five ExO attributes that help an organization connect with abundance in the world. Accessing existing untapped abundance is the basis for building an Exponential Organization. The five ExO attributes that look outside of the organization to connect you with abundance are: Staff on Demand, Community & Crowd, Algorithms, Leveraged Assets and Engagement.

Understanding the particular nature of each attribute and which ones best support your business model and objectives for scaling is the first step to becoming an ExO. Most important, SCALE attributes allow the organization to maintain a small resource footprint while using the techniques to grow rapidly and flexibly.

Where is there untapped abundance in the world that can contribute to the achievement of your MTP?

Where does your current business rely on scarce or limited resources? What would your business be if these resources became abundant and free?

The number of people connected through technology is anticipated to grow from three billion to between five and seven billion in the coming years. What opportunities does this create for your business?

SCALE

STAFF ON DEMAND   COMMUNITY & CROWD   ALGORITHMS   LEVERAGED ASSETS   ENGAGEMENT

Staff On Demand

Most of the bright people don't work for you, no matter who you are.

– Bill Joy, computer scientist

DESCRIPTION

If your business is growing exponentially—or if you want it to—you must continually improve your product or service. Your ability to adjust the composition, skill base and responsibilities of your workforce needs to keep pace. By not "owning" employees and the weight of their associated infrastructure, you can achieve agility and flexibility within your organization.

The Staff on Demand attribute relies on a pool of prequalified workers hired on an as-needed basis to conduct operational elements of your core business. Responsibilities range from simple tasks to complex work, and may even include mission-critical processes.

Drawing on resources beyond the confines of your organization and traditional hiring processes opens up the opportunity to access an incredible wealth and diversity of talent. The fresh perspectives generated by a global workforce provide a steady stream of insights, allowing you to learn and quickly improve your product or service. Use this attribute to access the brightest minds in your industry and to tap into unused capacity and potential.

An ExO applying the Staff on Demand attribute at its most extreme would see a relatively small core team conducting business almost entirely with external resources. Note that the scalability—sourcing resources at low-to-zero marginal cost—the Staff on Demand attribute permits is essential to the growth of an ExO.

S

54

Tips and considerations

■ Don't confuse the Staff on Demand attribute, which leverages external people, with the Leveraged Assets attribute, which as you'll see later, leverages external physical assets.

■ The Staff on Demand attribute is closely related to the Community attribute. (Staff on demand is a subset of your broader community.) Think about what distinguishes your relationship with each.

■ Accessing abundance in any form requires an interface to manage it (see the Interfaces attribute, covered in the next section). Use your staff on demand interface to engage your staff, provide them with the resources and tools they need, and provide feedback.

■ Dashboards, another ExO attribute covered in the next section, are fundamental to managing an external workforce at scale. Use dashboards to track results and provide visibility for your key metrics, along with setting clear performance indicators.

■ Identify what qualification, training and feedback will contribute to the quality of your external staff, and build this into the relationship using the Engagement attribute.

■ Measure contribution and reward high performers. Gathering automated peer and user reviews is a cost effective, real-time way to measure quality from each worker and to enable the best performers to be publicly recognized.

■ Every business can benefit from staff on demand in some form. Distinguish if you are building your business on the basis of the Staff on Demand attribute (as Uber has done, for example) or if you are simply using staff on demand services to achieve efficiencies in your existing business (i.e., to access temporary help with tasks when needed).

HOW TO IMPLEMENT

1 CREATE CLEAR TASK SPECIFICATIONS

Knowing and being able to clearly communicate what you are asking of your staff on demand is essential. Clear specifications allow a shared understanding of what the task is, when it has been completed, and when and how it will be compensated.

2 USE EXTERNAL PLATFORMS

Use one of the many existing staff on demand services available today to get started quickly. Start by leveraging external and temporary workforces to fill gaps in expertise and availability.

3 USE THE MTP TO RECRUIT THE BEST PEOPLE

Where a pre-existing platform doesn't exist, use manual processes to reach out to existing workforces. Your objective is to communicate your MTP and assemble an initial group of individuals whose passion is aligned with your purpose. Depending on the nature of the work, you may need to build qualification or certification processes for your incoming staff on demand.

4 CREATE AN INTERFACE TO AUTOMATE STAFF ON DEMAND ENGAGEMENT

Effectively managing your workforce—and the key to being able to scale it—requires the use of an interface to automate your interactions. Your interface should allow you to both collect and disseminate all the information related to the working relationship. Test the usability of your interface with your early members to improve it.

SAMPLE USE

Gigwalk

Gigwalk was founded in 2010 with the goal of "reinventing work in a mobile world." Gigwalk provides staff on demand (Gigwalkers) to help consumer brands and retailers seeking on-the-ground visibility into the conditions of their products or events post their needs as tasks, or "Gigs." Generally, users of this service wish to verify that their products are available on the shelf and displayed/priced correctly, or that marketing events are conducted accurately and on time.

A network of 1.2 million Gigwalkers use a mobile app to choose tasks to execute for payment, which is made via PayPal upon completion. All work is done through the app, including documenting results with geo-tagged photos. Each Gigwalker earns a performance score based on factors such as successful completion of Gigs and activity level. A higher score opens access to more complex and higher-paying Gigs.

When customers see that a Gigwalker is consistently doing good work for them, they can add that Gigwalker to a private workforce and direct Gigs specifically to this group.

EXPLORE!

Consider these companies from a Staff on Demand perspective. What are they doing to attract and retain a workforce? How have they built a business based on the Staff on Demand attribute?

Uber
TaskRabbit
Kaggle
Roamler

Upwork
(formerly Elance)
Fiverr
Topcoder
Eden McCallum

CHECKLIST FOR SUCCESS

Does an abundant supply of quality external talent exist to meet our needs?

Are we using available platforms to get started quickly?

Can we access our staff on demand quickly?

Are we clearly specifying tasks and expectations?

Have we established clear thresholds for successful completion of tasks?

Are we collecting objective feedback on an individual's work from peers and users?

Are we offering incentives to reward desirable behavior?

Are we maintaining engagement with our top performers?

S

Community & Crowd

If you build communities and you do things in public, you don't have to find the right people–they find you.

– Chris Anderson, founder, DIY Drones

DESCRIPTION

The world is a big place. What highly successful ExOs have in common is their ability to reach into the global public, draw together large groups of individuals who share their purpose and leverage them as resources. A compelling MTP and an enabling platform are the hallmarks of ExOs that do this well.

Community, in the ExO context, is made up of a large global group of individuals who are passionate about your MTP and are directly involved in the main functions of your organization. They are loyal to a shared goal and devoted to solving the grand challenges surrounding your organization's purpose.

In some cases, community is the foundation of the business. Companies like TEDx or Airbnb are entirely defined by the communities they have assembled. In other cases, community is adjacent to the core business and provides a valuable benefit complementary to the primary offering (such as the Apple

Support Communities). In the most advanced ExOs, community drives everything but the purpose.

Crowd is made up of an even larger global group of individuals—including infrequent users—who have some passive interest in your MTP but are not (yet) directly connected to your organization. Crowd can be used to provide ideation, validation and support for your ideas. Your goal is to make it easy and compelling for promising crowd members to move into community.

Leveraging shared passion for your MTP and providing a platform for peer-to-peer engagement opens your business to a world of opportunity. Crowdsourcing ideas and feedback, crowdfunding to finance new concepts, creating "prosumers" who build your product or service with you, and having ready markets for new offerings are examples of what can be achieved with the Community & Crowd attribute.

Tips and considerations

▌ Where are there existing communities and/or crowds that you can leverage?

▌ If you are an established business, your existing base of customers and followers is a valuable starting point from which to grow your community.

▌ An ExO does not create a crowd, but rather catalyzes crowd as a resource. (Leaders, trends or movements generally create communities and crowds that you can leverage.) An ExO provides a platform that enables members to better connect and grow together.

▌ Community members are drawn together by a sense of belonging, a common purpose and shared values. A strong MTP underlies the Community & Crowd attribute and is essential to draw community and galvanize participation.

▌ Community can play a powerful role in helping individuals to discover, refine and actualize their own personal MTPs, which creates deep, long-term engagement.

▌ Take a structured, incentivized approach to recruiting top contributors and drawing them closer. You must offer your community members value to maintain their engagement.

▌ Earning and retaining your community's trust is essential. Remember that your community is comprised of individuals who value the leadership, authenticity and transparency you demonstrate as their motivation to connect.

▌ Building and maintaining your community requires care. Pay close attention to your community's needs and demonstrate

responsiveness. Note that for every dollar spent establishing a community, it will take roughly $5 to maintain it.

▌ Use Community & Crowd to amplify your ability to rapidly generate, test and iterate ideas. Each group's responses will tell you what works well, what can be improved and what isn't working at all.

▌ The Community & Crowd attribute goes hand in hand with the Engagement and Interfaces attributes. How will you implement all three of these attributes together?

Multiple categories of individuals are contained within Community. Each layer has a different level of commitment to your MTP, is engaged to a different degree and requires a different type of attention.

Core Team/ Personal Network (where it begins)

Early Adopters (where it extends first)

Devoted Users/ Customers/Alumni

Staff on Demand

Vendors/Partners/Fans

Everyone Else

Community ▉

Crowd ▉

C

HOW TO IMPLEMENT

1 USE THE MTP TO ATTRACT AND ENGAGE EARLY MEMBERS

In the early stages, this process involves personal attention and manual processes as you reach out to existing groups and contacts individually to communicate the MTP and draw an initial group together. Find existing communities to leverage.

2 DEVELOP RELATIONSHIPS

Work with trial groups to develop your understanding of needs and preferences. Identify and build relationships with the strongest members (they will often find you) to gain valuable insights into further developing your community.

3 NURTURE THE COMMUNITY

Early stages of building community are like starting a fire with one match: you need to tend it carefully and fuel it with the right size, quantity and timing of inputs to coax a flame. Leadership must be authentic, transparent and come from your organization's executive level.

4 CREATE A PLATFORM FOR EARLY ADOPTERS

A great platform will be essential for future scaling. Make it easy and attractive for members to interact with you and each other. A key value to your community members is the ability to interact and collaborate with their peers. Test the usability of your first platform release with early members to improve it.

5 EXPAND THE REACH OF YOUR PLATFORM TO DRAW NEW MEMBERS TO THE ESTABLISHED COMMUNITY

Take your automated and tested platform public, beyond your initial test group, to reach a broader audience. Drawn by your MTP and the accessibility of your platform, people who share your purpose can now come to you at scale.

Creating, building and managing your community is different at each stage.

Crafting your MTP (the "spark") and attracting receptive community members early on are the first steps.

Developing your community requires careful tending and responsiveness to its needs and input.

Managing a well-established community requires leadership and attention.

CHECKLIST FOR SUCCESS

Are we using our MTP to attract and drive global community and crowd engagement?
Are the individual MTPs or purpose statements of community members in alignment with ours?
Is our community engaged and participating in creating value?
Are we using gamification to increase engagement within the community?
Have we established thresholds and clear expectations for our participating community and crowd members?
Have we attracted first movers in the field, including those with expertise that is scarce?
Are we receiving product/service feedback and market insight from our community and crowd?
Do we offer performance and engagement incentive prizes to move members from crowd into community?

SAMPLE USE

Wikipedia is a free online encyclopedia, written collaboratively by the people who use it. It is read more than 15 billion times each month, is ranked the fifth-most popular website and collectively holds more than 47 million articles in 298 language editions. Anyone is allowed to create or edit articles anytime, and thousands of changes and improvements are made hourly.

"Wikipedians" are the volunteers who write and edit Wikipedia's articles. They are encouraged to be bold and mandated to "find something that can be improved and make it better." Over 37 million users have registered usernames, which allows them to be contributors. This community is united in its desire to make human knowledge available to every person on the planet.

WIKIPEDIA
The Free Encyclopedia

EXPLORE!

Have a look at these companies from a Community & Crowd perspective. What are they doing to attract and increase participation?

Airbnb
DIY Drones
Xiaomi Global Community
TopCoder

Gustin
Lending Club
99designs
Purchx

Algorithms

Artificial Intelligence is not going to replace us, it's going to enhance us.
It already does.

– Ray Kurzweil, inventor, author and futurist

A

58

DESCRIPTION

As we plunge headlong into the Digital Age, and more and more elements of the physical world evolve to include some digital aspect, it is easy to see that algorithms—which offer the means to make sense of all that information—represent the very foundation of business survival.

An algorithm is simply a step-by-step set of instructions that is used to automate a task or solve a specific problem. The field of Artificial Intelligence (AI) explores how algorithms can be made "intelligent"—learning to solve problems without a predetermined set of instructions and creating new solutions to new problems without human intervention. AI enables computer systems to behave and/or "think" like humans—to solve complex problems and learn over time with improving performance.

Algorithms and AI learn by recognizing patterns in text, images, videos, voice and any other digital-based data. A system can also learn by itself through experience and/or analyzing previous use cases. Learning algorithms have existed for many years, but the current abundance of data and computing power are finally allowing them to provide real value and results to businesses. Science fiction is turning into "science reality."

ExOs use algorithms to automate what people are doing, so that as the business grows it isn't necessary to increase staff at the same pace. The current trend is to use Artificial Intelligence and algorithms to automate the operations of an organization. Increasingly, they will be used for the more complex tasks currently conducted by the core team and staff on demand and are further expected to reach the level of human intelligence in the next couple of decades.

The more sophisticated your use of algorithms, the better your ability to leverage the massive amount of information that current and emerging technology gives you the ability to capture. (Cisco estimates that by 2030, some 500 billion devices will be connected globally, each with embedded sensors that collect data.)

For an ExO, algorithms allow products and services to be fully scaled and improve quality by finding better solutions to problems—through decision support systems, for example. They allow for the mass manipulation of data to leverage its benefits, are easily updated, compensate for human biases and get better every day. Algorithms are your competitive advantage when doing business at scale.

Tips and considerations

◾ Data can be captured through multiple interfaces—by voice, visual and wearables, for example, in addition to text.

◾ Algorithms can be bought. You don't have to develop them all yourself. What third party algorithms and data would be of benefit to you?

◾ What data do you currently have access to that you are not leveraging?

◾ What public data sets can you leverage to enhance your private data?

◾ What additional data could you capture with more widespread use of sensors, and how could you benefit from it?

◾ Where can AI be used in combination with a human activity to create an enhanced outcome?

◾ What repetitive tasks can be automated? What knowledge worker roles can be automated? Where is human interaction critical to your market and thus should not be automated?

◾ Where can algorithms be used to enable the Autonomy attribute?

◾ Some of the tasks performed by your staff on demand may eventually be conducted by algorithms instead. How might algorithms and AI replace your need for staff on demand in the future?

◾ How will you leverage algorithms and AI when they operate at the level of human intelligence?

◾ How can the increasing volume of available data be used to achieve your MTP?

HOW TO IMPLEMENT

1 IDENTIFY THE NEED

What customer need are you solving? Keeping this end goal in mind is important in focusing your efforts. How will automated data-based decision-making address this need? Is this need in alignment with your MTP?

2 SOURCE EXPERTISE

Depending on the nature of your requirement and how integral it is to your core business, you will either want to create software development capability in-house, outsource it and/or employ staff on demand. Explore sources for third-party algorithms and data, such as Kaggle, IBM Watson Analytics and Amazon Web Services.

3 GATHER DATA ABOUT THE PROBLEM YOU WISH TO SOLVE

Identify where the data is originating—from people, sensors or public datasets—and determine with your technical team how best to automate its collection.

4 ORGANIZE THE DATA

A mountain of data is meaningless until you organize it in a way that allows it to be analyzed for insight. A process called ETL (Extract, Transform, Load) uses a programming tool to move data from the source database (where it was gathered) to a different database (where it can be evaluated).

5 APPLY ALGORITHMS

Now that the data is accessible, you can apply algorithms to automate processes, find solutions to new problems, extract insights, identify trends and tune new algorithms. By maintaining your focus on the customer need you want to address, you can execute an aligned solution.

6 EXPOSE DATA TO YOUR COMMUNITY

To truly scale and create value as an ExO, you may wish to open your application programming interface (API) to the public. APIs allow applications to easily communicate with and piggyback on other services. Opening your API will allow third-party developers to design products that are powered by your service, creating additional functionality for your product and fully immersing you in the realm of web-based opportunity.

CHECKLIST FOR SUCCESS

- Are we gathering enough data? Can we find external data sets to supplement internal data?
- Where could sensors be used?
- Are we measuring the right things?
- Is the quality of our data high enough (i.e., to avoid junk in, junk out)?
- Have we explored how to fully utilize our data?
- Are we continually updating and improving our algorithms?
- Are we applying algorithms to our routine, data-based decision-making?
- Are we using the analysis provided by algorithms to drive decision-making for our products or services?
- Are we managing the resulting cultural shift within the organization?

SAMPLE USE

NETFLIX

Netflix is the world's leading internet television network, with 104 million members in over 190 countries watching more than 125 million hours of TV shows and movies per day. Users are presented with a different experience each time they log in, thanks to a personalization algorithm. Based on viewing history, the algorithm resets every 24 hours to ensure that subscribers see content they are likely to watch.

Netflix recognizes that with an estimated 13,000 titles available at any given time, there's so much content that users can easily become overwhelmed. According to Business Insider, the company also knows it has about 90 seconds to convince viewers it has something for them to watch before they abandon the service and move on to something else. As a result, personalization is the key to retaining subscribers. To that end, the company has approximately one thousand staff members charged with customizing the product and personalization algorithm.

59

EXPLORE!

Have a look at these companies from the perspective of Algorithms. In what ways do algorithms underlie their business models?

Google
Apple's Siri
Amazon
FICO

Facebook
Airbnb
Uber
UPS

Leveraged Assets

Marriott wants to add 30,000 hotel rooms in 2014. We will do that in the next two weeks.

— Brian Chesky, co-founder and CEO, Airbnb

DESCRIPTION

Uber owns no cars, yet it manages one of the largest fleets of person-delivery vehicles on the planet, fleets that span dozens of countries. Airbnb owns no hotel rooms, yet in 2017 had four million listings worldwide—more than the top five hotel brands combined. These classic ExO examples illustrate how leveraging, rather than owning, physical property can dramatically change the economics of your business.

Renting, accessing or sharing assets, even those that are mission-critical, allow an organization to stay nimble and unencumbered. Marginal cost of supply is significantly lowered—to virtually zero in the case of a highly scaled model. By not owning physical property, you remove the costs associated with managing it, along with all related infrastructure costs.

Similar to Staff on Demand, the Leveraged Assets attribute gives you on-demand access to resources, replacing the need for ownership. For example, cloud computing stores your data on a provider's server, rather than on your own server or hard drive, and hackerspaces offer access to shared workspace and tools for projects.

Using customer assets is a powerful way to achieve leverage and create scalable products or services. Netflix uses its customers' devices to display movies, and Waze collects real-time traffic information from each user's smartphone or tablet, bypassing the need for dedicated devices or networks.

An ExO applying the Leveraged Assets attribute at its most extreme would have no owned physical assets, essentially eliminating asset-based fixed costs and providing the organization great flexibility.

L

60

Tips and considerations

▪ Leveraged Assets does not include the outsourcing of people, which is covered instead under the Staff on Demand attribute.

▪ Which assets on your organization's balance sheet could be shifted elsewhere?

▪ What assets do your customers own that could be of benefit to your business?

▪ Assets that are information-enabled or becoming commoditized are the most obvious candidates to leverage.

▪ Leverage cloud computing for information-based solutions and consider hackerspaces for hardware solutions.

▪ Real-time automated user reviews give you low-cost feedback on the quality of your leveraged assets.

▪ How does your use of leveraged assets allow you to create a scalable product or service?

HOW TO IMPLEMENT

1 UNDERSTAND YOUR BUSINESS MODEL AND OBJECTIVES

Every business can benefit from leveraged assets in some form. Distinguish if you are building your business on the foundation of leveraged assets (as Uber and Airbnb have done) or if you are simply using leveraged assets to achieve efficiencies in your existing business (such as accessing on-demand office space). A business founded fully on leveraged assets is one with true ExO potential, and the following steps apply.

2 IDENTIFY WHERE THERE IS AN ABUNDANCE OF ASSETS OF VALUE

Where is there spare capacity in the world that you could re-purpose, either inside or outside your current relationships? What untapped abundant resources could support your MTP?

3 DEVELOP RELATIONSHIPS

Identify early members of your leveraged asset community and work closely with them. You want to determine their needs and understand what value they place on the relationship.

4 CREATE AN INTERFACE

Effectively managing any abundance, leveraged assets included, requires the use of an interface to automate your interactions. Your interface should allow you to both collect and disseminate all information related to the working relationship. Test the usability of your interface with early adopters to improve it.

5 USE YOUR INTERFACE AND THE STRENGTH OF THE VALUE YOU OFFER TO DRAW NEW MEMBERS TO YOUR LEVERAGED ASSETS COMMUNITY

Take your automated and tested platform beyond your initial test group to reach a broader audience. The right people will come to you, attracted by the opportunity to participate in and benefit from a profitable business relationship.

CHECKLIST FOR SUCCESS	
	Is our use of leveraged assets allowing the business to scale?
	Can we easily access assets when we need them?
	Have we established clear requirements for participation?
	Are we measuring results?
	Are we collecting automated real-time user reviews?

SAMPLE USE

Zendrive is a company based in both the US and India that uses the sensors on a smartphone to measure and improve driving behavior. With an MTP of "Safer Drivers, Safer Roads," it provides road safety analytics to fleets, insurers and individuals. The company's vision extends beyond today's current driving models, including ride- and car-sharing services, to a future when autonomous fleets will have a need for real-time communication to monitor and analyze data to actively prevent collisions.

ZenDrive is hardware-free. The business is completely built on gathering and analyzing data gathered through sensors already built into its users' smartphones. No investment related to expensive standalone hardware or installation is needed. The company is simply leveraging the abundance of smartphones already in use.

EXPLORE!

Have a look at these companies from a Leveraged Assets perspective. In what ways have they either built a business without needing to incur investment in fixed assets or are they allowing others to do so?

Lyft/Uber
Airbnb
Getaround

WeWork
Waze
Amazon S3

Engagement

Growth without engagement is a leaky bucket.

– Nir Eyal, entrepreneur and author

E

DESCRIPTION

The most powerful motivators in creating value and action on a massive scale are a sense of belonging and engagement with a common cause. Your MTP is the starting point for attracting customers, crowd and community. Engagement is the use of techniques such as reputation systems, gamification, loyalty programs and incentive prizes to keep these groups interested, involved and increasingly committed to your shared purpose.

Through Engagement, you gain the loyalty of your customers and community, and create an effective means of converting crowd into community. Engagement allows you to know your customers, crowd and community more intimately, and better understand how to meet their needs.

What motivates each of these groups? Applying different engagement techniques provides the opportunity to leverage your marketing and experiment with different approaches. Create or share relevant content to help convert crowd to community. Use digital reputation systems to attract, motivate and create trust among community members. Positive feedback from fully engaged users can have a favorable compounding effect, creating virtuous cycles.

Service transparency plays a large role in customer engagement. FedEx and UPS let you track your package from shipment to delivery. Uber allows you to track the progress of your ride from dispatch to arrival. Many traditionally opaque business processes can be transformed by using transparency to allow the user a sense of agency and impact.

Gamification and incentivizing results are extremely effective engagement techniques. Many best-use cases for applying engagement techniques can be found in learning platforms and adapted for your business, including for improving your product or service. How will you compel people to use your product or service every day?

Tips and considerations

- Gamification is good way to engage community, with incentive prizes used to turn crowd into community.

- The Engagement attribute goes hand-in-hand with the Community & Crowd and Experimentation attributes, along with relying on your MTP to draw interest.

- Your employees are a valuable subset of your community. Use engagement techniques to draw on their unique perspectives and learn from your experiments with them. Where can you improve your company's internal culture?

- A plethora of innovation management software is available. Explore tools and platforms currently on the market that are specifically designed to engage your employees, customers and partners in sharing ideas.

- How can you use virtual currency or points effectively?

- Provide clear and authentic rules, goals and rewards. Reward results and provide instant feedback.

- Endeavor to elicit positive rather than negative emotions.

- Collaboration and "coopetition" (cooperative competition) drive faster innovation. Make it fun. Incentivize meaningful action. Ask questions that invite participation.

- Experiment and adjust as you take into account the feedback you are receiving.

HOW TO IMPLEMENT

1 ENSURE YOU HAVE AN MTP

A compelling, easy-to-understand MTP is an essential first step in attracting and engaging a community.

2 CLEARLY IDENTIFY YOUR CUSTOMERS, CROWD AND COMMUNITY

Identify the subsets within your customers, crowd and community. Select those you want to begin experimenting with and research what will appeal to their members.

3 DESIGN YOUR ENGAGEMENT TECHNIQUES

Make sure you set clear, measurable and objective goals. Are there incentives that encourage joining and becoming an active part of your community? Do your incentive competitions require breakthrough thinking or revolutionary products in order to win? Build in digital reputation systems to develop trust and community.

4 BEGIN WITH ENGAGEMENT EXPERIMENTS

Run engagement experiments with smaller test groups. Build on what you learn before scaling.

5 GATHER AND ANALYZE ALL USER INTERACTIONS

Effective use of Engagement requires ongoing evolution and an up-to-date understanding of who your users are, as well as what is—and isn't—working well for them. Your engagement activities will continually evolve based on the data you gather.

CHECKLIST FOR SUCCESS	
	Do we have a fully engaged community and crowd?
	Have we built trust?
	Are we creating customer loyalty?
	Are we improving the effectiveness of our marketing?
	Is gamification built into our core business processes?
	Are we designing products and services with engagement in mind?
	Do our engagement techniques challenge, leverage and motivate our community?

SAMPLE USE

XPrize is dedicated to achieving radical breakthroughs for the benefit of humanity. It is also an organization that believes in creating incentives to get the results it wants. Rather than spending money on seeking breakthroughs of its own, the company incentivizes the solution itself by challenging the world to solve specific problems. With prizes in excess of $1 million and guidelines that make the competition accessible to teams from a wide range of backgrounds, XPrize is spurring innovation and accelerating the rate of positive change.

EXPLORE!

Have a look at these companies from an Engagement perspective. In what ways are they motivating their communities?

Eyewire
Duolingo
Kaggle
Airbnb
Uber

Gigwalk
CarePay
Spigit
GitHub

63

IDEAS

IDEAS is the acronym for the five internal ExO attributes that help you to manage the abundance your Exponential Organization will reach by implementing the SCALE attributes. The five ExO attributes that focus within the organization are Interfaces, Dashboards, Experimentation, Autonomy and Social Technologies. Understanding the particular nature of each type of abundance you seek helps you determine which IDEAS attributes best support your business operations.

Where have you tapped into abundance with the SCALE attributes you've selected?

What corresponding IDEAS attributes will manage this abundance, thus enabling agility and adaptability?

IDEAS

INTERFACES

DASHBOARDS

EXPERIMENTATION

AUTONOMY

SOCIAL TECHNOLOGIES

Interfaces

There is an explosion of information happening, yet people demand quick access to relevant content that cuts through the clutter.

– **Anne M. Mulcahy, former chairperson and CEO, Xerox Corporation**

DESCRIPTION

How will your users—your customers, partners, staff and others—interact with your company? How will data be effectively exchanged? External abundance needs to be filtered and managed to be useful. Interfaces allow this to be done in an effective, targeted and seamless manner.

Interfaces are an automation of one or more SCALE attributes. They are the matching and filtering processes—using algorithms and automated workflows—that allow an organization to translate an abundance of data into meaningful information that can be acted upon. They are the bridge between the drivers of exponential growth (external) and the drivers for stabilization (internal).

Interfaces automatically direct actionable chunks of input to the appropriate internal departments for action. Automatic routing eliminates the limitations and errors common to manual processing and is essential in positioning your business for scaling.

Interfaces can either be what your users interact with or what other systems interact with. For users, the user interface (UI) is the visual part of the software application that they interact with. To be effective, the UI must be built with a good understanding of user experience (UX) needs to ensure it provides a delightful and easy way to engage with your product or service. For systems, application programing interfaces (APIs) are the code-based connections your systems will have with external (or internal) systems in order to gather and exchange data and functionality.

Tips and considerations

- Interfaces work in conjunction with one or more of the SCALE attributes.

- Use human-centered design thinking in the development of interfaces.

- Can your interfaces eventually become self-provisioning?

- How are you implementing the Algorithms attribute in conjunction with your interfaces?

- Your API can facilitate value exchange by filtering and integrating external data to create internal value, and by providing internal data to create external value.

- What user experience currently occurring in the physical realm could move to the digital realm with the use of emerging technologies?

HOW TO IMPLEMENT

1 IDENTIFY THE SOURCES OF ABUNDANCE YOU ARE ACCESSING

You need an abundance of outputs from your environment to create an abundance of inputs to your business.

2 HUMANIZE THE INTERACTION TO DEFINE THE RIGHT UX OR AUTOMATE THE INTERACTION TO DEFINE THE RIGHT API

What is an effective way to engage with your external sources? Experiment with manual interactions and mockups to test your hypothesis for how this will work. What you learn from these experiments will help you optimize the interactions.

3 CREATE STANDARDIZED PROCESSES

Define the flow of information and which actions are performed at each step. Experiment with manual processes to test your hypothesis for how this will work. Again, what you learn from your experiments will help you optimize the processes.

4 APPLY ALGORITHMS TO AUTOMATE PROCESSES

Interfaces need to become self-provisioning platforms to achieve scale. Creating effective algorithms to enable this is a core competency of your business.

5 TEST INTERFACES WITH PILOT POPULATIONS

Interfaces need to be effective before you scale globally. Create smaller-scale experiments in order to learn and optimize.

6 UPDATE INTERFACES REGULARLY

Continually monitor the effectiveness of your interfaces to build upon what you've learned.

CHECKLIST FOR SUCCESS

Will our interfaces allow the business to scale?
Do our interfaces create value?
How many of the SCALE attributes can we enable with Interfaces?
Are we measuring the effectiveness of our algorithms and automated workflows?
Do our interfaces engage users?

SAMPLE USE

CarePay is a Kenyan company with the MTP "Connecting Everyone, Everywhere to Better Healthcare." By linking funders, patients and healthcare providers through mobile technology, the company aims to transform the healthcare sector, first in Kenya and then out to the rest of the world.

Its M-TIBA platform is a "health wallet" (the interface), which is accessed by mobile phone and channels funds from public and private funders for health services directly to recipients. Use of these funds is restricted to conditional spending at selected healthcare providers across Kenya. With every transaction, a digital payment is combined with real-time medical and financial data collection to help make healthcare safer and more transparent for both patients and healthcare providers. To date, CarePay has contracted with more than 2,000 healthcare facilities across Kenya and is driving healthcare inclusion for millions of Kenyans.

EXPLORE!

Have a look at these companies from an Interfaces perspective. What are they doing that makes connection engaging for the user and valuable for the company?

Google (Adsense)
Airbnb
Uber

Apple App Store
LivePerso
Linden Labs
Pokemon Go

Dashboards

Measure what is measurable, and make measurable what is not so.

– Galileo Galilei

DESCRIPTION

Traditional annual or quarterly reporting cannot keep pace with the changes taking place in the current business environment. The hypergrowth that characterizes ExOs requires tight control frameworks and the ability to quickly course-correct. Information that influences your decision-making now needs to be available as close to instantly as possible.

Dashboards provide the real-time information you need to run your business. They reflect essential company and employee metrics, and allow short feedback loops to be implemented. The popular saying "what gets measured gets managed" applies here. In the case of ExOs, where growth is so rapid, dashboards are essential to allow management decision-making to keep up with the pace of change.

A dashboard is simply a screen that provides a visual representation of data that is important to the viewer. Dashboards are designed in a variety of formats to suit their particular purpose, but their function is to consolidate critical performance metrics all in one place, making it easy for users to stay updated on the information most relevant to their business.

Making dashboards accessible and transparent to everyone in the organization enables learning and motivation and can support a collaborative and open atmosphere.

Tips and considerations

▰ What metrics are valuable for you to know in real time?

▰ Define actionable metrics, which provide insight into what you can improve, and avoid vanity metrics, which don't. Similarly, distinguish between leading indicators, which are easy to influence, and lagging indicators, which are not.

▰ ExOs should implement dashboards focused on measuring key ExO attributes, such as Experimentation, and making progress in achieving your MTP.

▰ Dashboards need to be adaptable. You are measuring critical growth drivers—both internal and external data—in real time.

▰ Dashboards can help support the Autonomy attribute.

▰ Use dashboards to openly communicate across the organization. Everyone in the organization should participate in setting goals and providing data and feedback.

▰ Use dashboards in conjunction with Objectives and Key Results (OKRs) or real value Key Performance Indicators (KPIs). Explore the many online and print resources available for an in-depth treatment of these methods.

▰ Building a dashboard into your user interface can support customer engagement with your product or service but is not an example of applying the Dashboards attribute, which instead focuses on employing dashboards internally within your organization to support day-to-day decision-making.

HOW TO IMPLEMENT

1 IDENTIFY THE KEY METRICS FOR YOUR BUSINESS

Avoid traditional vanity metrics such as the number of registered users, number of downloads or page views. Instead, decide what's fundamental to the success of your operation. What are the hypotheses, key learnings and other elements for which you need data? What metrics give you information that you can act on?

2 IDENTIFY YOUR AUDIENCE(S)

Different metrics are relevant at different levels within your organization—strategy vs. operations, for example. Identify who will be using a particular dashboard and to what purpose, and design your dashboard to be invaluable to that audience. Dashboards are ubiquitous today, offering plenty of examples for inspiration as well as the resources needed to create them.

3 TRACK, GATHER AND ANALYZE DATA IN REAL TIME

Begin with customer metrics and then move on to employee metrics. Real-time access allows for short feedback cycles and increased speed of decision-making.

4 IMPLEMENT A GOAL-SETTING FRAMEWORK

Define Objectives and Key Results, or something similar, for individuals and teams company-wide to drive focus and results. In essence, "Objectives" define where you want to go and "Results" let you know if you have gotten there. Make improvements based on your learnings.

5 MAKE METRICS TRANSPARENT AND ACCESSIBLE

Everyone in the organization should have access to the key metrics. If they are to work, however, they must be accepted by employees as part of the company culture and perceived as adding value.

CHECKLIST FOR SUCCESS

Are we measuring business drivers?

Are we getting the information we need to make better decisions faster?

Does the data we're gathering lead to actionable next steps?

What problem does the data solve?

Is the measured benefit of the dashboard significantly greater than the resources required to gather and analyze the data?

What feedback are we getting from employees? Are the dashboards invaluable to them?

Are we a data-driven company? Are we supporting the day-to-day decisions of each team and allowing members to propose innovations, ideas and improvements based on their capacity to improve their performance indicators?

EXPLORE!

Have a look at these companies from a Dashboards perspective. For the first four examples, think about what real-time metrics would be essential to them. For the others, explore how they support the implementation of dashboards.

SAMPLE USE

Facebook knows that effective enterprise communication is fundamental for a fast-moving business. Supporting the productivity of over 25,000 employees demands an innovative approach to sharing information.

The internal tools team at Facebook created a framework to allow company dashboards to be easily created and customized. A dashboard creator may want to display statistics, such as the number of active users or the number of friendships created every day, or include internal news feeds that reflect employee activity, such as internal statuses from across the company or all code reviews done by engineers on a specific team.

As one example, Facebook's internal communication team created a company dashboard with information about product launches, company announcements, events, internal notes from people around the company, and an internal status update stream where people post topics of interest for discussion with coworkers.

Given the broad span of unique business needs across the employee base, customizable dashboards allow Facebook teams to monitor data trends and information relevant to them while promoting openness and transparency across the organization.

69

Facebook	Aha!
Twitter	Stocktouch
LinkedIn	Perdoo
ZenDrive	Tableau
Oracle	Geckoboard

Experimentation

The real measure of success is the number of experiments that can be crowded into 24 hours.

– Thomas Edison

DESCRIPTION

In their early stages, ExOs are similar to startups—both are still in search of a scalable business model. As Steve Blank advises, "In a startup, no business plan survives first contact with customers." Any new business model is not a set of actions to be executed, but rather a set of assumptions, or hypotheses, to be validated.

On the other hand, an ExO can also be an established organization trying to adapt to industry disruption—or perhaps even lead it. In this case, the ExO must continually come up with new ideas, such as new products, services or processes. All of these must also be considered hypotheses, which must be tested before executing at scale.

Traditional business or product plans are built on a vast number of assumptions about what the market needs. Experimentation is the act of validating your assumptions before making significant

investments. Each experiment creates a set of learnings that you then use to improve your product, service or process.

Whether an ExO is a new organization or an existing one, it must continually run experiments in order to learn how best to evolve. One of the best approaches to implementing Experimentation within an ExO is the Lean Startup methodology, which focuses on running fast feedback loops. These allow an organization to incorporate learnings and make adjustments before significant time and expense has been incurred on a given path.

Experimentation is done within multiple organizational departments, enabling a cultural acceptance of risk-taking. Risk-taking provides a strategic edge and results in faster learning. It keeps processes aligned with rapidly changing externalities and products aligned with real needs.

E

70

Tips and considerations

- How suited is your current culture to change? Are employees cooperative, supportive, motivated and open to transparency? These factors will support successful experimentation.

- Failure is an essential element of Experimentation. Areas where results fall short are where the learnings and opportunities for improvement lie. It requires a mindset shift to see failure as a positive (look what we learned!) rather than a negative (we didn't get top marks).

- Rewarding "good failures," those that offer insight and learning, help to instill experimentation as a core value within the organization and allow the attribute to be implemented without resistance or stigma.

- Align incentives for individuals and divisions with experimentation steps by, for example, measuring the number of experiments executed or the number of hypotheses evaluated.

- What is your external staff on demand telling you? This is a good group to experiment with, as they are invested enough in the business to offer unique insight and they have a direct interest in seeing improvements. At the same time, they are removed enough to be objective in their feedback.

- Existing customers and suppliers are easily accessible and effective groups to conduct experiments with. Follow the "get out of the building" mantra to test your assumptions!

- Design your products and services in a way that allows them to be easily iterated. Can you perform ongoing integration of customer feedback?

- Time-box your experiments, predict the results in advance, decide how to measure and use only falsifiable hypotheses. Avoid confirmation bias in the design of your questions.

SAMPLE USE

TATA MOTORS
Connecting Aspirations

Tata Motors, India's largest automobile company, operates globally through subsidiaries and partnerships. The company understands that securing a future in a rapidly changing business environment requires keeping pace with the advanced mobility solutions space.

Tata introduced TAMO, a separate and vertical division, as an open platform to network with global startups and leading tech companies. It was also designed to transform the experience of interfacing and interacting with customers and the wider community. Through the TAMO ecosystem, Tata can experiment with low-volume, low-investment vehicle models in order to provide fast-tracked proof of technologies and concepts. The results of these experiments contribute to the design of future mainstream products and services.

HOW TO IMPLEMENT

1 EDUCATE YOUR TEAM AND ALIGN INCENTIVES

Train your staff on the importance of asking questions, as well as on how to design good questions and find answers that bring value. Demonstrate your leadership support to create a culture that incentivizes and empowers staff to conduct rapid, quality experimentation—and even to fail in order to learn.

2 DEFINE YOUR HYPOTHESIS AND VALUE PROPOSITION

What are you testing? Will the outcome influence what you are currently doing? Continually test your underlying assumptions about the customer. Your Business Model Canvas is a compilation of every assumption you make in your business. Use it as a starting point for selecting hypotheses to test.

3 BUILD AND EXECUTE EXPERIMENTS TO EVALUATE YOUR HYPOTHESIS

Think through the design of your experiment. Are the results quantifiable? How will the results allow you to innovate? Form questions in creative ways in order to uncover real needs. Clearly define what determines success, including what thresholds need to be met.

4 GATHER AND ANALYZE DATA FROM THE RESULTS OF THE EXPERIMENTS

Track experiments and measure the results to capture learnings.

5 LEARN FROM DATA

What have you learned from your results? Did the data generated from the experiment validate or repudiate your hypothesis? Be ready to adapt or change course based on learnings, including evolving your business model.

6 ITERATE YOUR APPROACH

Where can you make adjustments to improve the quality of your experiment outcomes? Continually experiment with all aspects of your ideas, including the design and implementation of your experiments.

In essence, the Lean Startup process starts with a set of ideas and runs a Build -Measure-Learn loop to evaluate them:

BUILD

Depending on the stage of the idea, you can simply design a set of questions to ask customers or stakeholders about your new ideas (the Customer Development approach is great for this), or you can even build a first Minimum Viable Product (MVP). An MVP allows you to get a product to market faster and receive feedback sooner. Both approaches can be considered experiments.

MEASURE

One of the key principles of Lean Startup is to make data-driven decisions, which means data needs to be gathered about the experiment, regardless of whether it's an interview, an MVP or another kind of experiment.

LEARN

After analyzing the results of the experiment, you will be able to determine the validity of the hypothesis you are testing. Regardless of whether the hypothesis is validated or not, the learning that comes out of the experiment is invaluable. It allows the organization to further develop the initial idea and then repeat the Build-Measure-Learn loop.

The Build-Measure-Learn loop reduces your investment in new ideas—innovative products, for example—and reduces waste, since there's no need to spend time developing features for which you haven't confirmed a need. The faster and more frequently you can execute this three-step loop, the more you learn in a shorter period of time.

Variations on this process may be a good fit for your business. *Sprint: How to Solve Big Problems and Test New Ideas in Just Five Days*, by Jake Knapp of Google Ventures, outlines a design sprint that skips Build. *The Service Startup: Design Thinking Gets Lean*, by Tennyson Pinheiro, advocates beginning design sprints in Learn. When to introduce an MVP vs. a mock-up or prototype can also be explored.

CHECKLIST FOR SUCCESS

- Have we clearly defined assumptions that drive the business?
- Are we asking questions of value?
- Are our experiments generating valuable results?
- Are we continually growing and improving based on results?
- Is experimentation a core value in our organization?
- Have we defined a smooth, flexible process for capturing and leveraging new knowledge, including the use of a tool to categorize results?
- Are we including time for feedback and product improvement in our budgets and plans?

EXPLORE!

Have a look at these companies from an Experimentation perspective. What types of experiments do you think they benefit from?

Dropbox   Google X
Adobe   Amazon
General   Uber
Electric   Groupon

Autonomy

Those who say it can't be done should get out of the way of those doing it.

– Chinese proverb

DESCRIPTION

Increased speed of decision-making, accelerated innovation and rapid testing of ideas are examples of what teams can achieve when they are not only unencumbered by fossilized processes, rules and reporting structures, but also permitted to self-organize to meet shared goals.

Autonomy refers to the use of self-organized, multi-disciplinary teams that operate with decentralized authority. This approach stands in contrast to traditional organizations characterized by the rank and procedure of hierarchical structures. ExOs applying autonomy are characterized by flatter organizations with highly motivated self-starters who are empowered to innovate.

Autonomy can be applied in different ways. Within an organization, it enables core teams to operate with greater agility and flexibility, thereby allowing the organization to adapt more quickly to a dynamic environment. It can also be applied to staff external to the company (Staff on Demand), which allows them to operate more independently, thereby offering the organization greater potential for exponential growth.

Autonomy is not the removal of control; instead, it is the imposition of self-disciplined freedom for individuals and groups. It offers the benefits of increased agility and flexibility, faster reaction and learning times, and better employee morale.

Some common frameworks that support the Autonomy attribute are:

- **Agile product development frameworks** such as Scrum or Kanban support autonomy across product development teams. These frameworks are frequently used at software development companies but can be applied to any kind of company.

- **Objectives and Key Results** support autonomy and agility across organizations. They extend beyond product development activities to the entire organization, ensuring that the efforts of all teams and individuals are both cohesive and flexible.

- **Holacracy** is an example of a networked, rather than linear, organizational design and management model. It allows organizations to dynamically form teams to tackle temporary goals and challenges. Another example is Teal Organizations as described by Frederic Laloux in *Reinventing Organizations: A Guide to Creating Organizations Inspired by the Next Stage of Human Consciousness*.

- **Black Ops or Edge Teams** are examples of groups established at, or beyond, the boundaries of an existing organization with permission to make independent decisions relating to their work and projects. This increases the speed of decision-making and leads to more innovative, agile operations and breakthrough ideas.

72

Tips and considerations

- Teams benefit from a mix of long-term employees and more recent hires.

- Explore Holacracy and similar principles for ideas and inspiration.

- Accountability is still necessary with autonomy.

- How can the organization can achieve greater trust and role clarity, as well as lower the cost and effort of working together?

- Cultural acceptance is crucial to implementing self-organization within a company.

- Autonomy can be applied in conjunction with the Engagement attribute.

- Blockchain technology can be used to implement autonomy. It permits distributed nodes or people to interact without the need for a centralized control system.

HOW TO IMPLEMENT

1 DEFINE YOUR MTP

As with many of the ExO attributes, the MTP is essential to attracting the right employees and guiding decision-making.

2 IDENTIFY THE RIGHT PEOPLE

Self-starting employees and entrepreneurs are best suited for this innovative style of organization. New leadership models and skills are needed to support motivation, organization and innovation for agile frameworks and self-organized teams.

3 ESTABLISH TEAMS

Create a culture of small, independent and multidisciplinary teams. Hire talented and innovative self-starters.

4 IMPLEMENT FRAMEWORKS AND TOOLS

Define what level of autonomy the group has—its degree of freedom—and establish what the connection points are with the parent company. Set clear guiding principles based on the MTP and company values. Identify a framework for how the group will operate and exercise accountability.

5 COMMUNICATE OBJECTIVES

Define and communicate your goals for this organizational approach. Encourage staff to start new projects that fit your company's MTP, or to choose from a collection of ongoing projects.

6 IMPLEMENT DASHBOARDS

Create open and transparent dashboards to enable teams to make better data-driven decisions.

CHECKLIST FOR SUCCESS

Are our employees encouraged to make decisions on their own?
Is decision-making power distributed?
Does our culture support autonomy and independence?
Have we implemented peer accountability?
Are the roles in our organization dynamic?
Do we have a clear process for autonomous teams to manage risks and failures in an effective manner?

SAMPLE USE

Buurtzorg is a pioneering healthcare organization established in the Netherlands featuring a nurse-led model of holistic, neighborhood care that is innovating community care globally. After establishing a neighborhood office, 12-member teams—made up of registered nurses, licensed practical nurses and nursing assistants—introduce themselves to the local community and to GPs, therapists and other professionals in the area, thereby building their caseload through word of mouth and referrals. Each self-managing team decides how to organize the work, share responsibility and make decisions.

The model has improved quality of care (achieving the highest client satisfaction rates of any healthcare organization in the country), increased job satisfaction and lowered overall costs. Although its costs per hour are higher than those of other healthcare organizations, Buurtzorg has achieved a 50 percent reduction in the hours needed to care for the same number of patients.

A

73

EXPLORE!

Have a look at these companies from the Autonomy perspective. In what ways do they exercise or enable decentralized authority?

Enspiral
Medium
Zappos
Valve Corporation

ING Direct
Axosoft
Scaled Agile
Haier

Social Technologies

Alone we can do so little; together we can do so much.

– Helen Keller

S

74

DESCRIPTION

Social technologies are the tools that allow your community of employees, staff on demand, customers and others to communicate quickly and easily. These tools result in faster conversations, faster decision cycles and faster learning. The lag time between an idea being shared, accepted and implemented can be essentially eliminated.

The Social Technologies attribute is not about encouraging the use of social media for marketing. Instead, it is about improving internal operations by encouraging social interaction via technology—which includes communications, collaboration and workflow—and exploring how to do this well.

Social Technologies encompass communication tools (such as social messaging and discussion forums), collaboration tools (such as cloud-based document management for sharing and real-time editing) and workflow tools (to manage tasks and activity streams.) They allow your organization to benefit from an entirely digitized communication base. Tools create transparency and lower an organization's information latency—the time it takes for information to get from one place to another.

ExOs use the Social Technologies attribute within the organization to allow staff to collaborate in real time, drastically reducing cycle times. Teams stay connected and stabilized even in rapidly changing environments. Wikis, blogs, social networks and web conferencing are mainstream methods of collaboration, while Virtual Reality and Augmented Reality tools are rapidly emerging.

ExOs also use social technologies beyond the boundaries of their organizations to connect with customers and other members of community. Social environments can be created to drive information used for the development of your products and services in support of the Community & Crowd attribute. Products and services can be designed with the social element incorporated.

Tips and considerations

▉ A cooperative culture must be in place for Social Technologies to work. Is your work environment supportive, motivated and transparent? If not, what can you do to improve it?

▉ Enable both horizontal and vertical communication within the organization.

▉ How can emerging social tools such as telepresence, virtual worlds and emotional sensing be applied within the organization?

▉ What implications does the ability to work virtually have for your organization?

▉ The dynamics of communication and collaboration can dramatically change with the introduction of social tools. Company leadership and the marketing and PR departments, for example, may be accustomed to one-way communications. Social technologies create a shift to real-time, two-way and multi-directional communications.

▉ Use social technologies outside the boundaries of your organization to enable zero-latency communications with your customers in support of the Interfaces attribute.

▉ Building social technologies into your user interface can drive engagement, but is not an example of applying the Social Technologies attribute, which focuses on internal use.

▉ How will you use social technologies to manage abundance and grow your business? How, for example, can social tools be used to speed your development or acquire new customers?

▉ Building the correct social architecture and information flows into your organization to provide technology-enabled communication can be a massive driver of agility and innovation at scale. It can also keep things more human as an organization grows.

HOW TO IMPLEMENT

1 DEFINE YOUR MTP

An aspirational MTP must be in place for employees to collaborate in accordance with a common purpose.

2 ANALYZE THE CURRENT SOCIAL ENVIRONMENT

What are the existing social and community interactions? Who is communicating and how? Where are interactions missing that would be beneficial?

3 IMPLEMENT TOOLS

Leverage cloud-based social tools throughout your organization in accordance with what you've learned about your interactions. Experiment with the many tools available on the market to find ones that are a good fit for you. Consider not only communication tools, but also those that support collaboration and workflow.

4 TURN THE CAMERA ON

Are you fully utilizing the functionality of your tools? For example, are you using a service like Skype for Business—which has video capability—but only using it for audio calls? Video presence makes a big difference, enabling you to learn more about the people you are speaking with, receive nonverbal feedback and connect. Explore the full capacity of your tools to discover new ways of working together.

5 LEARN FROM YOUR EXPERIENCES

Where are you getting the most value from social tools? Which ones are people gravitating toward? What feedback are you getting from your employees and customers?

CHECKLIST FOR SUCCESS

Is our senior management leading the use of these tools?

Are we using social technologies to support our critical decision-making?

Are we supplementing our use of social technologies with periodic in-person connection for relationship-building?

Are our staff and customers readily adopting the social tools? Are they aware of them and trained in how to use them?

Is our Information Technology department supporting (and not blocking) the use of social tools?

Are we defining our products and services with the social element in mind?

EXPLORE!

Have a look at these companies from a Social Technologies perspective. How do they permit teams to collaborate?

SAMPLE USE

TED

Although TED is headquartered in New York, its technology team includes developers who live across other states and countries. While a distributed workforce allows the company to access talent wherever it resides, good virtual collaboration is essential.

TED's tech team makes use of a full complement of available social technologies:

- GitHub to collaborate on code
- Dropbox to store shared assets
- Google Docs for notes on group thinking and works in progress
- Skype and Google Hangouts for smaller meetings
- BlueJeans for videoconferencing
- A group wiki for collectively planning agendas
- Chat for one-on-one conversations
- Flowdock for internal team chatter and transparent conversations

Staff are issued a MiFi—a portable WiFi hotspot—to make sure that everyone has a top quality connection at all times. The team makes customizations along the way and polls staff periodically to understand its pain points. Everyone recognizes the value of in-person connection and gathers together as a team to discuss goals and ideas a few times a year.

75

Yammer (communication)
Slack (collaboration)
Trello (project management)
Asana (work tracking)
Dropbox (file sharing)
Zoom (video conferencing)
Aha! (product roadmaps)
Sansar (virtual reality)
Skype (video conferencing)
Evernote (organization)
Google Drive (collaboration)
Google Hangouts (communications)
Flowdock (group chat)
Vidyo (video conferencing)
Join.me (video conferencing)
Poll Everywhere (interaction)
Medium (publishing)
GitHub (coding)
99Designs (design)

ExO Canvas

Having read the previous pages, you should now be familiar with the different ExO attributes that Exponential Organizations implement in order to reach and manage abundance. Next up, we present the ExO Canvas, a simple, one-page tool that will help you easily design—and improve—your Exponential Organization.

The ExO Canvas is a management template that helps visionaries, innovators, top executives and entrepreneurs design agile organizations by leveraging exponentially accelerating technologies. Use the ExO Canvas to design a new ExO or to implement the ExO framework within an existing organization.

How flexible or agile is your organization? Is it an ExO? These are the questions the ExO Canvas was designed to help you answer. It will guide you toward becoming an ExO, one that is both flexible and agile.

The ExO Canvas provides a one-page overview of all of the attributes that make up the ExO model. In addition to establishing a simple and clear foundation for either designing a new ExO or creating ExO initiatives within an existing organization, the ExO Canvas helps ensure that the full scope of an ExO is considered. It provides an opportunity to think through not only which attributes you will employ but also—more specifically—how each attribute will be implemented.

We have found the ExO Canvas to be an effective tool to take a business model as expressed by a Business Model Canvas and facilitate its transformation into an Exponential Organization business model. In addition, when used in the early stages of ideation, it can be a key driver for learning about the potential applications of exponential technologies relevant to your organization.

The ExO Canvas was co-created by a group of over 100 ExO practitioners from around the world. A full list of the creators is available at www.exocanvas.com. There you will also find a downloadable version of the ExO Canvas.

Moving from left to right across the ExO Canvas, you'll first use the SCALE attributes to connect with a world of abundance. Next, as you move on to the IDEAS attributes, you'll put that abundance to work through experimentation and implementation. Through these methods, you now have the potential to create your own new abundance. Keep in mind that this process is guided by an overarching MTP that defines the core purpose of the organization's existence.

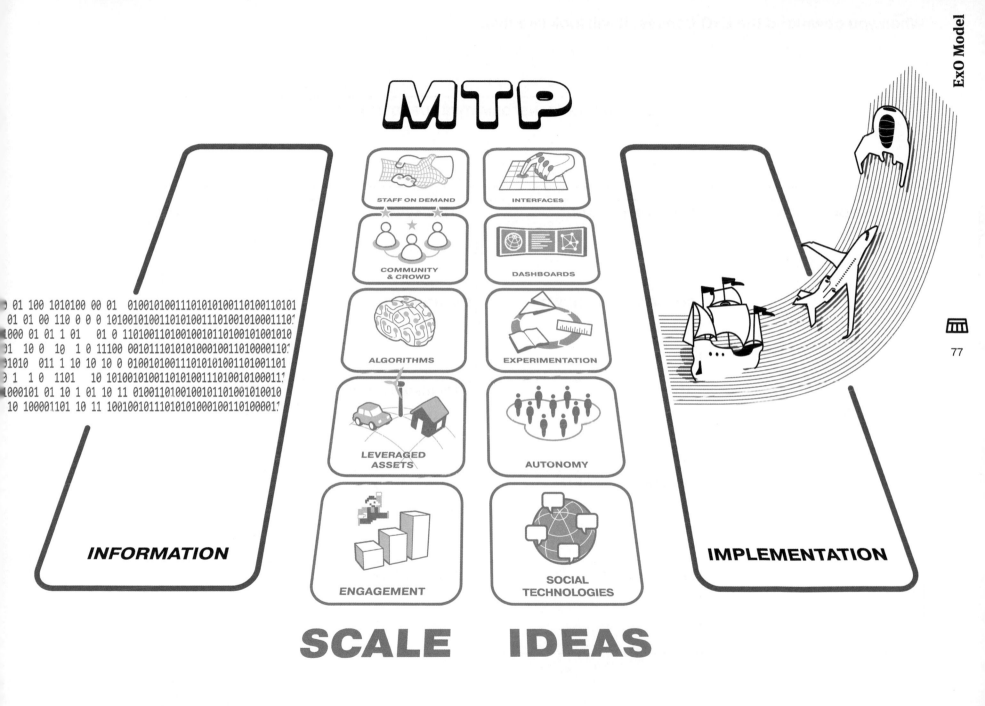

MTP

STAFF ON DEMAND

INTERFACES

COMMUNITY & CROWD

DASHBOARDS

ALGORITHMS

EXPERIMENTATION

LEVERAGED ASSETS

AUTONOMY

ENGAGEMENT

SOCIAL TECHNOLOGIES

INFORMATION

IMPLEMENTATION

SCALE   IDEAS

77

When you download the ExO Canvas, it will look like this:

MASSIVE TRANSFORMATIVE PURPOSE (MTP)			

INFORMATION	STAFF ON DEMAND	INTERFACES	IMPLEMENTATION
	COMMUNITY & CROWD	DASHBOARDS	
	ALGORITHMS	EXPERIMENTATION	
	LEVERAGED ASSETS	AUTONOMY	
	ENGAGEMENT	SOCIAL TECHNOLOGIES	

USING THE EXO CANVAS

If you're working with the ExO Canvas in a group, print blank copies of the ExO Canvas on as large a scale as is practical. You'll find that a wall-sized version is great to work with when brainstorming with larger groups. For smaller groups, A0 paper size is best; just make sure there's enough room to populate each of the sections on the ExO Canvas with sticky notes.

Each section of the ExO Canvas will eventually be covered with sticky notes, so have plenty of markers available for all members of the group. Before you begin, remind everyone to keep the entries short enough to fit on the notes.

For easy reference, give everyone a copy of the ExO Canvas, which should be pre-populated with prompting questions for each attribute (as available on the www.exocanvas.com website). Having ideas to work with will stimulate the thinking process.

At the top of the ExO Canvas, write out the MTP that you're currently considering. All subsequent entries will be in support of this particular MTP.

Next, think about where and how to access the untapped abundance in the world that will help you achieve your MTP. (For example, Airbnb used an abundance of unused rooms.) As outlined earlier, the five attributes listed on the left-hand side of the ExO Canvas (acronym: SCALE) are different ways of accessing that abundance.

Think about the sources of information or data that enable you to connect your SCALE attributes to abundance. That's the block you will find on the left of the ExO Canvas, next to the SCALE attributes. Consider what information or data you have, what you need, where it will come from and how you will collect it.

Once you've identified sources of abundance, turn your attention to the five attributes on the right-hand side of the ExO Canvas (acronym: IDEAS), which offer different approaches to managing the abundance. Think about the dependencies between the attributes and the order in which you want to implement them. For example, once the Community & Crowd attribute is defined, move on to Engagement.

Finally, consider what key milestones and tasks are needed to move forward with either implementing the ExO attributes within your current organization or building a new ExO. These steps should be discrete and measurable. Use the Implementation block on the right-hand side of the ExO Canvas to capture the steps.

The ExO Canvas you create for each MTP will go through many cycles of development as you proceed through an ExO Sprint. Quick iterations of ideas and the rapid development of the ExO Canvases are important. Remember that this is the early stage only; nothing needs to be polished.

Save early versions of your ExO Canvases. You may end up using components of them down the road.

TIPS FOR USING THE EXO CANVAS

An **MTP** is mandatory for any Exponential Organization and serves as your starting point.

Begin by thinking about **how to reach** abundance (SCALE attributes) and then **how to manage** it (IDEAS attributes).

Remember **to balance the number of SCALE and IDEAS attributes.** Due to the overlapping relationship between SCALE and IDEAS, you will need attributes from each set, and you may want to aim for a similar number.

Think about the **dependencies between attributes**. For example, if you want to use the Staff on Demand attribute from the SCALE set, you will likely require Interfaces and Dashboards from the IDEAS side of the page. Similarly, Autonomy points to a need for Dashboards and Social Technologies, and so on.

Experimentation is a given, at least during the early stages of your ExO. This attribute is fundamental to achieving a mindset of ongoing learning.

You don't need to implement all of the ExO attributes, but a **minimum of four are required** to build a true ExO.

There is a tendency **to use the ExO attributes as a simple checklist**. (Community? Check! Interfaces? Check!) Instead, use the ExO Canvas as a tool to move beyond casual use and to define specifically how each attribute will be implemented.

Now that you understand the components and interdependencies of the ExO model—the MTP, the five SCALE attributes that enable you to access global abundance externally, and the five IDEAS attributes to help you manage that abundance internally—what's next?

The ExO Sprint is a 10-week process that allows you to put the ExO model to work for you. Consider the ExO attributes as the ingredients for transformation and the ExO Sprint your recipe. The next section of the book will guide you through the ExO Sprint by providing a series of assignments, direction and support for defining your ExO initiatives and achieving your exponential transformation.

ExO
Sprint

ExO Sprint

Ready to implement the ExO model in order to transform your business and achieve exponential results?

There's no question that Exponential Organizations are the businesses that succeed the most in this age of exponential technologies, but let's be honest: Implementing the ExO model is not an easy task. Without the right process in place, many challenges—including your company's own immune system—will conspire to prevent your organization from achieving the transformation you desire.

In this section, we will describe how to run the 10-week ExO Sprint—step by step and week by week. After running the ExO Sprint, not only will your business be resistant to disruption, it will also be in a position to leapfrog current innovators and take a leadership spot within your industry. Or even invent a new one!

Challenges to Transformation

Applying the ExO framework to an existing organization is not easy, and you face a number of challenges on your way to transformation. In the following pages, we describe these challenges and outline how running the ExO Sprint process in full enables you to address them.

If you are an established organization, you may want to transform your business model to connect with abundance by becoming a platform, creating your own ecosystem or choosing another abundance-based model. To find the right approach, experiment with new business models without risking your current organization.

FINDING THE RIGHT BUSINESS MODEL

Traditional business models are based on scarcity: value is derived from selling a product or service that is in limited supply. However, as mentioned earlier, exponential technologies are generating an abundance of everything—from information to energy—so the main challenge that all industries face is finding new business models that work for abundance. Examples include:

UBER

Product as a service
A system that allows consumers to buy less and rent more. A good example is Uber, which users call on only when they need a car. Uber is able to leverage an abundance of both drivers and clients to provide its service.

Sharing economy
People rent out unused resources, which encourages sharing and cuts down on waste. In the case of Airbnb, for example, individuals lease homes or rooms they are not using. Airbnb is able to leverage an abundance of places to rent.

99designs

Platform
Online software that connects and automates the processes between consumers and producers. An example is 99designs, an online graphic design marketplace that allows someone looking for a design (e.g., a logo) to post a request and have designers compete for the job. 99designs accesses an abundance of designers in order to offer its clients a wide range of designs.

Ecosystem
Beyond platforms, ecosystems connect different services and solutions to offer comprehensive value to the members of the ecosystem. Recently, emerging ecosystems have been extending the platform model.

Successful global companies are building their own ecosystems, within which a number of companies exist. Not all of these companies have clear business models, but all contribute value to the ecosystem. For example:

- **Google** built its own ecosystem by creating entities such as Gmail, Google Maps and Google Drive.

- **Facebook** built its ecosystem by buying entities such as Instagram, WhatsApp and Oculus.

The real challenge is discovering the right business model for a certain organization or industry. Or—even more difficult—the right shape and configuration of the ecosystem for a given organization or industry.

ECOSYSTEM

ECOSYSTEM

THE CORPORATE IMMUNE SYSTEM WILL ALWAYS ATTACK INNOVATION

You may already be familiar with the business model that your organization should implement in order to connect with abundance. That's great, but picking the right business model is the easy part. The challenge you will inevitably face is that any time a large organization attempts to innovate or transform itself, the corporate immune system—certain employees and processes hard-wired to prevent organizational transformation—will always attack. (We are sure everyone can relate to this.)

The corporate immune system does its job for a good reason: established organizations usually have a working business, which is important to maintain. The goal here isn't to kill the immune system; instead, it is to manage it.

The ways in which an organization introduces innovation tends to magnify the immune system problem. Organizations often ask external consultants what needs to be done to achieve transformation. Or they invest in or buy external startups to integrate into the main body. Either way, the organization's immune system will attack any and all initiatives.

Why? Because the corporate immune system reacts to whatever it considers foreign DNA.

Balance innovation and risk by keeping the current business model as it is and running disruptive projects outside the main organization.

Execute the transformation process with existing employees so that the organization's DNA remains intact. Also, if you choose to buy an external startup, operate it outside the main organization, keeping it as a new entity within the greater ecosystem (as Facebook has done).

IT'S ALSO ABOUT PEOPLE TRANSFORMATION

Key employees must be heavily involved in the transformation process. They should learn new concepts, practice using the new tools and generate their own transformation ideas. The new environment and changes will occasionally—even often—prove uncomfortable, so the leadership team must offer the employees their full support.

Transforming an organization is not only about the organization itself, but also about updating the mindset and knowledge base of the people who work for it. As an issue, this one is strongly linked to the challenge posed by the corporate immune system. In order to tackle the latter, you must first address the former: transform your organization's antibodies (its white cells) into organizational champions—red blood cells dedicated to driving innovation.

EXISTING EFFICIENCY-ORIENTED CULTURE, MANAGEMENT AND PROCESSES

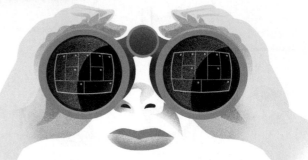

Established organizations are focused on efficiency; their purpose is to maximize profits. Such management practices and processes don't work, however, when the goal is disruptive innovation.

Why? By definition, early stage disruptive businesses don't even have a clear business model. As a result, the focus isn't on efficiency but rather on searching for the right model. As Steve Blank said, "A startup is a temporary organization searching for a scalable and replicable business model."

To run innovation and transformation processes, use search-oriented innovation methodologies such as Customer Development, Design Thinking and Lean Startup.

YOU DON'T LEARN HOW TO PLAY BASKETBALL FROM A BOOK

The following books outline some of the search-oriented methodologies previously mentioned: *The Lean Startup*, by Eric Ries; *Four Steps to the Epiphany*, by Steve Blank; and, of course, *Exponential Organizations*, by Salim Ismail, Michael Malone and Yuri van Geest.

Nonetheless, in the same way that nobody really learns how to play basketball from a book, your team won't understand how to implement these methodologies simply by reading about them. It's crucial that your team members own and run the transformation process themselves, which means they'll need to adopt a hands-on approach to truly learn how it works.

THE SMARTEST PEOPLE DON'T WORK FOR YOU

Regardless of your organization's size, there will be always more people outside your organization than within. This fact has two important implications: First, you won't always have access to the most knowledgeable person for any specific issue. Second, your customers, who have the answers to key questions about whether your innovation will succeed or fail, aren't necessarily available either.

Open your innovation and transformation processes to the community in order to gain insight and validation and to discover what is required to successfully implement your innovative initiatives. To quote Steve Blank again: "Get out of the building!"

LACK OF SPEED (AND ENGAGEMENT)

The primary focus of an organization is to run its existing business, not to transform itself. As a result, innovative activities are always second-tier priorities. This slows the progress of disruption and transformation.

At the same time, running one-day workshops or small programs is not effective either. While such short-format programs are a great way to get people excited and open their minds, they don't change behavior.

Use a "learning by doing" approach whereby your team gains knowledge about the different methodologies and executes the transformation process with the support of an external facilitator or coach (with this book operating as the playbook).

Run a process that is neither too short nor too long. The goal is to achieve behavioral change and long-term engagement while sustaining enough energy to see the process through to the end.

ExO Sprint Approach

The ExO Sprint has been designed to address all of the above challenges and offers practical solutions and suggestions for tackling each.

The processes outlined in this book are a culmination of the authors' experiences running innovation and transformation projects for the past 15 years, initiatives that have involved more than 200 innovation consultants who have provided invaluable feedback.

In addition, the ExO Sprint has been successfully applied across a variety of industries and to many companies worldwide, including Procter & Gamble, Stanley Black & Decker, HP Inc. and Visa.

By running an ExO Sprint, organizations will discover the right business model, which will then enable them to connect to abundance. They will also be equipped to manage the corporate immune system's compulsion to block innovation and change, learn how to implement the right innovation-oriented methodologies and use a learn-by-doing approach to build internal capabilities within the organization.

All in just 10 weeks!

DISCOVER THE RIGHT ABUNDANCE-BASED BUSINESS MODEL

The outcome of an ExO Sprint is a set of ExO initiatives that will both improve the existing business model to make it more adaptable to external industry disruption and generate next-generation organizations that have the potential to lead their industries.

NEUTRALIZE THE CORPORATE IMMUNE SYSTEM

To prevent a corporate immune system attack, have existing employees design and execute the transformation process rather than bringing in outside consultants. Allowing employees to come up with their own ideas will ensure implementation of the resulting initiatives, thus reducing the immune system response.

Another way to mitigate the immune reaction is to implement incremental innovation (initiatives that maintain the existing business model) within the company and develop all disruptive initiatives (those that involve a new business model) outside the company.

SUPPORT PEOPLE IN THEIR TRANSFORMATION EXPERIENCE

An ExO Sprint is an intensive experience and generally entails asking people to work in a completely different way than they are used to operating. During the course of an ExO Sprint, participants will need to engage with new tools and disciplines. They will also be required to validate imperfect ideas with clients, develop those ideas in the face of limited information and a high level of uncertainty about next steps, and prepare prototypes within days.

Our experience has shown that ExO Sprint participants embrace the experience . . . eventually. It may, however, take the entire process for them to get there. As a result, it's important to be aware that participants will go through an intensive process, one that—although it will change their mindset forever, and for the better—will require psychological support, both from the company's leadership team and the staff running the ExO Sprint.

USE SEARCH-ORIENTED INNOVATION METHODOLOGIES

The ExO Sprint supports the use of search-oriented innovation methodologies—Blue Ocean Strategy, Customer Development, Lean Startup and Design Thinking—in combination with traditional management methodologies.

SUPPORT LEARNING BY DOING

Running an ExO Sprint is a learning experience. Participants will learn about the principles, the process and the outside world as they complete the weekly assignments. Their mindset will shift as they practice and refine new methods of working, communicating and forming ideas. As a result of their experience, members of a completed ExO Sprint will serve as ambassadors in implementing ExO principles throughout the organization.

LEVERAGE EXTERNAL TALENT

While using the organization's employees is crucial to circumventing the corporate immune response (in addition to many other benefits), involving outside coaches and advisors in the ExO Sprint maximizes the value of the outcome by drawing on external input and knowledge.

FINISH IN 10 WEEKS

In order to cement new habits among the participants, the ideal time span for the ExO Sprint is 10 weeks.

ExO Sprint Structure

The ExO Sprint is conducted in three main phases, each with sub-components.

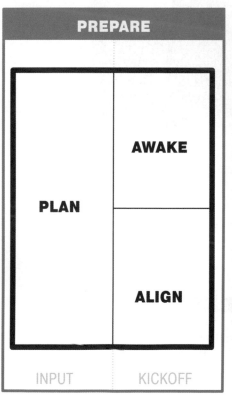
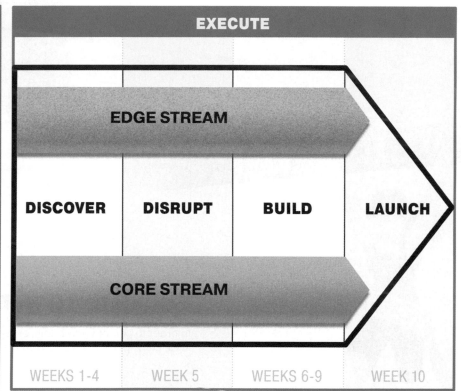
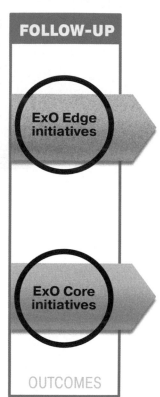

PREPARE		EXECUTE				FOLLOW-UP
PLAN	AWAKE	EDGE STREAM				ExO Edge initiatives
		DISCOVER	DISRUPT	BUILD	LAUNCH	
	ALIGN	CORE STREAM				ExO Core initiatives
INPUT	KICKOFF	WEEKS 1-4	WEEK 5	WEEKS 6-9	WEEK 10	OUTCOMES

PREPARATION PHASE

Focus on making sure all needed elements are in place before beginning the 10-week process.

PLAN

The organization defines the scope of the ExO Sprint and decides on key participants.

AWAKE

The organization understands the difference between linear and exponential thinking and makes sure participants understand the importance of running an ExO Sprint.

ALIGN

ExO Sprint participants receive training on the methodologies and tools they will need to execute the ExO Sprint, including the ExO model.

EXECUTION PHASE

The ExO Sprint is a 10-week process. During this phase, participants generate ideas and develop a set of ExO initiatives designed to transform the organization—and even the industry. Two streams run in tandem throughout this stage: The Core Stream is focused on innovation—adapting to external industry disruption without changing the existing business model (so as to avoid triggering an immune system reaction). The Edge Stream is focused on disruption—on creating the next generation of organizations (new businesses outside of the existing organization), which will eventually lead the industry. Both streams are coordinated for a coherent and comprehensive outcome.

DISCOVER

During the first five weeks, participants come up with ideas for the transformation process, evaluating them as they go in order to identify the best options.

DISRUPT

The best ideas are presented at the halfway point of the ExO Sprint, a session designed to obtain feedback, improve the initiatives and select the best ones for further development.

BUILD

Throughout the second five weeks, participants build prototypes around the top-ranked initiatives.

LAUNCH

At the close of the final week, participants present the top initiatives to the company's leadership team and secure funding for those that are ultimately approved.

Note that the 10 weeks that comprise the core of the ExO Sprint are designed in such a way that the team generates as many ideas as possible during the first half of the ExO Sprint, with the second half dedicated to the most promising initiatives. This follows the innovation best practice of generation/synthesis.

FOLLOW-UP PHASE

The resulting ExO initiatives are implemented. Some will be set up within the existing organization, others on the edge (i.e., outside the organization).

EXO EDGE INITIATIVES

EXO CORE INITIATIVES

ExO Initiatives (Core vs. Edge)

The outcome of the ExO Sprint will be a set of ExO initiatives that will transform the company into an Exponential Organization, or even a set of them.

As outlined before, the ExO Sprint entails two different work streams: The ExO Core Stream generates initiatives to adapt the current organization to external industry disruption, while the ExO Edge Stream generates initiatives that will disrupt the market by launching new Exponential Organizations.

During the 10-week process, ExO Sprint participants will come up with a lot of different ideas, some of which will result in initiatives. In this section, we explain how to differentiate between ExO Core Initiatives and ExO Edge Initiatives. We will also describe some of the subtypes to help ExO Sprint participants better understand the implications of each kind of initiative in order to achieve the best possible results.

You can differentiate between the two types of ExO initiatives—Core and Edge—by asking and answering one question. You will then be able to differentiate among the different subtypes of ExO Core/Edge Initiatives by asking and answering a second question.

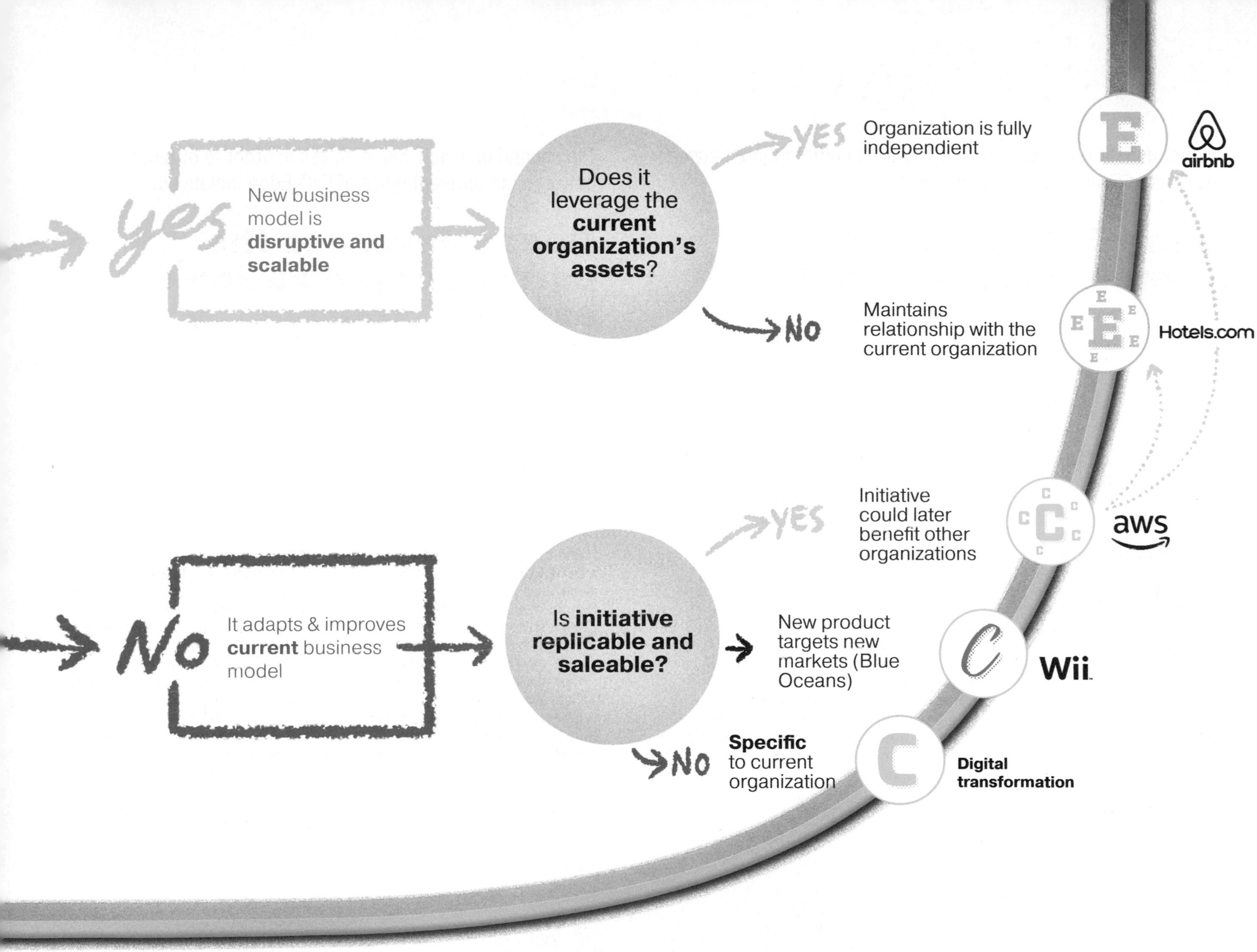

yes

New business model is **disruptive and scalable**

Does it leverage the **current organization's assets**?

→ YES → Organization is fully independient

→ **No** → Maintains relationship with the current organization

No

It adapts & improves **current** business model

Is **initiative replicable and saleable?**

→ YES → Initiative could later benefit other organizations

→ New product targets new markets (Blue Oceans)

→ **No** → **Specific** to current organization

airbnb

Hotels.com

aws

Wii

Digital transformation

The first question you must to ask in order to differentiate between ExO Core Initiatives and ExO Edge Initiatives:

Is the ExO initiative a new business model?

The second question you must ask in order to differentiate between the different types of ExO Edge Initiatives:

Does it leverage the current organization's assets?

If the answer is yes, and this new business model is disruptive (i.e., it challenges how the industry or current organization works) and scalable (it can reach a global scale quickly), the project will be an ExO Edge Initiative. Note that if the business model is different but not disruptive/scalable, even though the initiative might not result in an Exponential Organization, you can still develop it as an ExO Edge Initiative. The important thing is not to build anything within the current organization that uses a different business model. That, of course, will trigger the corporate immune system to attack.

If the answer is no, and the initiative is in line with your existing business model, the project will be an ExO Core Initiative. There are several ways to improve the existing business model, including launching a new product or service (with the same business/revenue model) or improving the current service or operations of the company by applying exponential technologies and/or ExO attributes.

If the answer is no, the initiative is a **Pure Edge Initiative**, meaning it will become an independent Exponential Organization whose growth will not be constrained by the original organization's (or other, similar organizations') assets or size. An example of an ExO Pure Edge Initiative would be an Airbnb-type business launched by an existing hotel chain, since this new platform wouldn't leverage existing assets, instead relying on those of others (i.e., private owners' houses and rooms).

If the answer is yes, the initiative is a **Linked Edge Initiative** and will maintain a relationship with the main organization (and perhaps other, similar organizations), leveraging some of that organization's assets such as existing clients, facilities, physical assets and data. An example of an ExO Linked Edge Initiative might be a hotel chain that launches an online portal similar to Hotels.com, offering available rooms to internet users. The new company, operating at the edge of the parent organization, could then use its platform to team up with competitors and offer their rooms as well.

When it comes to ExO Core Initiatives, the question to ask in order to differentiate among the different types:

Is it a replicable and saleable initiative for other organizations?

If the answer is yes, —meaning that you could both implement the ExO initiative within your existing organization and eventually sell it to other organizations—you have an **Edge Core Initiative**. For example, Amazon Web Services (AWS), which is today used by companies all over the world, grew out of an internal project initiated by the company to develop a set of network services to improve its own IT infrastructure. Amazon subsequently launched AWS as a new business to address the same need in other organizations. The takeaway? ExO Core Initiatives initially developed within a company can evolve into ExO Edge enterprises that can be further developed beyond the parent organization.

If the answer is no, because the ExO initiative is specific to your current organization and implementing it elsewhere wouldn't result in a scalable business model, you have a **Pure Core Initiative**. An example: running a digital transformation project to digitalize all paper records. Another example: using AI-based algorithms to automate an organization's various processes.

ExO initiatives can also be new products or services developed under an organization's existing business model. Usually these new products or services, called **Blue Core Initiatives**, tackle new markets. In fact, launching new product or service represents an opportunity for an organization to follow a Blue Ocean Strategy (outlined in greater detail later in the book) and create new markets where competition is limited or even nonexistent. A great example is the Nintendo Wii, which moved beyond a focus on complex graphics in video games and found a new and highly profitable customer segment in aging baby boomers drawn by the ability to physically interact with onscreen golf, tennis, baseball and additional gameplay.

Last but not least, note that these are simply guidelines to help ExO Sprint participants classify and shape their ExO initiatives in accordance with the individual ExO Sprint streams.

> Think of the Edge and Core Streams as ExO Wild and ExO Mild, respectively. You will be leaving the box far, far behind as you create your ExO Edge Initiatives. ExO Core Initiatives, on the other hand, have constraints, as they need to both respect the current business model and maintain the organization's existing assets.

ExO Sprint Roles

During an ExO Sprint, key roles are filled both from within and outside the organization.

As noted earlier, people from within the organization are key to maintaining the DNA of the company; their presence will help suppress the corporate immune response. Remember: organizational transformation is all about transforming the people who work for the organization.

At the same time, you'll also need to recruit people from outside the organization if you are to access the necessary knowledge and expertise required to run your ExO Sprint. As outlined before, there's no way all the smartest and most talented people in the world already work for you. As a result, you'll need to connect your project to the external community.

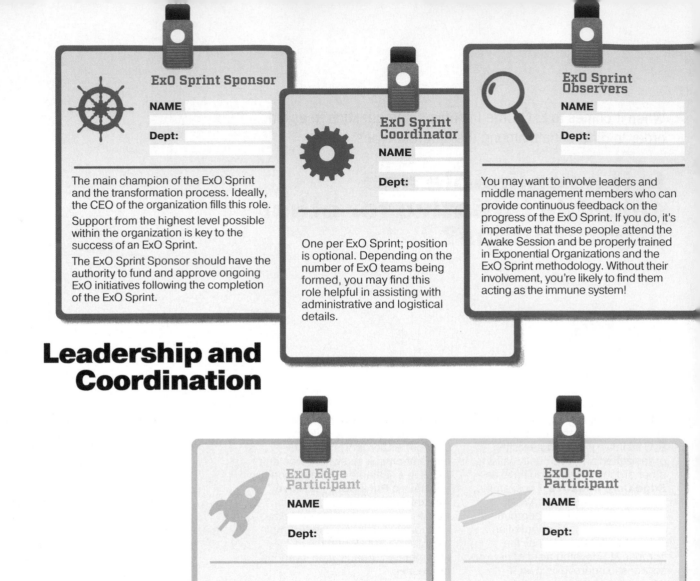

Leadership and Coordination

ExO Sprint Sponsor

NAME

Dept:

The main champion of the ExO Sprint and the transformation process. Ideally, the CEO of the organization fills this role.

Support from the highest level possible within the organization is key to the success of an ExO Sprint.

The ExO Sprint Sponsor should have the authority to fund and approve ongoing ExO initiatives following the completion of the ExO Sprint.

ExO Sprint Coordinator

NAME

Dept:

One per ExO Sprint; position is optional. Depending on the number of ExO teams being formed, you may find this role helpful in assisting with administrative and logistical details.

ExO Sprint Observers

NAME

Dept:

You may want to involve leaders and middle management members who can provide continuous feedback on the progress of the ExO Sprint. If you do, it's imperative that these people attend the Awake Session and be properly trained in Exponential Organizations and the ExO Sprint methodology. Without their involvement, you're likely to find them acting as the immune system!

Team Members

ExO Edge Participant

NAME

Dept:

A member of an ExO Edge team, which is comprised of four to six members.

ExO Core Participant

NAME

Dept:

A member of an ExO Core team, which is also comprised of four to six members.

External Support

The team running the ExO Sprint will benefit from complementary support from and access to external resources.

ExO Head Coach

NAME

One per ExO Sprint. Oversees execution and provides support to individual ExO Coaches. Ensures that results are cohesive and that objectives are met. Has a good understanding of the ExO model and approach.

ExO Coaches

NAME

One per team. Facilitate the process by supporting individuals in understanding and successfully completing exercises and assignments.

ExO Disruptors

NAME

Those with a strong understanding of innovation in general and about the ExO model in particular. Can provide teams with feedback about their ExO initiatives during the Disruption Session and Launch Session. Should be independent of the organization and its leadership.

External Advisors

NAME

Respond to particular requests for topic-specific insight and expertise in exponential technologies and ExO attributes. Should be available throughout the course of the ExO Sprint and depending on the specific needs of the team.

ExO Speakers

NAME

ExO expert(s) able to deliver a "shock and awe" talk at the Awake Session and/or Disruption Session(s). Position is optional.

ExO Trainer

NAME

Runs the Align Session to train the ExO Sprint participants on the ExO framework, processes and tools that they will use during the ExO Sprint. Position is optional.

Setting up your ExO Sprint Teams

What **external** resources do you need to support your ExO Sprint teams?

For each ExO Sprint team, you need an **ExO Coach** for daily and weekly support.

What **internal** resources do you need to structure your ExO Sprint teams?

If you are a
LEADING ORGANIZATION

that wants not only to transform yourself but also to transform your industry (and perhaps even create new industries), you'll need:

Two Edge teams and two Core teams, each with between four and six members. Note that you can run an ExO Sprint with more or fewer teams (e.g., one Edge team and one Core team), or with a different balance of Edge/Core teams (e.g., one Edge team and three Core teams), depending on your goals. However, experience has taught us that setting up two Edge teams and two Core teams is generally the best approach.

A project sponsor representing the highest level of the organization impacted; sponsor should have the authority to make funding decisions at the close of the ExO Sprint.

A project coordinator to provide project cohesion and manage administrative and logistical details.

You need an **ExO Head Coach** who will oversee, coordinate and support all ExO Coaches.

You need a set of **ExO Disruptors** for the Disruption Session and the Launch Session.

We also recommend providing your ExO Sprint teams with access to external ExO Advisors, specialists offering expertise in different technologies, industries and innovation methodologies.

If you are an
ESTABLISHED ORGANIZATION

that wants to keep your business safe by transforming it to adapt it to external industry disruption, you'll need:

Two Core teams, each with between four and six members. Note that you can run the ExO Sprint with more or fewer teams (one or even four Core teams), depending on your goals. However, experience has taught us that setting up two Core teams is generally the best approach.

A project sponsor representing the highest level of the organization impacted; sponsor should have the authority to make funding decisions at the close of the ExO Sprint.

A project coordinator to provide project cohesion and manage administrative and logistical details.

If you are an
ENTREPRENEUR

who wants to disrupt an industry by launching a new business with a goal of becoming an Exponential Organization, you'll need:

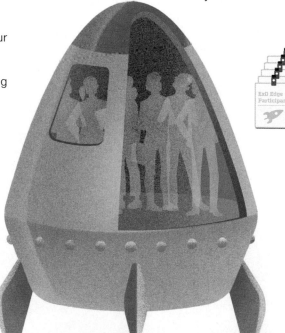

One Edge team (made up of between four and six members) focused on a single MTP.

IT Tools Supporting the ExO Sprint

One of the primary aims of the ExO model is to increase organizational agility by implementing new technologies. The ExO Sprint is a perfect opportunity for teams to experiment with social technologies and discover their benefits firsthand.

Given the pace and intensity of the ExO Sprint assignments, teams must be able to share files and collaborate in real time. If the ExO Sprint teams are geographically dispersed, tools for virtual communication and collaboration are essential.

The experience and outcomes of an ExO Sprint reach entirely new levels with access to relevant resources and when using the right tools to support the process.

Here are some tools that can help you run your ExO Sprint more successfully and that enable teams to organize and connect.

www.slack.com

Slack is a tool for messaging and more that can help your ExO Sprint team members share resources and easily communicate.

Main feature for the ExO Sprint:

Communication

Google Drive

www.google.com/drive

Google Drive is a file storage and synchronization service. It allows users to store files on their servers, synchronize files across devices and share files. Google Docs, Google Sheets and Google Slides enable team members to collaborate on Sprint assignments concurrently.

Main features for the ExO Sprint:

Document management and collaboration

zoom

www.zoom.us

An enterprise video communications system, Zoom offers an easy-to-use and reliable cloud-based platform for video and audio conferencing, chat and webinars across mobile, desktop and room systems.

Main features for the ExO Sprint:

Scheduled and ad hoc video conferencing communication

Keep in mind that these are only a few examples of the many tools that can help you to run an ExO Sprint. Feel free to use others as well.

 **exolever**

www.exolever.com

ExO Lever is a global transformation ecosystem that provides certified ExO staff on demand (ExO Coaches, ExO Advisors, etc.) and other resources for running an ExO Sprint. Its platform also offers tools designed to encourage team collaboration.

Main features for the ExO Sprint:

Access to certified ExO staff on demand

ExO resources

ExO tools

ExO processes

Communication

File management

Preparation Phase

It's time to think big—to go outside your comfort zone to where the magic happens.

Innovators, particularly young innovators, are building new products and services that can disrupt entire industries, or even create new ones. Examples include Danit Peleg, who designed the first 3D printed fashion collection when she was 25, and Jack Andraka, who as a 15-year-old conducted award-winning work on a potential method to detect the early stages of pancreatic and other cancers.

Now it's your turn. Start dreaming…It's the only way to achieve anything!

Running a successful ExO Sprint depends on setting the right foundation. Use the preparation phase to define the goals for the ExO Sprint and make sure all elements and logistics are in place to achieve them.

The preparation phase typically takes between two and eight weeks depending on the scope of the ExO Sprint and the size of your organization.

Plan

What do we want to accomplish ?

To reinvent the industry and transform our organization so that it's able to adapt to external industry disruption. Creating ExOs will allow us to build a new global ecosystem.

If so, run the full ExO Sprint with Edge teams and Core teams.

To transform our organization so that it's able to adapt to external industry disruption, which will help us to adapt our organization to existing ecosystems.

If so, run the ExO Sprint with two Core teams.

SCOPE DEFINITION

What are we trying to transform ?

The organization as a whole, including all markets and industries in which it is positioned.

A specific business unit focused on a particular industry.

To launch an ExO or multiple ExOs in order to transform the industry.

If so, run the ExO Sprint with one Edge team focused on the ExO(s) you want to build and launch.

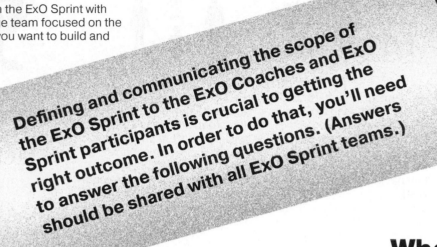

Defining and communicating the scope of the ExO Sprint to the ExO Coaches and ExO Sprint participants is crucial to getting the right outcome. In order to do that, you'll need to answer the following questions. (Answers should be shared with all ExO Sprint teams.)

What's our playground

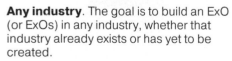

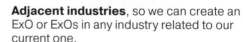

Any industry. The goal is to build an ExO (or ExOs) in any industry, whether that industry already exists or has yet to be created.

Note that this approach will provide outcomes (new ExO Edge Initiatives) far beyond those feasible with your existing business.

Adjacent industries, so we can create an ExO or ExOs in any industry related to our current one.

This option gives you the opportunity of leveraging existing assets or relationships that will aid your foray into adjacent industries.

Our current industry, with a goal of creating an ExO.

If you are also trying to reinvent an industry, any ExOs you launch as the result of the ExO Sprint might well disrupt your own organization. Nonetheless, this would still represent a successful outcome, because if you don't disrupt, someone else certainly will. In fact, the best thing you can do is disrupt your own organization, thereby creating the next leading enterprise within your industry.

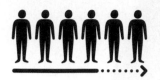

Optimal team size is four to six participants per team.

10-20 hrs

All team participants should be available to spend a minimum of 10 hours per week on the ExO Sprint (we recommend approximately 20 hours per week). The workload should be spaced throughout the week.

Each team should select a coordinator to represent the group and ensure that assignments are progressing on schedule. Some teams may choose to rotate this role weekly, which gives each team member the opportunity to take on the role once or twice during the 10-week process.

Having two Edge teams and two Core teams not only creates friendly competition but also adds to the range of resulting initiatives.

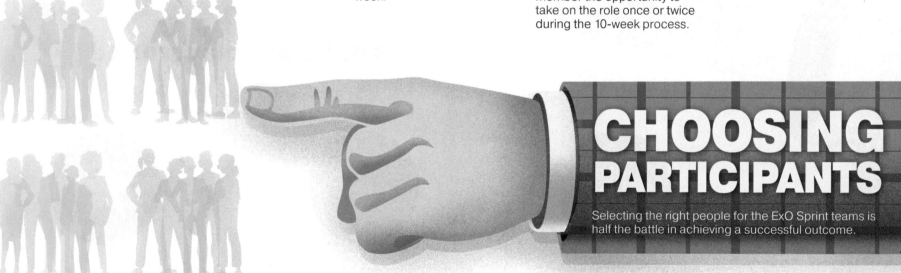

CHOOSING PARTICIPANTS

Selecting the right people for the ExO Sprint teams is half the battle in achieving a successful outcome.

Form as many teams as you feel is practical for your organization. Anywhere from two to six teams is generally a good number, although experience has shown that four teams (two Edge and two Core) seems to be optimal. Remember that each team consists of anywhere from four to six people and is focused on either the Edge Stream or the Core Stream.

When you were considering the number of staff to commit to the ExO Sprint, what came up for you? Did it feel as though you were pulling too many senior people away from their daily commitments for too long? What does that tell you about where current priorities lie for running existing operations as opposed to making space for a project designed to prevent disruption?

Each team will require different kinds of people and talent:

CORE STREAM TEAMS REQUIRE:

Senior leadership and middle management members who can lead the resulting initiatives at the conclusion of the ExO Sprint.

EDGE STREAM TEAMS REQUIRE:

Young leaders, creative thinkers and intrapreneurs who are enthusiastic about innovation. In general, the younger, the better, although keep in mind that great candidates can also be found among more senior employees.

People with previous entrepreneurial experience. If you are running the ExO Sprint for an existing organization, include entrepreneurs from outside the organization who can provide different points of view and facilitate disruptive thinking.

Members from different areas of the organization.

Personnel with different areas of expertise.

People who can jump into managing the ExO Edge Initiatives that grow out of the ExO Sprint. Remember that these initiatives will result in new companies operating at the edge of the main organization.

Optional: One or more entrepreneurs from outside the organization. Input from beyond company walls results in more disruptive ideas.

SETTING A SCHEDULE

Create a schedule of dates and daily flow before launching your ExO Sprint. Ensuring that all participants are committed to the schedule is crucial to its smooth execution.

Key events to schedule:

Awake Session

The ExO Sprint kickoff. We highly recommended conducting the kickoff as an in-person session; the event takes anywhere from one hour to a full day.

Align Session

Optional as an in-person meeting. Session can be either a set of in-person training sessions to educate participants about the processes and tools that they will use during the ExO Sprint, or a series of learning activities (online research, reading books and/or watching videos).

Disruption Session

The midpoint of the ExO Sprint. Teams share their initiatives with other ExO Sprint participants, the company's leadership team and a panel of ExO Disruptors to receive valuable feedback and input for improvement.

Launch Session

Teams present the final version of their ExO initiatives to the company's leadership team. Initiatives are then selected and funded for continued development.

Scheduling Tips

 Maintain focus and momentum by scheduling the 10-week ExO Sprint away from major holidays and traditional vacation periods.

 Avoid scheduling the 10-week ExO Sprint during an organization's busy season.

 If the ExO Sprint does overlap with seasonal holidays or vacations, put it on hold as needed until everyone is back at work. It's best to pause the ExO Sprint for a week to accommodate a major public holiday, as the weekly workload can be too heavy for short weeks, when many employees take vacation time.

 Although not mandatory, it's a good idea to fit the ExO Sprint within a particular quarter.

Weekly Meetings

 ### Weekly assignment communication:

Each team receives a weekly assignment. We recommend posting assignments every Monday morning.

Team meetings:

 Each team should arrange a set of meetings to check progress and assign work. We recommend at least 30 minutes for meetings or calls at the beginning of each workday to track progress and define next steps for the day.

Assignment delivery:

Each team will deliver its assignment to the team's ExO Coach, who will review it and provide feedback. Feedback should focus on process, not content, and may include next steps to improve delivery for the following week. We recommend the ExO Coach receive updates every Thursday. The ExO Coach should then conduct a one-hour call with the team on Friday to review deliverables and provide feedback.

CREATING SPACE

It's best for ExO Sprint participants operate outside their usual habits and patterns. You also want to encourage them as they come together as a new group with a mandate to craft the organization's future. Support this cohesion and mandate by creating a functional, dedicated and appealing workspace— its walls papered with work in progress—that encourages creativity. This can be as simple as providing a meeting room for the team's private use or as elaborate as creating an off-site workspace.

A dedicated space gives ExO Sprint participants a place to meet and promotes interaction between members of different teams. It is also likely to prompt conversations with employees outside the ExO Sprint, drawing interest and giving team members a chance to share, discuss and test the ideas they're working on.

In addition to the physical space, setting up a virtual space is also critical. Virtual space creates a foundation for working productively and collaboratively. Ensure that ExO Sprint participants have easy access to video conferencing, messaging and document sharing with real-time document collaboration. Use of these social technologies is integral to the ExO Sprint process and is standard to ExOs in general.

Not all teams will be located together in one space. For geographically distributed teams, the virtual space and tools are even more important. To establish and cement personal connections, however, it's important that ExO teams gather in person for the Awake Session and the Align Session. It's also helpful if they are able to spend time together before the Disruption Session and Launch Session presentations.

EMBRACING GUIDING PRINCIPLES

1 Inspiring creativity and boldness

2 Thinking beyond the existing organization

3 Working in collaboration across hierarchy and function

4 Embracing speed, feedback, experimentation, constant learning and new methods

5 Respecting everyone's ideas. Every idea is a good idea!

6 Using new tools to communicate and being open to new patterns of working together

An ExO Sprint introduces a different process, one that will likely be new to your organization. Creating the mindset to thrive in the midst of change requires commitment to the following principles.

7

Understanding that "failure" holds valuable learning

8

Being okay with sharing and seeing prototypes and MVPs—by definition, they're flawed and unrefined!

9

Challenging personal boundaries

10

Allowing yourself to be uncomfortable

11

Understanding that failure and frustration is part of the process

READINESS CHECKLIST

Are you ready? Before starting an ExO Sprint, make sure that you are able to answer all questions from the planning phase.

1 **What is our playground? Is it our own industry? Any industry? Adjacent industries?**

_____
_____
_____

2 **What are we trying to transform? The whole organization? A specific business unit?**

_____
_____
_____

3 **What do we want to accomplish? Do we want to reinvent the industry and our organization? To transform our organization? To launch a new ExO? To launch multiple ExOs?**

_____
_____
_____

4 **Do we have a list of participants for all teams?**

☐ Yes   ☐ No

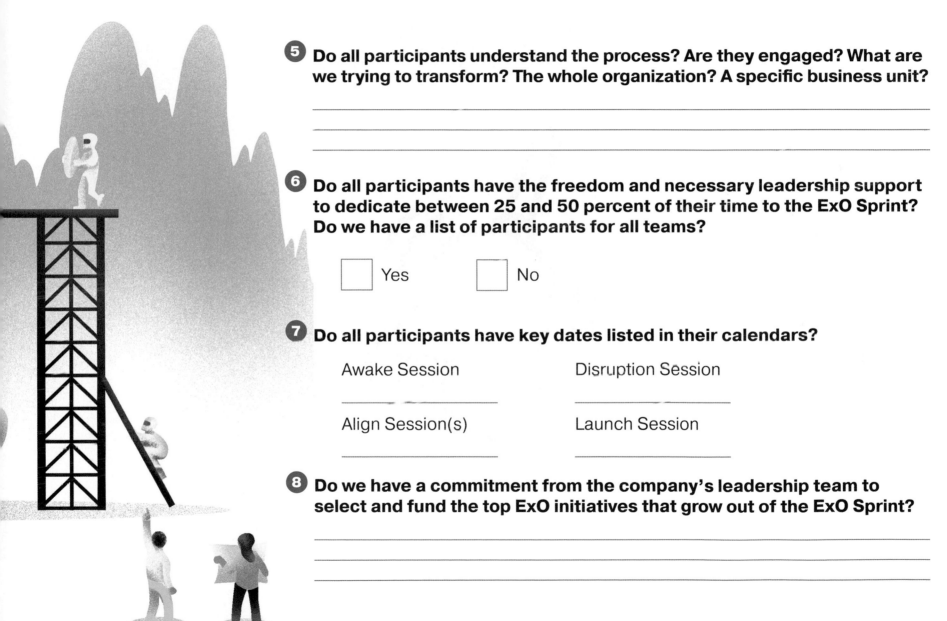

⑤ Do all participants understand the process? Are they engaged? What are we trying to transform? The whole organization? A specific business unit?

_____

_____

_____

⑥ Do all participants have the freedom and necessary leadership support to dedicate between 25 and 50 percent of their time to the ExO Sprint? Do we have a list of participants for all teams?

☐ Yes   ☐ No

⑦ Do all participants have key dates listed in their calendars?

Awake Session   Disruption Session

_____   _____

Align Session(s)   Launch Session

_____   _____

⑧ Do we have a commitment from the company's leadership team to select and fund the top ExO initiatives that grow out of the ExO Sprint?

_____

_____

_____

Awake

AWAKE

One of the key elements of the ExO Sprint is making your organization aware of what's happening in the world and what to do about it. Time to awaken the organization!

The goal is to ensure that the members of your organization understand why it's so important to transform the enterprise. Everyone involved in the process should comprehend how external industry disruption might affect the industry, the difference between linear and exponential thinking, the tremendous opportunities exponential technologies bring in the form of abundance and how to take advantage of that abundance by building Exponential Organizations.

The format of this session should be an in-person event, focused on Exponential Organizations, emerging technologies and industry disruption. It might also include hands-on exercises to facilitate understanding.

Who should attend? An organization's stakeholders, the top leadership, mid-level managers and all ExO Sprint participants. Anyone else interested should be invited as well. The more people within the organization who get the message, the wider awake it will be as a whole.

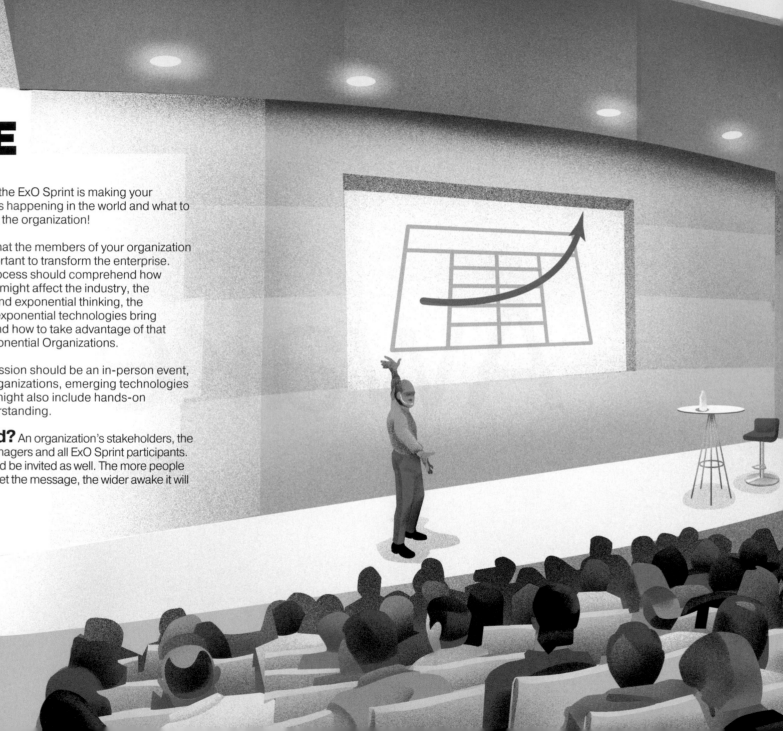

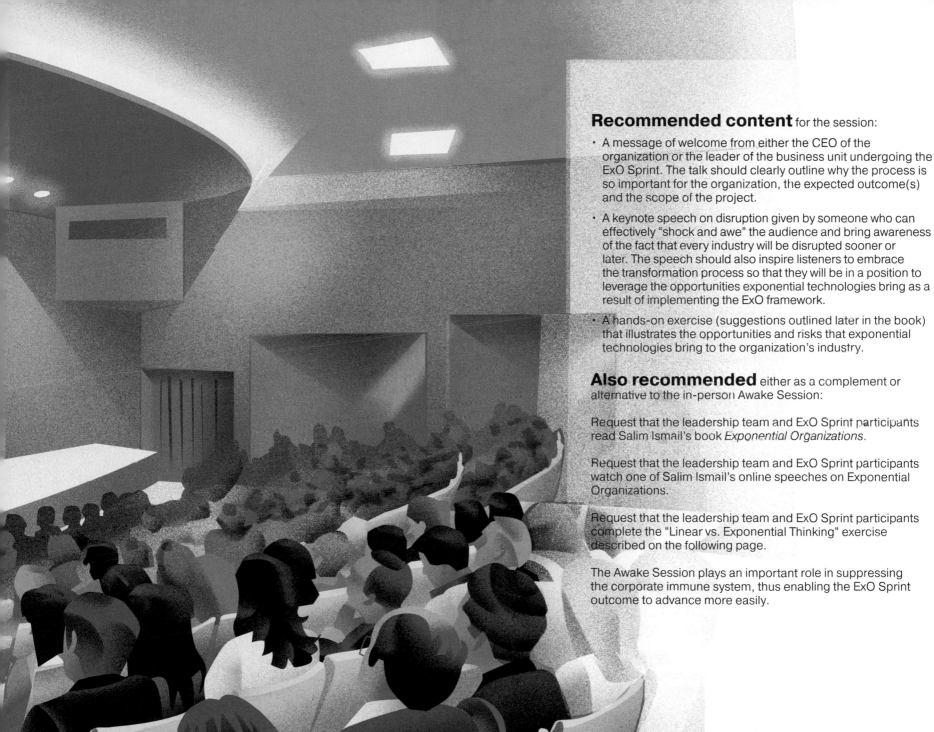

Recommended content for the session:

- A message of welcome from either the CEO of the organization or the leader of the business unit undergoing the ExO Sprint. The talk should clearly outline why the process is so important for the organization, the expected outcome(s) and the scope of the project.

- A keynote speech on disruption given by someone who can effectively "shock and awe" the audience and bring awareness of the fact that every industry will be disrupted sooner or later. The speech should also inspire listeners to embrace the transformation process so that they will be in a position to leverage the opportunities exponential technologies bring as a result of implementing the ExO framework.

- A hands-on exercise (suggestions outlined later in the book) that illustrates the opportunities and risks that exponential technologies bring to the organization's industry.

Also recommended either as a complement or alternative to the in-person Awake Session:

Request that the leadership team and ExO Sprint participants read Salim Ismail's book *Exponential Organizations*.

Request that the leadership team and ExO Sprint participants watch one of Salim Ismail's online speeches on Exponential Organizations.

Request that the leadership team and ExO Sprint participants complete the "Linear vs. Exponential Thinking" exercise described on the following page.

The Awake Session plays an important role in suppressing the corporate immune system, thus enabling the ExO Sprint outcome to advance more easily.

Awake

EXERCISE: Linear vs. Exponential Thinking

The goal of this exercise is to ensure that the organization's leadership team and all ExO Sprint participants understand exponential thinking and its implications.

Description

According to Moore's Law, the performance of anything powered by information technologies doubles, on average, every two years. Looked at from a theoretical point of view, it's easy to understand that technologies evolve in an exponential way. Meaning, for example, that the computing power of our phones may double every couple of years.

However, because our brains work in a linear way, it can be difficult for humans to grasp exponentials. For example, if you want to know how many meters you will travel taking 30 linear steps (one meter per step), the answer is easy: 30 meters (one step, 1 meter; two steps, 2 meters; three steps, 3 meters; and so on). But if you want to know how many meters you'll advance taking 30 exponential steps, the answer is not as easy to calculate: one step, 1 meter; two steps 2 meters; three steps, 4 meters; four steps, 8 meters; and so on, for a total of 1,073,741,824 meters. Who knows where you'll land after taking those 30 exponential steps. (You'd need a calculator to figure out that they equate to more than 26 trips around the world!)

Assuming a 1-meter-long stride, 30 linear steps...

Assuming a 1-meter-long stride, 30 exponential steps will take you around the world more than 26 times

The key point about exponential technologies is understanding the implications they can have for your organization and industry. The result is often impossible to predict, but you should at least have the right mindset to understand the implications of exponentials.

Experts often fail at predicting the future of their fields. Why? They make a linear correlation from the past to the future and mistakenly assume that straight-line growth, rather than exponential growth, will continue.

■ Exercise

Apply linear thinking to the examples below and use exponential thinking to consider the implications. Next, take an exponential view in considering the implications.

Example	Linear Thinking	Exponential Thinking	Implications of Exponentials
How many meters will you advance if you take 30 linear steps of 1 meter each? What if the steps are exponential instead?	If you take 30 linear steps, you'll advance 30 meters from your starting point.	If you take 30 exponential steps, you'll advance 1,073,741,824 meters from your starting point.	Thirty exponential steps will take you around the world more than 26 times, which means it's almost impossible to figure out exactly where you will end up.
In early 2018 Boeing drones could carry as much as 200 kg of cargo; in 2017 they carried just 100 kg. How much might they carry in another eight years?			
The first full genome was sequenced in 2001 for $100 million. That sequencing could be done for less than $1,000 in 2017. How much might it cost in another 10 years?			
Cost per room for a new economy-rate hotel (based on a traditional, linear business model) averages $90,000. How much might it cost Airbnb (an Exponential Organization) to add a new room to its platform?			

Taking into account an exponential evolution, drones should be able to carry up to 50,000 kg eight years from now. Consider also that batteries should evolve at an exponential rate, which means that in just a few years, we're likely to see drones capable of carrying containers weighing some 30,000 kg.

In just a few years, the ability to sequence DNA will be cheap (and fast) enough to enable access to DNA-based medicine, also known as personalized medicine. Such technological advancements will render current medical diagnostic methods and treatments obsolete.

By applying the ExO approach—and the Leveraged Asset attribute, in particular—Airbnb can reduce the cost of supply to almost zero. The implications of using exponential technologies to disrupt the hotel industry are enormous (which is why in 2017 Airbnb became the largest hotel chain in the world).

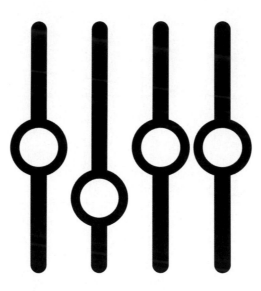

Align

ALIGN

Before starting your transformation journey, you need to master the tools and processes that will make you successful.

The goal of the Align Session is to provide ExO Sprint team participants with the knowledge and confidence needed to define and develop ExO initiatives throughout the 10-week process. Equally important is to provide the company's leadership team with the knowledge and training to manage disruptive innovation and new Exponential Organizations.

The ideal format entails in-person training sessions. Training consists of a mix of theoretical sessions and hands-on exercises to help participants learn by doing. Another option is to have the ExO Sprint participants and leadership members learn via online research, documents, books and videos.

Who should participate? At a minimum, all ExO Sprint participants should receive Align training. It's also recommended that the company's leadership team receive the same training (or at least a pared-down version).

Recommended content:

ExO Sprint participants should be familiar with the following:

CONCEPTS

- Exponential Organizations
- ExO Attributes
- ExO Core Initiatives vs. ExO Edge Initiatives

TOOLS:

- ExO Canvas
- Business Model Canvas
- Blue Ocean Strategy Canvas

PROCESSES:

- Build-Measure-Learn Loop
- Customer Development Process

RECOMMENDED READING:

- *Exponential Organizations: Why New Organizations Are Ten Times Better, Faster, and Cheaper Than Yours (And What to Do About It)*, by Salim Ismail
- *Abundance: The Future Is Better Than You Think*, by Peter Diamandis
- *The Lean Startup: How Today's Entrepreneurs Use Continuous Innovation to Create Radically Successful Businesses*, by Eric Ries
- *Business Model Generation: A Handbook for Visionaries, Game Changers, and Challengers*, by Alex Osterwalder
- *The Startup Owner's Manual: The Step-by-Step Guide for Building A Great Company*, by Steve Blank

The management team will need to cultivate an exponential mindset and understand the ExO framework. It should thus be familiar with:

CONCEPTS

- Exponential leadership (linear vs. exponential mindset)
- Exponential Organization management (search vs. execution)
- Balancing innovation/risk: ExO Core and ExO Edge processes

RECOMMENDED READING:

- *Exponential Organizations: Why New Organizations Are Ten Times Better, Faster, and Cheaper Than Yours (And What to Do About It)*, by Salim Ismail
- *Abundance: The Future Is Better Than You Think*, by Peter Diamandis

As an alternative to in-person training—

and recommended as a complement to it—ExO Sprint participants can complete the following exercises, which explore the concepts, processes and tools recommended for executing an ExO Sprint.

EXERCISE: ExO Core/Edge Initiatives Ideation

The goal of this exercise is to help ExO Sprint participants understand the difference between ExO Edge Initiatives and ExO Core Initiatives.

Description

Both ExO Edge Initiatives and ExO Core Initiatives will be generated during the course of an ExO Sprint. While the goal with ExO Edge Initiatives is to create new and scalable businesses that have the potential to disrupt an industry by leveraging exponential technologies, ExO Core Initiatives help an existing organization adapt to external industry disruption and become more agile.

■ Exercise

Choose a sample organization (not your own) for the following exercises. It's best to choose a company that offers a product or service, such as a bank or retail business; B2C business models are comparatively easy to analyze from the outside.

The idea is to generate ideas for ExO initiatives that will help the organization adapt to external industry disruption (ExO Core Initiatives), and to create new and scalable business models that can disrupt an industry by leveraging exponential technologies (ExO Edge Initiatives).

ExO Initiative Name	Brief Description	ExO Initiative Type	Impact

EXERCISE: ExO Canvas Design

The goal of this exercise is to have ExO Sprint participants practice applying the ExO Canvas to a real use case.

Description

As described earlier, the ExO Canvas is a tool to help visionaries, innovators, top executives and entrepreneurs design new Exponential Organizations on one page. The ExO Canvas requires an MTP and makes use of the 10 ExO attributes.

■ Exercise

Using one of the ExO initiatives defined in the previous exercise, fill in the ExO Canvas, taking into consideration applicable ExO attributes.

We recommend using an ExO Edge Initiative so that you can think about how to connect this new organization to abundance (using the SCALE attributes). Next, consider how to manage it (applying the IDEAS attributes).

MASSIVE TRANSFORMATIVE PURPOSE (MTP)

INFORMATION	STAFF ON DEMAND	INTERFACES	IMPLEMENTATION
	COMMUNITY & CROWD	DASHBOARDS	
	ALGORITHMS	EXPERIMENTATION	
	LEVERAGED ASSETS	AUTONOMY	
	ENGAGEMENT	SOCIAL TECHNOLOGIES	

EXERCISE: Business Model Canvas Design

The goal of this exercise is to provide ExO Sprint participants with a basic understanding of what a business model is and how to design one using the Business Model Canvas.

Description

By definition, a business model describes how an organization creates, delivers and captures value so that it is a profitable (or at least a sustainable) entity.

The Business Model Canvas, originated by business theorist and entrepreneur Alex Osterwalder, is a tool for developing new—or documenting existing—business models on one page. It is made up of nine elements, or blocks:

 Customer Segments: The different groups of people or organizations an enterprise aims to reach and serve.

 Value Proposition: The bundle of products and services that create value for a specific Customer Segment.

 Channel: How to communicate with and reach each Customer Segment to deliver a Value Proposition.

 Customer Relationship: The types of relationships a company establishes with specific Customer Segments.

 Revenue Streams: The cash a company generates from each Customer Segment.

 Key Resources: The most important assets required to make a business model work.

 Key Activities: The most important things a company must do to make its business model work.

 Key Partners: The network of suppliers and partners that make the business model work.

 Cost Structure: All costs incurred to operate a business model.

For more information, check out the book *Business Model Generation* by Alex Osterwalder.

■ Exercise

Using one of the ExO Edge Initiatives defined earlier, fill in the Business Model Canvas. Further define the initiative while thinking about how the different ExO attributes can be applied.

Key partners	Key activities	Value propositions	Customer relationships	Customer segments
	Key resources		**Channels**	

Cost structure	Revenue streams

EXERCISE: Blue Ocean Strategy Canvas Design

The goal of this exercise is to provide ExO Sprint participants with a basic understanding of the Blue Ocean Strategy and how to use the Blue Ocean Strategy Canvas.

Description

Blue Ocean Strategy is a marketing theory focused on product innovation. It stems from the idea that every industry offers opportunities to move from ultra-competitive battles around price and features (Red Ocean) to a new market reality in which competition is either nonexistent or very limited (Blue Ocean).

The Blue Ocean Strategy Canvas is a X/Y graph designed to give you an immediate snapshot of how your business, product or service stacks up against the competition. The horizontal X axis lists product attributes, or factors of competition. The vertical Y axis evaluates each product's attributes/factors of competition.

The basic idea of the Blue Ocean Strategy Canvas is to group the product/service attributes of the X axis in four categories. It's a good idea to organize the Y axis as follows:

- **Raise:** The factors of your competitors' product or service that you want to bring well above the current industry standard with your own product or service (e.g., "Price" in the Nintendo Wii graph).

- **Eliminate:** Competitor attributes that you want to eliminate from your product/service (e.g., "Hard Disk," "Dolby 5.1," "DVD" and "Connectivity" in the Nintendo Wii graph).

- **Reduce:** The existing attributes of the product/service of your competitors that you want to reduce in yours (e.g., "Processor Speed" in the Nintendo Wii graph).

- **Create:** The attributes you want to create for your product/service that don't yet exist (e.g., "Motion Controller" and "Large Public" in the Nintendo Wii graph).

To illustrate: the Nintendo Wii found a new market among older consumers (i.e., Blue Ocean) after simplifying its video game devices and adding motion sensors.

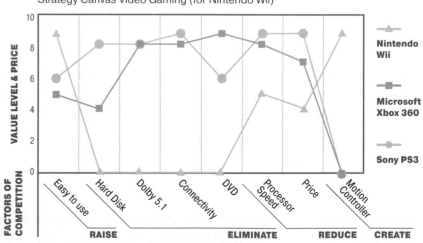

Strategy Canvas Video Gaming (for Nintendo Wii)

For more information, check out the book *Blue Ocean Strategy* by Renée Mauborgne and W. Chan Kim.

■ Exercise

Using the Blue Ocean Strategy Canvas for your case study, find an uncontested market for a hypothetical new product or service. Compare it with at least two competitors.

Blue Ocean Strategy Canvas

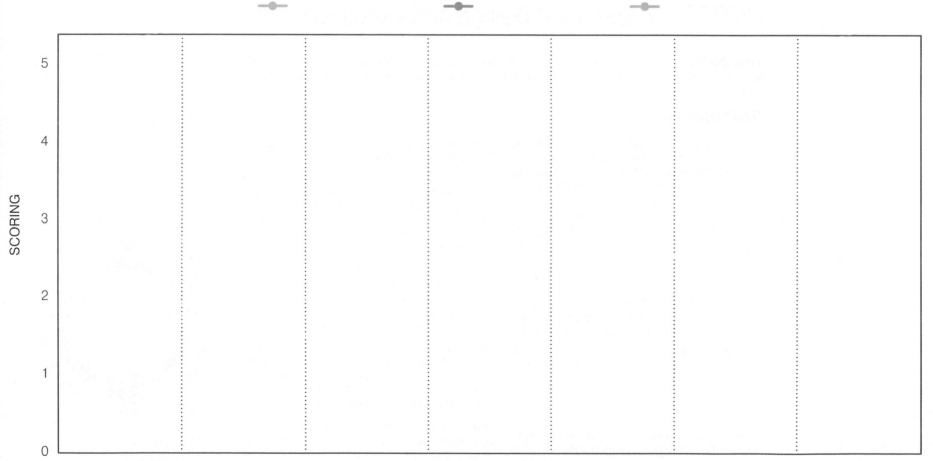

SCORING

5

4

3

2

1

0

FACTORS OF COMPETITION

Align

139

Preparation Phase

EXERCISE: Experiment Design and Execution

The goal of this exercise is to introduce the Experimentation attribute and provide ExO Sprint participants with the basic knowledge and experience needed to design and run experiments that will help them evaluate their ExO initiatives.

Description

By definition, any new innovative idea (such as an ExO initiative) is composed of a set of hypotheses. When designing a Business Model Canvas or an ExO Canvas, it's important to remember that each of the elements may be nothing more than a hypothesis. It's thus crucial to test the key hypotheses that are most relevant to a successful outcome. For example, when thinking about a new business, begin by testing the hypotheses linked to Customer Segments and the Value Propositions.

A great way to identify key hypotheses and design evaluation experiments is to follow the Customer Development model created by Steve Blank. The process is quite comprehensive, but in short: pick one Customer Segment as a hypothesis and design an interview for it.

- Ask potential customers about their needs and pain points in order to ascertain whether or not you're on the right track.

- Query potential customers on what they see as the perfect solution to their needs; they may offer ideas you've never considered.

- Describe your Value Proposition to determine whether or not potential customers like your proposed solution.

- After the interview, validate or invalidate the Customer Segment hypotheses according to whether or not the interviewees have the problem you think they do. You'll also validate or invalidate the Value Proposition hypotheses based on whether or not the interviewees like your solution.

- For more information, check out the book *Four Steps to the Epiphany* by Steve Blank.

Another good (and complementary) way to evaluate and evolve innovative ideas is to use The Lean Startup's Build-Measure-Learn loop, which should be continually executed throughout the different stages of a project. The goal here is not to validate that your ideas are right (remember: take all ego out of the equation), but to learn the truth.

Build: The first order of business is to define your ideas (hypotheses) and build experiments to test them. In the early stages, experiments might consist of little more than interviews with potential clients or stakeholders. Later experiments will result in a prototype—or even a final product.

Measure: Once you have built or designed something, it's time to test it. You'll interview potential clients and then measure the percentage who liked your ideas (hypotheses). In later executions of the loop, you'll build a Minimum Viable Product (MVP) and measure its performance.

Learn: Once all information has been gathered, you'll need to make data-based decisions about whether your ideas (hypotheses) have been validated. Regardless of the outcome, any learning is great progress. Remember that the goal is not to validate specific ideas, but to learn as much as possible in a relatively short period of time. After completing this step, you'll revisit the build stage, iterating based on your learnings and continuing to build your project.

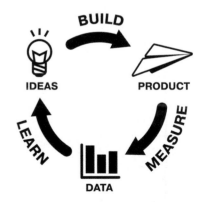

For more information, check out *The Lean Startup* by Eric Ries.

■ Exercise

Using the Business Model Canvas and one of the ExO Edge Initiatives defined earlier:

· Pick one pair from the Customer Segment/Value Proposition hypotheses.

· Design an interview (an experiment) to test the selected hypotheses. The interview should include a list of questions and evaluation criteria—usually a percentage of the Customer Segment and the Value Proposition that will indicate whether the hypothesis can be validated.

· Run the experiment to test the hypothesis.

BUILD		MEASURE		LEARN
Hypothesis	Experiment Description	Evaluation Criteria	Experiment Results	Key Learnings

Execution Phase

This next section outlines a week-by-week process that will guide you through the ExO Sprint. Remember that there are two streams in an ExO Sprint—Edge and Core—and whether you do one or both depends on your objectives.

Are you a leading organization wanting not only to transform yourself but also the industry or industries in which you operate? Perhaps even create new industries? If so, assignments for both the Edge Stream and Core Stream apply.

Are you an established organization wanting to keep your existing business safe by adapting it to external industry disruption? If so, skip ahead to the Core Stream assignments.

Are you an entrepreneur wanting to disrupt an industry by creating an Exponential Organization from the ground up? A local business looking to scale globally? In these cases, only Edge Stream assignments apply.

Regardless of your path, at the end of 10 weeks, you will have created a validated set of ExO initiatives and/or new ExOs, as well as a clear understanding of how to implement them.

When you select ExO Sprint participants, you will also decide how many Edge and Core teams to form. The number of teams determines the number of resulting initiatives. Each team will complete individual weekly assignments and come together as a group at the beginning, midpoint and end of the ExO Sprint.

As you will see, each week's assignments include a list of tasks and a resource guide that will aid in those tasks.

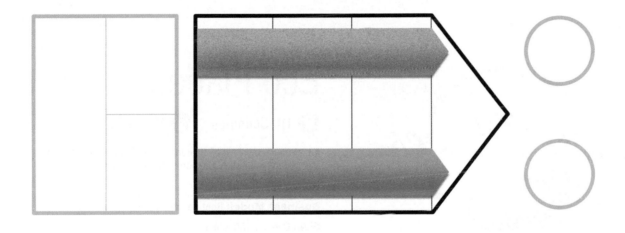

SAMPLE CASE STUDY

To help illustrate how to execute an ExO Sprint, we have created a fictitious case study. Although the tasks outlined are a simplification of those you will need to complete for your own ExO Sprint, the case study's ExO development is designed to aid understanding of the weekly assignments.

ORGANIZATION:

Eco Places

 110 Countries   10 weeks

An international chain of environmentally friendly hotels, Eco Places runs more than 500 hotels around the world

Industry: Hospitality

Business Model: Renting proprietary hotel rooms

Size: Over 25,000 rooms

Locations: 110 countries

THE EXO SPRINT:

The company's goal is to establish a leading position in the hospitality industry. After running the Preparation phase, the leadership team defined the following approach for its ExO Sprint.

SCOPE

What does Eco Places want to accomplish?

Transform the company into an organization able to keep up with external industry disruption and reinvent the hospitality industry. The company will run a full ExO Sprint encompassing both the Edge Stream and Core Stream.

What is Eco Places trying to transform?

The organization as a whole, as well as the hospitality industry.

What is the playground?

The hospitality industry, with a goal of creating ExOs within that industry.

PARTICIPANTS AND EXO TEAMS

The ExO Sprint Sponsor:
Eco Places' CEO

24 ExO Sprint Participants, organized in 4 teams:

2 ExO Edge teams, 6 members per team

2 ExO Core teams, 6 members per team

1 ExO Head Coach
overseeing the execution of the ExO Sprint and helping the ExO Coaches

4 ExO Coaches,
one per team

4 ExO Disruptors
who will provide feedback at both the Disruption Session and Launch Session

Note: This case study could be applied to any other kind of hotel chain (traditional, boutique, bed and breakfast, etc.). You don't need to go with an eco-type project to make an exponential impact and change the world for the better. Any organization can run an ExO Sprint!

EXECUTION
EDGE STREAM

Execution [Edge Stream]

The Edge Stream creates next-generation global organizations equipped to lead an existing or new industry.

FEATURES

The Edge Stream requires adopting a different mindset. While an established corporation requires control over execution and is predominantly focused on improving efficiency, creating an innovative organization requires search-based methodologies geared toward finding the right value proposition and business model capable of disrupting a specific industry.

OPPORTUNITIES

- Establish a global presence in an existing industry where you once only had a local impact

- Disrupt an existing industry, overtaking current competitors along the way

- Reinvent an existing industry

- Create a new industry

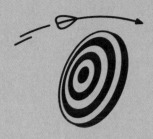

CHALLENGES

· Push people to think outside the box. We recommend bringing in entrepreneurs from outside the industry.

· Embrace failure as an inevitable part of the process and keep experimenting and iterating ideas until you find the right fit for the market.

INPUTS

· An industry or set of industries on which the new ExOs will focus. It is also possible to execute the Edge Stream without any framework, allowing teams to come up with new ExOs for any industry.

· A team of people willing and eager to spend the next 10 weeks creating new initiatives designed to build the future of an industry.

OUTPUTS

An early stage ExO or set of ExOs that will eventually disrupt and lead an industry. ExO Edge Initiatives will include:

· A high-level and detailed description of the new ExO

· A set of experiments and lessons learned

· A development roadmap

· A prototype

· Potential first clients (early adopters)

WEEK 1

Explore

WHY THIS WEEK?

The world changes every day. Exploring it can be an exciting learning experience—one that may even surprise you!

Many executives spend most of their time dealing with internal issues and never look at what's happening beyond the organization. Don't be one of them!

The biggest opportunities can be found at the intersection of global challenges (problems that need to be solved), exponential technologies (which can solve those problems) and business models (which monetize and grow your organization).

This week's assignment sets the foundation for the Edge Stream. It helps you gain a strategic overview of the world's greatest challenges along with the most important technologies that may disrupt your industry, either now or in the future. How is your industry already being reshaped? By looking "outside the building" you will gain an understanding of non-traditional and disruptive business models coming into use.

TASK 1 Explore global challenges

DESCRIPTION

Think about and research issues the world is facing, as well as the global trends related to the scope of your project (either specific to your industry or in general).

Research social needs and trends.

Social issues
- Education
- Poverty
- Energy
- Environmental
- Health
- Peace
- Human rights
- Children
- Justice

Trends
- Market
- Consumer behavior
- Competitors
- Suppliers
- Social changes
- Politics

TOOLS

Use the template in this section.

RESOURCES

Look for information about social issues on the websites of international institutions and nongovernmental organizations.

www.un.org

https://www.ngoadvisor.net/top100ngos/

TIP

Pay attention to the news! It will highlight some of the main trends facing the world in general and your industry in particular.

TASK 2 Learn about exponential technologies

DESCRIPTION

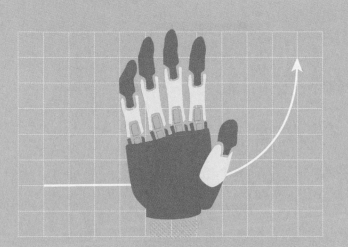

Most exponential technologies will impact your industry, either directly or indirectly. At the same time, disruption will bring new opportunities that you can and should leverage.

Consider how some of the following emerging/exponential technologies may impact (or have already impacted) your industry. Keep in mind that the list is not conclusive, since new technologies emerge every day.

- Artificial intelligence
- Robotics
- 3D printing
- Virtual reality and augmented reality
- Biotechnology and bioinformatics

- Blockchain and Bitcoin
- Nanotechnology
- Drones
- The Internet of Things
- Quantum computing

Search the internet for terms and phrases such as "disruptive technologies for [X] industry," which should yield lots of great examples.

TOOLS

Use the template in this section.

RESOURCES

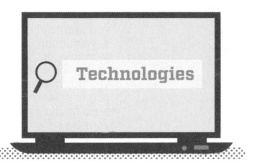

Look for recent articles on tech-focused websites. Even if the articles don't address your industry specifically, you may find connections and potential applications. Websites to review include:

MIT Technology Review:
www.technologyreview.com

Singularity University Hub:
www.singularityhub.com

Disruption Hub:
www.disruptionhub.com

Wired:
www.wired.com

TechCrunch:
www.techcrunch.com

TASK 2   Learn about exponential technologies

TIP

Subscribe to the weekly newsletters tech-focused sites offer. They will keep you apprised of the latest developments in emerging technologies. A quick scan each week keeps you informed and allows you to research further if a particular topic catches your eye.

TIP

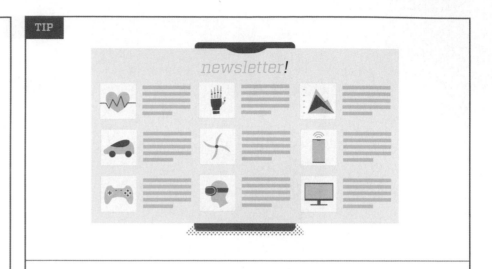

Avoid reports coming out of your own industry—or at least don't focus on them exclusively. They are usually geared toward improving an existing industry rather than re-inventing it, which is what you are trying to do.

TIP

Create Google Alerts to receive news related to specific keywords.

TIP

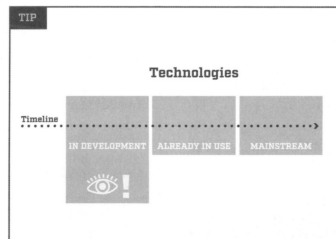

The technologies you research will be in various stages of moving into the mainstream. Some will already be in active use, while others will still be in development. Consider timing in terms of market impact and remember that "experts" generally make forecasts based on linear projections. Don't overlook exponential doubling patterns when they are in the early stages but keep in mind that they can be deceptive, since at the very beginning the exponential curve may be too flat.

TASK 3 — Learn about disruptive startups

DESCRIPTION

Technology by itself doesn't have any value to users. To be successful, organizations need to implement the right business model, which is the way to create, deliver and retain value.

Research new startups in your industry and other industries that are successfully executing new and disruptive business models. The goal is to discover new ways of doing business in your target industry.

Look for disruptive startups and new business models both within your industry and outside it. The Next Big Thing can come from anywhere.

Search the internet for terms and phrases such as "disruptive startups for [X] industry." We found lots of great examples!

TOOLS

Use the template in this section.

RESOURCES

Search startup-focused websites, where you will find articles about new and different startups. Remember that you are not looking for startups focused just on your industry. Instead, you're looking for new business models that can be applied to your industry. Good websites to check out:

TechCrunch:
https://techcrunch.com/

AngelList:
https://angel.co/

Gust:
http://www.gust.com

Entrepreneur:
https://www.entrepreneur.com

TIP

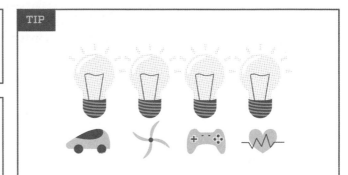

There are countless startups finding new ways to disrupt industries. Many of these approaches can be applied to your industry as well. Use them as inspiration for your own industry.

TIP

Ask yourself the following questions, ignoring the constrains of specific industries:

- What new and different ways of doing business are shaking things up?
- How are traditional businesses being bypassed as startups increasingly connect directly with consumers?

TEMPLATES for delivery

Eco Places

Global Challenges	Risks	Opportunities	Timing
Description here...	How the industry would be impacted...	What the world would look like if this problem were solved...	When the impact of the trend will manifest...

Exponential Technology	Risks	Opportunities	Timing
Name and/or description here...	How this exponential technology can disrupt your industry...	How this exponential technology can bring new business opportunities...	When this exponential technology may impact the industry...

Disruptive Startups and Business Models	Risks	Opportunities	Timing
Company name and business model description...	How it can disrupt your industry...	How to implement this business model in your industry...	When this new business model might disrupt your industry...

TEMPLATES for delivery (populated with sample entries for the Eco Places example)

Global Challenges	Risks	Opportunities	Timing
Description here...	How the industry would be impacted...	What the world would look like if this problem were solved...	When the impact of the trend will manifest...
Many people can't afford to travel	Market limited due to the financial constraints of many consumers.	Hotels achieve abundance.	Now
Consumers want personalized services	Consumers looking for nontraditional hotel options.	A world with a higher level of personalization.	Now
Sharing economy	Owners rent available space.	Better use of resources.	Now
Eco trend	Trend has a limited lifetime.	Existing eco communities can be leveraged.	Now
Many consumers unfamiliar with eco products/services	Some consumers perceive eco as a lower quality industry.	Offer promotions to encourage consumers to choose eco travel.	Now

Exponential Technology	Risks	Opportunities	Timing
Name and/or description here...	How this exponential technology can disrupt your industry...	How this exponential technology can bring new business opportunities...	When this exponential technology may impact the industry...
Internet	Allows sharing economy and P2P business models.	Allows hotels to better reach clients and develop new business models.	Now
Artificial Intelligence & Robotics	Automate majority of hotel's operations and increase competition.	Help hotels better understand clients and personalize services.	Within next 2 years
Drones	Market reduction due to new types of hotels.	Provide new ways of traveling.	Within next 5 years

TEMPLATES for delivery (populated with sample entries for the Eco Places example)

Eco Places

Disruptive Startups and Business Models	Risks	Opportunities	Timing
Company name and business model description...	How it can disrupt your industry...	How to implement this business model in your industry...	When this new business model might disrupt your industry...
Airbnb (sharing economy leverages assets)	Airbnb (or any other similar startup) could offer customers eco-type accommodations.	Launch a sharing economy P2P platform.	Now
Uber (on-demand staff)	Staff on demand could allow competitors to be more responsive to market needs.	Implement the Staff on Demand attribute.	Now
Cratejoy (subscription business model)	Market reduction if other hotel chains launch a subscription model.	Launch subscription business model.	Now

Suggestions for the week...

The perfect flow for this week:

Spend the first four days researching the assignments.

| Sun | Mon Tue Wed Thu | Fri | Sat |

Review your findings with your ExO Coach on the fifth day.

Start all research with an open mind. No preconceived ideas allowed!

Step outside your comfort and knowledge zones and explore unknown areas.

Never stop researching and learning, even when the ExO Sprint has ended.

Discover new insights by talking to others. Seek connections beyond your usual circle to gain a broader perspective.

WEEK 2

Ideate

WHY THIS WEEK?

You have at your fingertips the opportunity to invent the future and make the world a better place.

Exponential technologies allow us to generate an abundance of anything. At the same time, there are countless global challenges that need to be addressed. In fact, the biggest business opportunities are usually related to the biggest problems the world faces.

As Thomas Edison said, "To have a great idea, have a lot of them." So, this week you will generate as many ExO Edge Initiative ideas as possible in order to ensure success.

Imagine the next generation of Exponential Organizations leading a variety of industries and making the world a better place, all by leveraging exponential technologies and implementing disruptive business models.

This week's assignment allows you to unleash your creativity. It's time to dive into the future and define the most disruptive ideas for your industry and organization. Let those billion-dollar ideas flow! Starting with an expansive list of ideas will provide both inspiration and a wealth of options as you move forward.

TASK 1

Define multiple Massive Transformative Purposes (MTPs)

DESCRIPTION

The starting point for defining an Exponential Organization is to ask yourself why you want to be in this world. Then describe what the world would look like if your project were successful. Keep in mind that your task is to define a set of MTPs—one is not enough!

Run an ideation session, using such techniques as brainstorming, "what-ifs" and visual thinking.

RESOURCE

Review the MTP section for ideas on how to implement a good MTP for your organization.
➡ Pg. 40

TIP

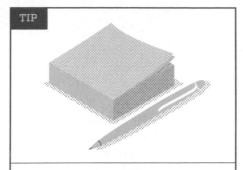

A set of sticky notes and a pen are all you need for a brainstorming session.

TIP

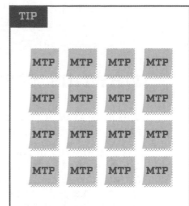

Remember that you are in the generation phase of the ExO Sprint; the more ideas for MTPs you generate, the better.

TIP

The underlying purpose here is not only to transform the industry but also to have a positive impact on the world. MTPs reflect and communicate this purpose.

TIP

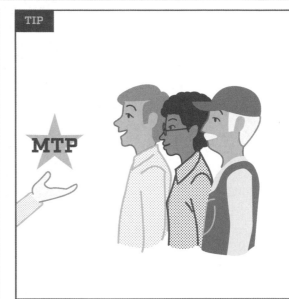

Remember that the MTP should be something you can share with customers, employees, investors and others.

TASK 2 Define problem/solution pairs for each MTP

DESCRIPTION

Now that you have a set of MTPs, the next step is to think about specific problems and solutions related to those MTPs. Your task is to identify at least 10 pairs of problems/solutions relating to the previously defined MTPs. You can have one or more problem/solution pairs per MTP. Note that each problem/solution pairs with an ExO Edge Initiative.

Depending on the relationship with the main organization, you must choose between the different types of ExO Edge Initiatives:

Linked Edge: Maintains a relationship with the main organization (and perhaps other, similar organizations), leveraging some of that organization's assets, such as existing clients, facilities, physical assets and data. An example of an ExO Linked Edge Initiative might be a hotel chain that launches an online portal similar to Hotels.com, offering available rooms to internet users. The new company, operating at the edge of the parent organization, could then use its platform to team up with competitors and offer their rooms as well.

Pure Edge: No relationship with the main organization, so growth is not constrained by the original organization's assets. For example, if a hotel chain had launched the Airbnb platform, this would have been a new business that did not leverage any of the existing hotel's assets but only the assets of others (the houses and rooms of property owners).

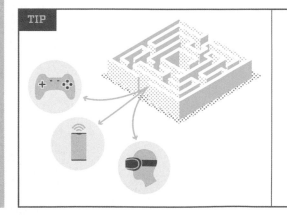

TASK 2   Define problem/solution pairs for each MTP

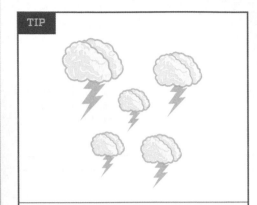

Run an ideation session, defining the problem through brainstorming and storytelling and using "what-ifs" to come up with solutions.

Team dynamics will quickly become apparent in the first weeks of the ExO Sprint. Ensure that everyone on the team (regardless of his or her position within the company) has the opportunity to contribute ideas during brainstorming sessions.

P S   P S
P S   P S
P S   P S
P S   P S
P S   P S

The minimum number of problem/solution pairs you should define is 10, but feel free to come up with more. In addition, realize that a problem may have more than one solution, meaning you may end up with more than one pair with the same problem.

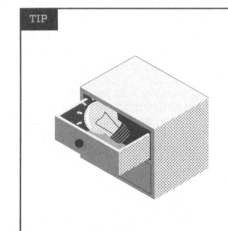

You want to avoid using the ExO Sprint as a vehicle to advance existing projects, so use this week to determine if any of the ideas your team has come up with existed anywhere in the organization previously. And if you do choose to advance a pre-existing idea, the company's leadership team must be in agreement.

TEMPLATE for delivery

Eco Places

MTP	ExO Edge Initiative Name	Problem	Solution
Unlock Eco	AirEco	Eco-friendly travelers desire a variety of eco experiences. In addition, many privately held eco properties are going unused.	Build a platform to connect eco homeowners with eco travelers. Leverage unused eco properties and follow a sharing-economy approach to rent them.
Democratize Eco	LocalEco	Many people can't afford to stay in hotels when they travel.	Build regional communities to provide eco hotel guests with local experiences. In exchange, offer free accommodation nights to participating community members, which will increase accessibility to the service.
Eco Always	Eco Places as a Service	Eco travelers appreciate suggestions on new places to stay. They also want discounts.	Monthly subscription service that offers customers a 2-night stay at a variety of eco hotels at a reduced rate.

Suggestions for the week...

The perfect flow for this week:

Spend the first two days of the week defining MTPs.

Review results with your ExO Coach on the fifth day.

| Sun | Mon Tue | Wed Thu | Fri | Sat |

Over the next two days, create problem/solution pairs for the previously defined MTPs.

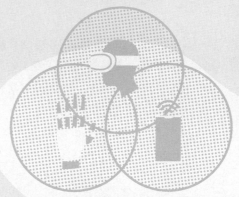

Consider the intersections of different technologies and industries to create new and original ideas.

Feel free to come up with more problem/solution pairs than suggested. We have seen teams generate more than 60!

The goal of the Edge Stream is to create next-generation organizations that over time will come to lead their industries. Ideas you generate at this stage can target your organization's existing industry, an adjacent industry or an industry that has yet to be created. Think beyond your own industry as you brainstorm ideas.

MTP

The key to building a successful ExO is to start with an MTP, which allows you to explore disruptive solutions for a variety of problems.

×4

The more ExO Edge Initiatives (which at this point include an MTP and a problem/solution pair) you generate, the better! You will need to present a minimum of four initiatives at the Disruption Session, so it's better to work on as many as possible now, since some may not survive the experimentation stage.

We know it can be hard to develop and manage so many ExO initiatives, so if you need to skip certain elements, that's fine. At this stage, it's better to generate a lot of ideas even if they have yet to be fleshed out than to be left with only a small number of initiatives, no matter how meticulously detailed.

WEEK 3

Share

WHY THIS WEEK?

Experimentation is crucial to any innovative project.

Steve Blank got it right when he said, "No business plan survives first contact with customers." Any innovative business plan is just a set of hypotheses, so instead of immediately executing them, you must first evaluate them. Innovative business plans start by defining the problem you want to solve and then move on to the solution you intend to build for that problem. So, the first set of hypotheses to evaluate are the problem/solution pairs defined last week. This is what is called the Problem/Solution Fit.

This week, you will focus on running experiments to evaluate your hypotheses—the ExO equivalent of Steve Blank's "Get out of the building!"—which will allow you to gain experience using the Experimentation attribute.

Based on what you learn, your team will select the four most promising ideas to develop further in the coming weeks.

TASK 1

Define key hypotheses and design experiments

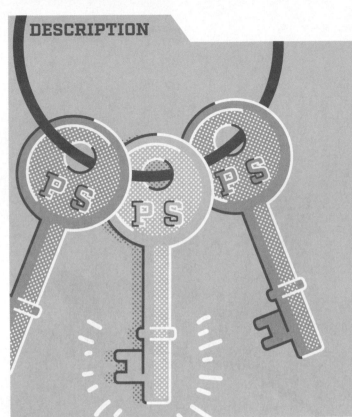

DESCRIPTION

The problems and solutions you have previously defined are a set of hypotheses, which now need to be evaluated. However, you won't have time to evaluate all of them, so focus just on those key hypotheses that will enable your ExO initiative to succeed.

As you know, your goal is to build an organization that leverages cutting-edge technologies and the ExO attributes to become exponential. The first step is to find a real problem to solve, which is why you'll run experiments focused on value generation; later phases will focus on scaling the organization.

At this early stage of the project, the best thing you can do is to run a version of Steve Blank's Customer Development technique, which calls for asking people whether or not they have a specific problem and whether or not they like your solution (Product/Solution Fit).

- **Identify the key hypotheses to evaluate at this stage:** Most will center on whether your clients/users have the problem you think they have, and whether or not they like the solution you propose to implement. But you can have other kinds of hypotheses as well, such as whether your target market is big enough or whether it's technically feasible to build the solution under consideration.

- **Design an experiment to evaluate the key hypotheses.** It's a good idea to design an interview geared toward gathering actual data about the previously defined hypotheses and the evaluation criteria you will use to either validate or invalidate each hypothesis.

TOOLS

Use the template in this section.

RESOURCE

Go to the Align section and check out the exercise for experiment design. ➡ **Pg. 128**

TASK 1 Define key hypotheses and design experiments

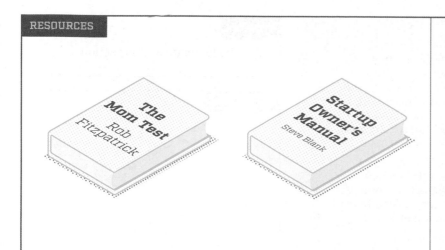

Two helpful books that outline how to conduct interviews with potential customers are Rob Fitzpatrick's *The Mom Test: How to Talk to Customers*, and Steve Blank's *The Startup Owner's Manual*. In short, you'll want to ask people about a specific problem (without mentioning the solution) and then, to elicit feedback, explain your solution. We recommend focusing in particular on the section in Blank's book that discusses the Customer Discovery phase.

TIP

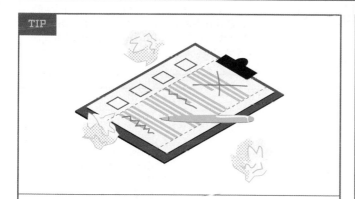

Think through the design of your experiments before beginning them. Results should allow you to uncover real needs, not just answer the question, "Is this a good idea?" How you construct the interview questions is also important. How will the results allow you to improve the initiative? Clearly define what will determine the success of an experiment, including what thresholds need to be met.

TIP

Prioritizing experiments is key, since you may have so many hypotheses to evaluate that you won't have time to run experiments on all of them. In general, you want to focus on evaluating the key hypotheses that are critical for the success of your business, such as technology viability, customer segments, value proposition and revenue sources.

TASK 2   Run experiments to evaluate the ExO initiatives

DESCRIPTION

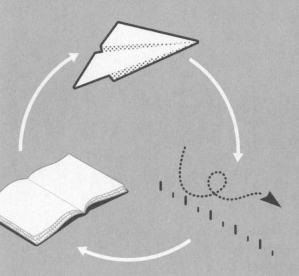

The next step is to run the experiments that you have defined. At this stage, most of the experiments will consist of interviewing potential clients (to evaluate problems/solutions) and/or tech people (to evaluate product feasibility), so reach out to arrange calls or meetings. Your goal with these interviews is to gather actual data.

After running the experiments, it's important to spend time analyzing the results. You will evaluate all hypotheses, refine the ExO initiatives based on what you've learned and make a final evaluation of the improved ExO initiatives.

The Build-Measure-Learn loop, which complements the Customer Development process, provides a set of useful guidelines that will help you evaluate your hypotheses, which is your primary goal at this juncture.

TOOLS

Use the template in this section.

RESOURCE

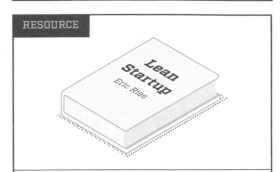

Eric Ries' *The Lean Startup* introduces the Build-Measure-Learn loop and is a great reference for how to run these processes.

TIP

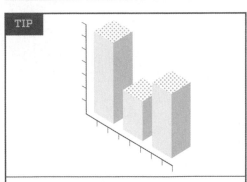

Your number one asset at this point is actual data, since the goal of the Build-Measure-Learn loop is to base all your decisions on solid data and not on opinions or intuition.

TIP

Ask for honest feedback. Invalidating a hypothesis is not bad; it's part of the innovation process. Remember that the primary goal is to learn!

TIP

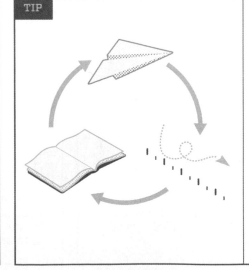

Keep in mind that most (if not all) ExOs implement the ExO attribute Experimentation. Following Lean Startup principles and the Build-Measure-Learn loop will ensure your organization is always focused on learning.

TEMPLATE for delivery

Define and run experiments (Problem/Solution Fit)

Eco Places

ExO Initiative Name	BUILD		MEASURE		LEARN
	Key Hypotheses	Experiment Description	Evaluation Criteria	Experiment Result	Key Learnings
AirEco	Eco travelers desire a variety of destinations and experiences.	Interview 10 potential clients using an interview template based on Customer Development.	At least 60% of potential clients should validate our hypotheses.	80% of potential clients validated our hypotheses.	**Hypothesis Validated** Most potential clients validated the hypotheses. We also discovered that the majority of the respondents are young eco travelers. Conclusion: young eco travelers are our customer segment.
	Owners of eco properties are willing to rent to eco travelers.	Interview 10 potential owners of rental properties using an interview template based on Customer Development.	The responses of at least 60% of potential owners of rental properties should validate our hypothesis.	Only 30% of potential owners of rental properties indicated they would rent their properties.	**Hypothesis Invalidated** Even though the hypothesis was invalidated, more than 70% responded that they were willing to rent their properties if we provided staff to take care of the rental process.

Suggestions for the week...

The perfect flow for this week:

Use the first day of the week to identify key hypotheses, design experiments, arrange interviews and build surveys.

Use the fourth day to gather results and identify key learnings.

Sun	Mon	Tue Wed Thu	Fri	Sat

Over the next three days, perform experiments (conduct interviews, send surveys, etc.).

Spend the fifth day reviewing results with your ExO Coach.

Interviews are always preferable to surveys, since they provide greater insight, especially when you ask open-ended questions. If you want to evaluate multiple ideas, however, surveys are often the only option.

The idea is to run experiments for all the problem/solution pairs you have defined. If you have one or two problem/solution pairs per team member, we recommend assigning one or two initiatives per team member. If you have more than two initiatives per team member, consider running a much bigger but more superficial experiment by sending surveys to potential clients rather than conducting direct interviews.

In order to evaluate different types of hypotheses, you may need to reach out to external advisors who are specialists in your industry or in a specific technology or methodology.

Always remember that getting out of the building and talking to real customers is the best way to turn your hypotheses into facts.

You may have different ExO Edge Initiatives that share the same customer segment. In that case, ask the different groups of people about the various ExO Edge Initiatives at the same time.

WEEK 4
Select

WHY THIS WEEK?

Up until now, you have been working on several ExO Edge Initiatives in order to explore as many opportunities as possible. It's now time to begin selecting the best ones based on the experiments you ran and what you learned from them.

Take into account that next week you will present your best ideas to a panel that will include ExO Disruptors (people from outside the organization who have experience either in your industry or with innovation in general) for feedback on the work you've done so far.

This week's primary assignment is to work on the presentations for the upcoming Disruption Session, which entails a five-minute pitch for each of the four initiatives. You will present your project to your company's leadership team, the other members of the ExO Sprint and a select panel of ExO Disruptors, who will provide feedback.

TASK 1 — Select the four most promising ideas

DESCRIPTION

Your first task is to pick the best four ideas to present at the Disruption Session. In order to do that you will evaluate them according to the previous week's results (based on experiments and key learnings) and the following criteria:

- **The MTP**: Is it really massive? Does it inspire people? Did you learn something about it during the experiments?

- **The problem you are trying to solve**: Is it global? Was it validated by your experiments?

- **The solution you are considering building:** Is it scalable? Is it disruptive? Is it feasible, or will it be in the future due to exponentials? Was it validated by your experiments?

TIP

All decisions should be data-based, so select projects with strong evidence to support them.

TIP

All non-selected ExO initiatives should be filed away for possible development in the future. Even if specific initiatives do not qualify as real ExO Edge Initiatives, other divisions of the organization might value your research and want to take over implementation (which is beneficial in quelling the immune system).

TIP

To test how disruptive your initiative is, ask yourself the following: If someone else were enacting this ExO Edge Initiative now, how would our organization be impacted?

TIP

Give each initiative a compelling title that makes it easy to understand. You should also include a one-line description.

TIP

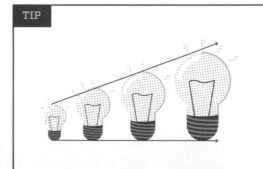

To test how scalable your initiative is, ask yourself the following: In a favorable scenario, would it be possible to scale this new company to reach a $1 billion valuation within the next five years?

TASK 2 Design the ExO Canvas

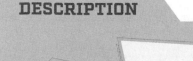

DESCRIPTION

In order to ensure your organization will become exponential by reaching and managing abundance, fill out an ExO Canvas, which will make you think about how to leverage each of the 10 ExO attributes. You will design an ExO Canvas for each of the problem/solution pairs defined in the previous step. Each is a potential ExO!

Run a brainstorming session using the blocks in the ExO Canvas as steps for the ideation process.

TOOLS

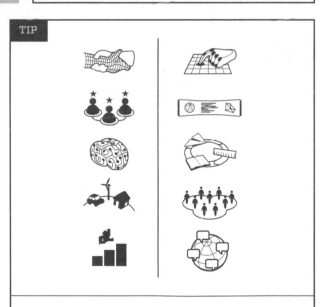

Use the ExO Canvas template. → Pg. 78

RESOURCE

Review the ExO Canvas section to refresh your memory on how to define each of the different ExO attributes. → Pg. 76

TIP

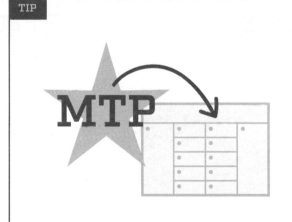

Remember to include the MTP in your ExO Canvas. Each of the problem/solution pairs you defined in the second step should be connected to one of the MTPs generated in the first step.

TIP

Remember to use the SCALE attributes to reach abundance, and the IDEAS attributes to manage abundance.

TASK 3 Define your business model (optional)

DESCRIPTION

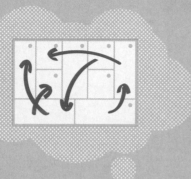

A business model is the way an organization creates, delivers and retains value. If you have enough time, it's a good idea to start thinking about and designing the business model for your ExO Edge Initiatives. (If you can't do it now, there will be time for this project in a few weeks.)

Since you are working on early stage ExO initiatives that will change very quickly as you learn more about them, use the Business Model Canvas to define your business model.

TOOLS

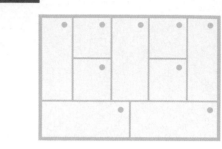

Use the Business Model Canvas template in this section.

RESOURCES

Go to the Align section and review the exercise on business model design. ⤷ Pg. 136

RESOURCE

The book *Business Model Generation* by Alex Osterwalder will help with your Business Model Canvas.

TIP

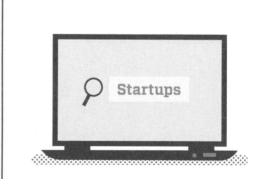

Remember those disruptive business models you researched the first week? Review them for inspiration!

TASK 3 Define your business model (optional)

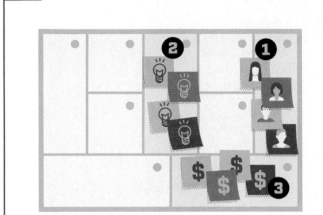

TIP

Begin defining your customer segments with sticky notes, using a different color for each customer segment. Next, define the value proposition for each customer segment, continuing with the same color-coding. Finally, define and color-code your revenue model, making sure that you include a clear way to make money. Continue the process for the remaining canvas blocks. Use a separate color for generic items (related to the business as a whole and all customer segments).

TIP

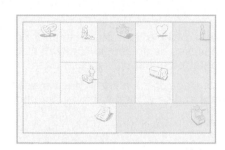

Defining the business model is optional at this stage, so don't feel any pressure if time is an issue. If you can manage it, however, we recommend defining the three main blocks of the Business Model Canvas: Customer Segments, Value Proposition and Revenue Model.

TIP

Both for-profit and nonprofit organizations must have a business model.

TIP

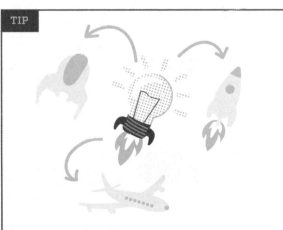

Remember that everything included in the Business Model Canvas should be considered a hypothesis that can change at any point in the future.

TIP

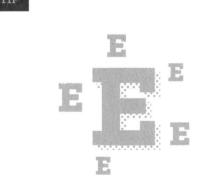

For an ExO Linked Edge Initiative, keep in mind that you may need to include your organization (and perhaps other, similar ones) as a Key Partner.

TASK 4

Create an extended elevator pitch for each ExO Edge Initiative

DESCRIPTION

You will create a five-minute pitch for each of the ExO initiatives to be presented. You will also develop a presentation in support of each pitch.

At this stage of the process (idea-stage initiatives), we recommend composing an elevator pitch—a summary of your idea that could conceivably be delivered during a standard elevator ride. An elevator pitch is usually delivered in 60 to 90 seconds, but in this case, you're going to a write a five-minute version.

The elevator pitch should include the following items:

 MTP

Explain why your organization exists.

 Problem

Describe the problem you want to solve.

 Solution

Present the solution's differentiating factors and discuss how your solution will both disrupt the industry and be scalable.

 ExO Attributes

Discuss the ExO attributes you will use most, identifying those that will help the organization reach abundance and those that will help manage it.

 Business Model (optional)

If you have had the chance to think about it, explain how you aim to generate, deliver and retain value. In other words, how you are going to make money.

TASK 4   Create an extended elevator pitch for each ExO Edge Initiative

TOOLS

Use the Elevator Pitch Script in this section.

RESOURCES

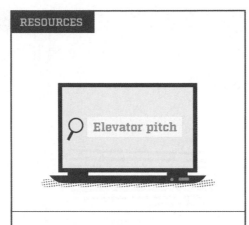

There are countless websites dedicated to describing how to prepare and deliver elevator pitches.

RESOURCE

Check out the Pitch Canvas, an online brainstorming tool that helps entrepreneurs visualize an entire pitch on one page.

TIP

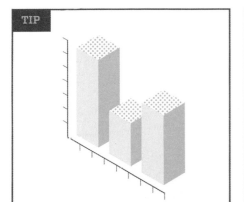

Include actual data from the experiments in your pitch. Awesome ideas are valuable but validated ones are even better.

TIP

Storytelling is a great way to present an elevator pitch.

TIP

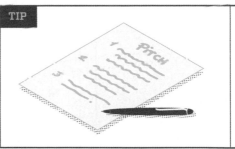

Get your pitch down on paper so you can practice it repeatedly.

TIP

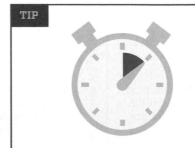

Time management is important, so create a pitch you can deliver in five minutes without having to rush.

TASK 5 Create a presentation in support of the pitch

DESCRIPTION

Consider creating slides to accompany your extended elevator pitch.

If you opt for a visual presentation, keep it simple, using only a few inspiring and informative images and graphs.

My MTP

TOOLS

Use the presentation template in this section.

TIP

A good book to help you prepare is Garr Reynolds' *Presentation Zen: Simple Ideas on Presentation Design and Delivery*, which describes using simplicity and storytelling to reach an audience.

TIP

Whenever possible, use pictures instead of text for your slides. You want people to listen to what you have to say rather than be distracted reading your slides.

TIP

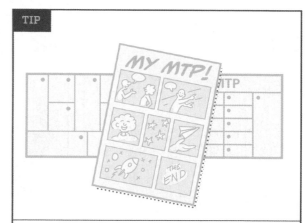

Using the ExO Canvas and the Business Model Canvas to design your ExO initiatives is helpful. However, you don't need these canvases to describe the individual pieces during your presentation. Instead, explain them in other, more visual and creative ways.

TASK 6 Practice your pitch!

DESCRIPTION

You will be presenting a large number of ideas, so your delivery must be concise and to the point. The more you practice, the better you will do.

Practice, practice, practice!

RESOURCES

Your pitch, your voice and your passion.

RESOURCES

External feedback is great at this point, so share your presentation with your team and anyone else you can.

TIP

Time management is important, so practice as much as possible.

TIP

A relaxed and natural delivery is key, so again, practice as much as possible.

TEMPLATE

ExO Canvas for AirEco

Eco Places

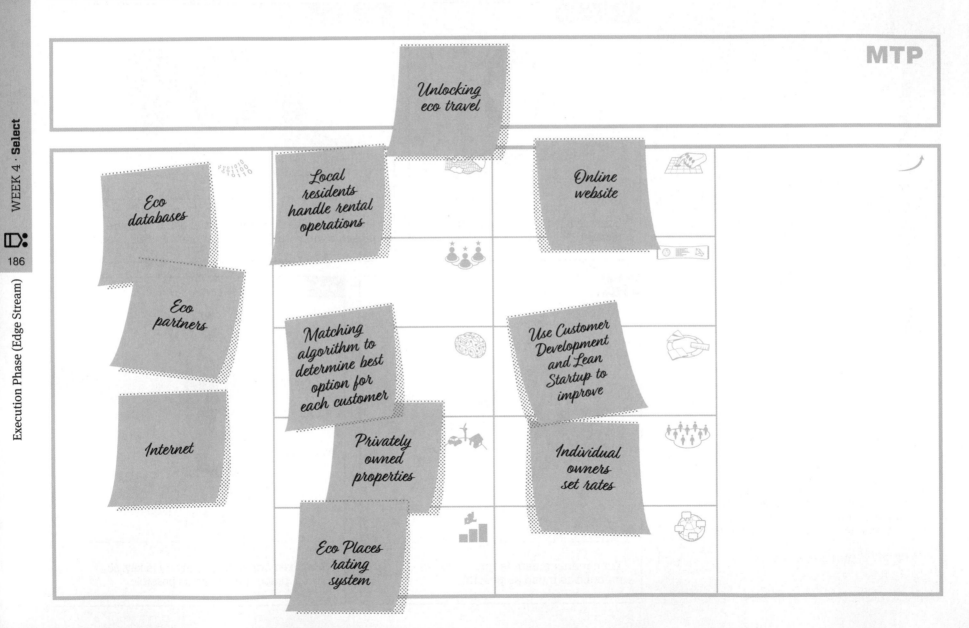

MTP

Unlocking eco travel

Eco databases

Local residents handle rental operations

Online website

Eco partners

Matching algorithm to determine best option for each customer

Use Customer Development and Lean Startup to improve

Internet

Privately owned properties

Individual owners set rates

Eco Places rating system

TEMPLATE

Business Model Canvas for AirEco

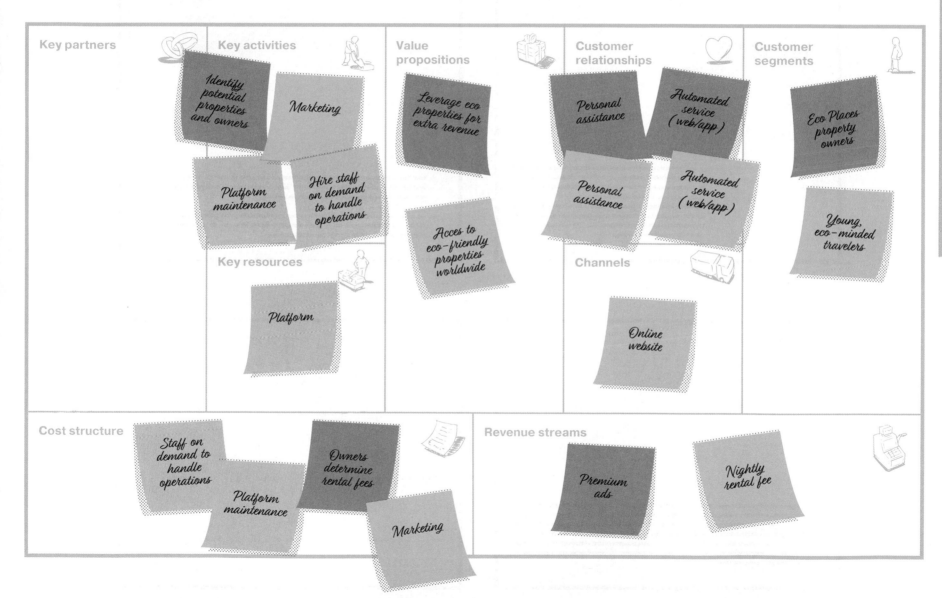

Key partners

Key activities

Identify potential properties and owners

Marketing

Platform maintenance

Hire staff on demand to handle operations

Key resources

Platform

Value propositions

Leverage eco properties for extra revenue

Acces to eco-friendly properties worldwide

Customer relationships

Personal assistance

Automated service (web/app)

Personal assistance

Automated service (web/app)

Channels

Online website

Customer segments

Eco Places property owners

Young, eco-minded travelers

Cost structure

Staff on demand to handle operations

Platform maintenance

Owners determine rental fees

Marketing

Revenue streams

Premium ads

Nightly rental fee

PRESENTATION

Your template should include the following slides or sections:

My MTP

MTP

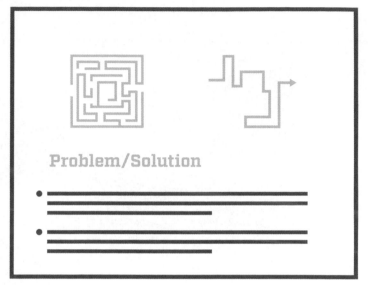

Problem/Solution

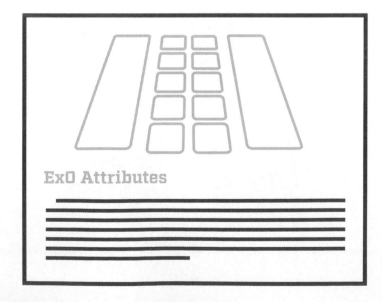

ExO Attributes

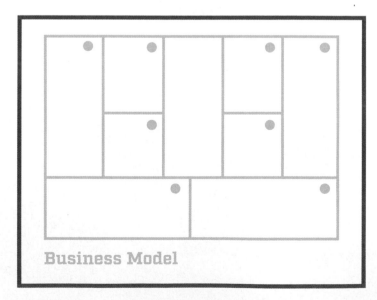

Business Model

MTP

Every ExO Edge Initiative must open with an MTP presentation.

Note that you may have several ExO Edge Initiatives sharing the same MTP. If so, explain the MTP first, followed by each of the ExO Edge Initiatives.

In general, use just one slide to introduce the MTP.

Problem/Solution

Introduce the problem before the solution.

Once the problem has been outlined, introduce the solution in an innovative way. A sample use case can be an effective way to illustrate your solution.

Use one slide for both the problem and the solution, or a different slide for each.

ExO Attributes

Since you are building new ExOs, you must show how you plan to reach abundance (using the SCALE attributes) and how you will manage it (using the IDEAS attributes).

You may also want to present the ExO Canvas and explain something about each of the ExO attributes as they are applied to the ExO Edge Initiative.

Business Model

You need to show not only how you will create value for users (although this may already be clear from the previous sections), but also how you plan to retain this value.

Include the Business Model Canvas on one slide or (perhaps even better) use a couple of slides to explain the foundation of the business model.

Suggestions for the week...

The perfect flow for this week:

Spend the first day prioritizing and selecting the ideas you will present and assign people (or groups) to build each of the presentations.

On the fifth day, present the pitch to your ExO Coach for feedback. Continue iterating and practicing the presentation in advance of the Disruption Session.

| Sun | Mon | Tue Wed | Thu | Fri | Sat |

The next two days should be devoted to building the presentations.

Spend the fourth day practicing the presentations with the team, using internal feedback to improve it. We recommend looking ahead to next week's assignment, where you will find pitch techniques.

Include actual data from your completed experiments. A great performance is always a plus, but in the end it's only a nice deck. There is always more value in providing data and insights (e.g., testimonials) from actual clients or users to illustrate what you have learned.

Running additional experiments is a good idea if you have the time. The more data you have, the better—especially in the case of any ExO initiatives that were iterated after some of your hypotheses were invalidated. You now have the opportunity to run more experiments on any new ExO initiatives (which are actually new hypotheses).

WEEK 5

Disrupt

WHY THIS WEEK?

It's time to disrupt the industry before someone else beats you to it!

This week's assignment provides an opportunity to present your most promising ExO initiatives to a group of disruptors, who will then provide feedback on how to improve them.

Remember: failure is part of the process. If some ExO initiatives are rejected post-presentation, don't take it personally. It's better to fail fast and cheap now than to fail later after having invested a lot of time and money.

Based on the feedback you receive, you may end up killing some of your ExO Edge Initiatives. On the flip side, you may well create new ones that will complement your portfolio. Always keep your eyes and ears open for new opportunities!

TASK 1 Prepare the scenario and logistics

DESCRIPTION

Create the right environment for the presentations.

You can deliver the presentations either in person or online depending on everyone's location and the parameters of your budget. If the Disruption Session is held in person, consider decorating the space to create a unique atmosphere. If you conduct it online, test the video conferencing system in advance. Also note that if the ExO Sprint is running both an ExO Edge Stream and an ExO Core Stream, the Disruption Session will include teams for both streams.

TIP

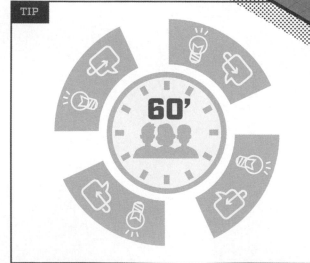

60'

Follow an established agenda for each presentation, allowing 60 minutes for each team to present all four of its ExO initiatives, with a short break between presentations. Present each of the four ExO initiatives within five minutes, followed by five minutes of feedback.

TIP

AGENDA

Time management is the key to presenting effectively. Communicate your agenda in advance, including the order of the presentations.

TASK 2 Present

DESCRIPTION

The big moment has arrived! It's time to present your ExO Edge Initiatives for feedback.

Each team will have 60 minutes to present its ExO initiatives and receive feedback.

The audience for the presentations: the company's leadership team, the other ExO teams and a group of disruption experts made up of three to five people from outside the organization who have specific experience in your industry or of innovation in general.

TIP

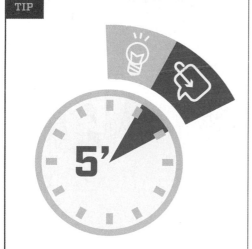

After each presentation, the audience will provide a total of five minutes of feedback. We recommend limiting this part of the session to feedback only, with no questions allowed. At this stage, the goal is not to sell the initiatives but to learn.

TIP

Record all presentations for later review.

TASK 3 Gather feedback

DESCRIPTION

Take note of all feedback received from your peers and the disruption experts. Everything you hear is valuable. Keep in mind that this set of presentations, combined with the feedback you'll receive, is yet another aspect of the experiments you've been running, and is included to improve your ExO initiatives.

Classify the feedback into different categories, one of which may include new hypotheses. Also remember to gather feedback about potential ExO initiatives.

TOOLS

Use the feedback template in this section.

TIP

You will likely receive two types of feedback:

- **A focus on the ExO framework:** ExO Disruptors knowledgeable about the ExO approach are well equipped to offer advice on moving forward so as to gain the maximum benefit from the ExO process.

- **A focus on content:** Feedback relates to the ideas themselves and sometimes includes opinions about the problem you are working to solve or the solution you are trying to create. Such feedback doesn't necessarily affect your approach; it can simply provide additional data points for evaluating your hypotheses.

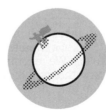

TASK 4 Debrief with the leadership team

DESCRIPTION

You will have a debrief meeting with the management team to determine which of the ExO Edge Initiatives is aligned with the general direction the company's leadership wants to go.

TIP

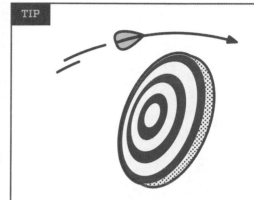

Remember that although you may have come up with amazing initiatives, some may ultimately fall outside the scope of what the company's leadership team has defined for the ExO Sprint.

TIP

We recommend that the ExO Head Coach meet with the leadership team separately to facilitate the decision-making process.

TIP

The leadership team may be inclined to select the ExO initiatives it wants to see move forward, but we suggest the group limit itself to recommendations (to avoid acting as the corporate immune system) and leave the ExO Sprint teams to make their own decisions. That said, be prepared for the possibility that the leadership team may make the final call.

TIP

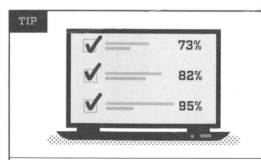

Provide the leadership team with actual data when it comes to feedback. For example, providing disruptors with an online survey to complete during the in-person presentations ensures comments and feedback are captured for later review at the leadership debrief meeting.

TASK 5 Narrow the number of initiatives down to three

DESCRIPTION

It's time to select the most promising initiatives and take them to the next level. Digest the feedback received in the Disruption Workshop and during the meeting with the leadership team and pick the top three ExO initiatives (or those the management team chose).

TIP

The leadership team may have already made a decision about which initiatives to back or kill. If so, accept the decision and try not to be too disappointed if more ExO initiatives than anticipated were scratched off the list. Rejection and failure are part of the process, so don't take it personally. Just keep being awesome!

TIP

Picking the top three initiatives is not just a matter of choosing the ones that received the best feedback. There may be other reasons: something strategic, perhaps, or a gut feeling.

TIP

Remember that you can create new ExO Edge Initiatives based on the feedback received during the Disruption Session. The goal is simply to have three ExO Edge Initiatives by the end of the week.

TASK 6

Improve the selected initiatives based on the feedback received

DESCRIPTION

Review the work you've done on the ExO Edge Initiatives so far and refine them after taking into account all feedback. If you have any new ExO Edge Initiatives, draft as many of the main elements (MTP, problem/solution pairs and the ExO Canvas) as you can and use the following weeks to catch up.

TIP

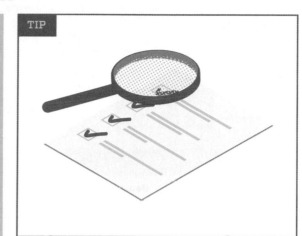

Follow the previous weeks' assignment descriptions to refine your initiatives.

TIP

Are you thinking big enough? The goal with the Edge Stream is to create a next-generation industry. Do your ideas qualify?

TIP

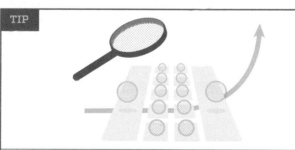

The Disruption Session can highlight where participants need to do further work to fully understand the ExO model and concepts. Take time this week to address any gaps in understanding. For example, does everyone on the team have a good grasp of the ExO attributes? Do they understand what it means for an initiative to be scalable? Do they see where their MTPs can be improved? Revisiting some of the initial concepts might have greater impact now that the team has experience applying them.

TIP

At this point of the ExO Sprint, we recommend splitting the team into subgroups and assigning each subgroup one or two initiatives. For example, if there are six team members, you can split the team into three groups of two team members and assign an ExO Edge Initiative to each. No matter how you organize the groups, it's important that all team members offer feedback on all initiatives, regardless of their level of involvement.

PRESENTATIONS AGENDA

Eco Places

  Welcome

 1 **60'**
ExO Edge Team 1 presentations (60-minute time slot per team)

 Short break

 2 **60'**
ExO Edge Team 2 presentations (60-minute time slot per team)

 Break

 **1** **60'**
ExO Core Team 1 presentations (60-minute time slot per team)

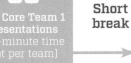 Short break

 2 **60'**
ExO Core Team 2 presentations (60-minute time slot per team)

 CLOSE
Closing and next steps

 ExO Sprint Leader meets with organization's leadership team

Feedback Form

	General Feedback	Alignment With Leadership Objectives?
AirEco	Initiative well received; suggestions offered.	
MTP	People love it!	
Problem	Disruptors and leadership team agree that rates are unaffordable for some travelers.	
Solution	Disruptors suggest increasing the market by creating a means of access for those who cannot typically afford the rooms.	Yes
ExO Attributes	Disruptors suggest leveraging the Community attribute.	
Business Model	Universal agreement that solution is feasible; suggestion made to increase market reach (Key Partners).	
[Initiative Name Here]		
MTP		
Problem		
Solution		
ExO Attributes		
Business Model		
Other Feedback (General, Other Projects, etc.)	Leadership didn't like all initiatives; some are killed.	

Suggestions for the week...

FINAL TIPS

The requirements for determining the right ExO Edge Initiative:

Global

Understand that you are building an Exponential Organization (or multiple organizations) with a Massive Transformative Purpose, so all initiatives must have the potential to reach a global market.

Disruptive

Unless the existing industry is disrupted in some way, it will be impossible to outperform current market players and become a global organization.

If possible, schedule the presentations during the latter half of the week so that teams will have enough time to improve their pitches based on the feedback received the previous week.

Designate one team member in charge of writing down all feedback. Feel free to assign a different team member for each initiative. Just make sure all feedback is captured.

After the presentations, discuss your initiatives with the attendees (the management team, members of other teams and the ExO Disruptors) and request additional feedback.

As always, remember that failure is a part of the process, so try not to get upset about any negative feedback. It's better to know sooner rather than later that you may need to change, hold off on or even kill one or more of your initiatives.

If some (or even all) of your ExO initiatives are rejected following the Disruption Session, don't take it personally! This is just part of the process. We have worked with teams whose ExO initiatives were all killed off during the Disruption Session but by the end of the ExO Sprint their new or improved initiatives were the most highly rated. Consider this session a learning exercise and an opportunity to improve your initiatives and process.

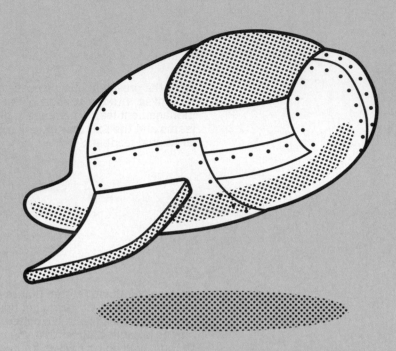

WEEK 6
Prototype

WHY THIS WEEK?

It's time to take your ExO initiatives to the next level!

This week's assignment is to formally define the assumptions underlying your ideas and prepare to test them further.

If you don't already have one, start by defining your ExO Edge Initiative business model so that you can build something that both generates value and retains it.

Next on the agenda is to begin building a Minimum Viable Product (MVP) that will facilitate learning more about your value proposition.

Are you worried you won't be able to accomplish all this in only one week? You can!

TASK 1 Define your business model

DESCRIPTION

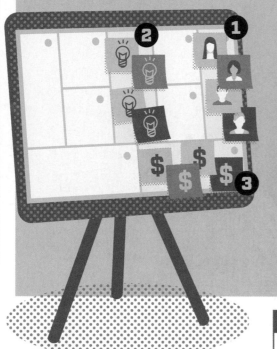

A business model is the way an organization creates, delivers and retains value. If you haven't defined a business model for your ExO Edge Initiatives before, now is the time to do it. If you already have a business model in place, this exercise will allow you to improve it based on what you've learned.

Since you are working on early stage ExO initiatives that will change frequently as you learn more about them, use the Business Model Generation technique to define your business model.

Begin defining your customer segments with sticky notes, using a different color for each segment. Next, define the value proposition for each customer segment, continuing with the same color-coding. Third, define your revenue model, keeping the color coding intact and making sure you outline a clear way to make money. Do the same for the remainder of the Business Model Canvas blocks. Use different color sticky notes for generic items (related to the business as a whole and all customer segments).

TOOLS

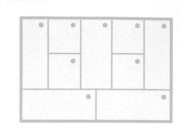

The Business Model Canvas template in this section.

RESOURCE

Go to the Align section of the book and check out the business model design exercise. ➡ Pg. 136

RESOURCE

Alex Osterwalder's book *Business Model Generation* will help with your Business Model Canvas.

RESOURCE

Another great book is *Value Proposition Design*, also by Alex Osterwalder, which includes the Value Proposition Canvas. Although not mandatory reading for this week, we think you'll find it helpful.

TASK 1 — Define your business model

RESOURCE

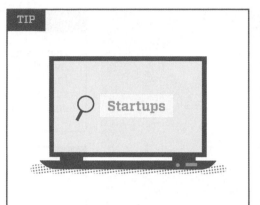

The Product/Market Fit Canvas

Yet another resource for further defining a product is the Product/Market Fit Canvas, which was co-created by more than 150 innovators around the world: www.productmarketfitcanvas.com. Again, this is not mandatory for this week, but it will complement your efforts.

TIP

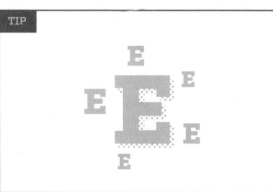

Startups

For inspiration, review the disruptive business models you researched the first week.

TIP

Regardless of whether you are a for-profit or nonprofit organization, you will need a business model.

TIP

Remember that everything included in the Business Model Canvas is a hypothesis and subject to change.

TIP

For ExO Linked Edge Initiatives, keep in mind that you may need to include your organization as a Key Partner. Consider including other, similar ones as well.

TIP

MTP

We recommend reviewing and improving your ExO Canvas based on the recent progress of your ExO initiatives.

TASK 2

Identify the key hypotheses you want to evaluate with your MVP

DESCRIPTION

Eric Ries, who launched the Lean Startup movement, defines an MVP as "a version of a new product which allows a team to collect the maximum amount of validated learning about customers with the least effort." In terms of an ExO project, the idea is to use the MVP concept to build something that will help you learn about your initiatives. Before designing and building your MVP, consider the outcome—i.e., think about what you want to learn as a result of building and testing your MVP.

The next step is to identify the key hypotheses to evaluate—those that are critical for success and to scale the business. At this stage, most of the hypotheses will be found in your ExO Canvas and your Business Model Canvas.

- **ExO Attributes:** whether the different ExO attributes you have defined are the right ones, or even if it's realistic to implement them.

- **Feasibility of the product:** whether your product or service will actually work in the way you think it will (especially if it's based on new technologies).

- **Value Proposition:** whether clients like your value proposition.

- **Revenue Model:** whether or not clients are willing to pay for it.

TOOLS

Use the template in this section to identify and evaluate the hypotheses. At this stage you only need to fill in the Build column (or columns), including the key hypotheses you're evaluating and the experiment design details. The table's Measure and Learn columns will be fleshed out in the coming weeks.

TIP

Each ExO is different so think about the critical factors that will make your business a success or not; these are the primary hypotheses to evaluate.

TIP

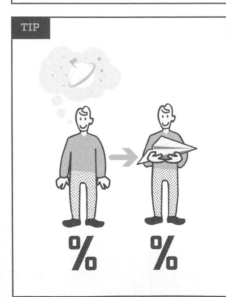

To define the success criteria of the sales experiment, define meaningful metrics for the process. The right metrics are usually expressed as a percentage that reflects the conversion rate of potential customers from one phase to another. Example: percentage of visitors who buy the product. This is known as Innovation Accounting. We encourage researching this concept more online, since it could be helpful in developing your ExO Edge Initiatives.

TASK 3 Define your Minimum Viable Product (MVP)

DESCRIPTION

You don't need to build a full product or service to start learning and selling. There is no need to waste time and money building something that no one will want to use or pay for. Instead, experiment with a Minimum Viable Product (MVP).

Before developing that MVP, determine the minimum number of features required to launch a test version of your product or service.

Eric Ries' book *The Lean Startup* is a good source for learning about MVPs and the foundations underlying the concept.

1 Define the consumer/user experience of your product or service based on the problems you detected, as well as on your defined value proposition.

2 List all features that your product or service needs in order to solve your customer's problem.

3 Weigh each feature using the ICE approach. ICE is an acronym for the three primary factors to consider when setting priorities: Impact (in terms of value for the user), Cost (in terms of money) and Effort (in terms of time). Award each factor a value between 0 and 2, with 2 representing the highest value (greatest impact, lowest cost and least effort), and 0 the lowest value (least impact, highest cost and greatest effort).

4 Prioritize the features according to their total ICE value. The features with the highest ICE scores should be included at the top your MVP list.

5 Analyze the results and define how the first version of the MVP might look according to:

- The key hypotheses you need to evaluate Remember that the primary goal of the MVP is to learn, so take these hypotheses into account before defining your next experiment, which is to build your MVP.

- ICE prioritization and the key hypotheses that you need to evaluate.

- For this first version of the MVP, you will likely need to add or delete features. Some may be required for technical reasons, while others could take too long to develop and thus should be removed for now.

Remember that your goal here is not to have the best product— or even a product that clients love—but to develop a product that allows you to learn. To that end, include learning-oriented features and add-ons that will result in further feedback.

TASK 4 Build Your MVP!

DESCRIPTION

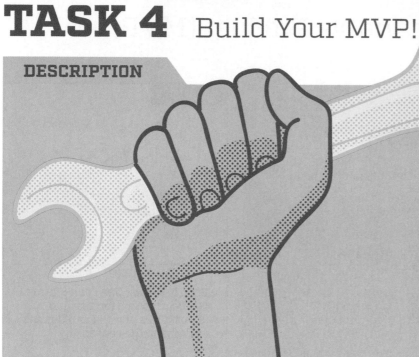

Build your first MVP based on the business model you defined earlier, including demonstrating your value proposition.

There are several techniques you can use to build your MVP. Some are focused on building an actual product, others on simply presenting the idea to potential clients. You will need to pick the one that works best for your product or service based on the amount of time you have to build the MVP. To that end, consider combining the following techniques:

Landing Page

Develop a landing page that shows and describes your MVP. (You can also describe the complete version of the product or service, although we recommend focusing the landing page on the key features of the MVP.) In addition to describing your product or service—either the MVP or a complete version—encourage clients to pre-order. Another option is to run A/B testing, which consists of building two different versions of the landing page, each with a different value proposition, and see which visitors prefer.

RESOURCES

Visit www.launchrock.com and www.landerapp.com for help in creating a landing page.

HOW MUCH YOU WILL LEARN

A bit: how much clients like the value proposition of your product/service and its price based on the number of pre-orders the website receives and the actual data you gather from the analytics of website usage.

Video

Create a video that shows and promotes your MVP.

RESOURCES

Use a professional video creation service or online tools such as www.animoto.com or www.goanimate.com.

HOW MUCH YOU WILL LEARN

A bit more: how clients like your product/service value proposition based on their reactions after watching the video. Getting clients to pre-order results in data about the price and revenue model.

TASK 3 Build Your MVP!

Wireframes

Build a set of wireframes or digital designs that will help illustrate what your product will look like.

RESOURCES

Use any rapid prototyping tool such as www.invisionapp.com, www.justinmind.com or even PowerPoint.

HOW MUCH YOU WILL LEARN

Even more: how clients like your product/service value proposition based on their reactions and interactions with the wireframes. Getting clients to pre-order also provides data about the price and revenue model.

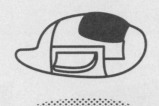

Working prototype

Build a prototype that includes only the key features you want to learn more about. This is actually the real MVP, and in many cases it's possible to build it in just a few days. Remember, it doesn't have to be perfect; it just needs to be something that will help you learn over a several-day period.

HOW MUCH YOU WILL LEARN

A lot: how easy or hard it is to build and deliver the actual product or service, how clients like the value proposition of your product or service, and what the user experience is like based on interactions with the prototype. Getting clients to pre-order provides data about the price and revenue model.

RESOURCES

Eric Ries' book *The Lean Startup* offers great ideas on how to build MVPs in just a few days. Another good book is *MVP*, by Paul Vii, which provides tips for creating an MVP using Agile Development Methodologies.

TIP

Compiling a list of prioritized features and the number of hours that each will take to develop will tell you whether or not it is possible to have a prototype ready within the next week.

TEMPLATE for delivery

Business Model Canvas for AirEco

Eco Places

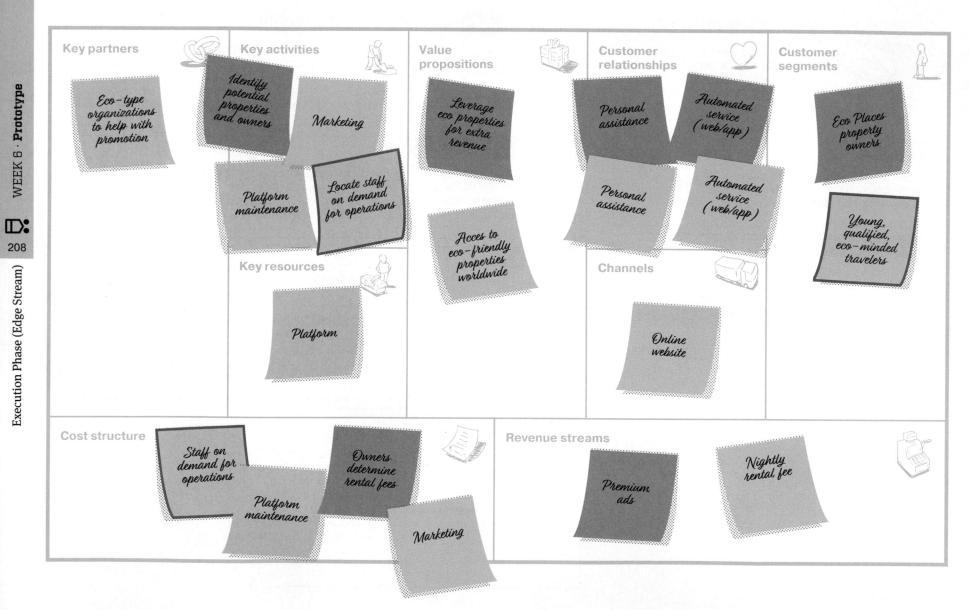

Key partners

Eco-type organizations to help with promotion

Key activities

Identify potential properties and owners

Marketing

Platform maintenance

Locate staff on demand for operations

Key resources

Platform

Value propositions

Leverage eco properties for extra revenue

Acces to eco-friendly properties worldwide

Customer relationships

Personal assistance

Automated service (web/app)

Personal assistance

Automated service (web/app)

Channels

Online website

Customer segments

Eco Places property owners

Young, qualified, eco-minded travelers

Cost structure

Staff on demand for operations

Platform maintenance

Owners determine rental fees

Marketing

Revenue streams

Premium ads

Nightly rental fee

TEMPLATE for delivery

ExO Canvas for AirEco

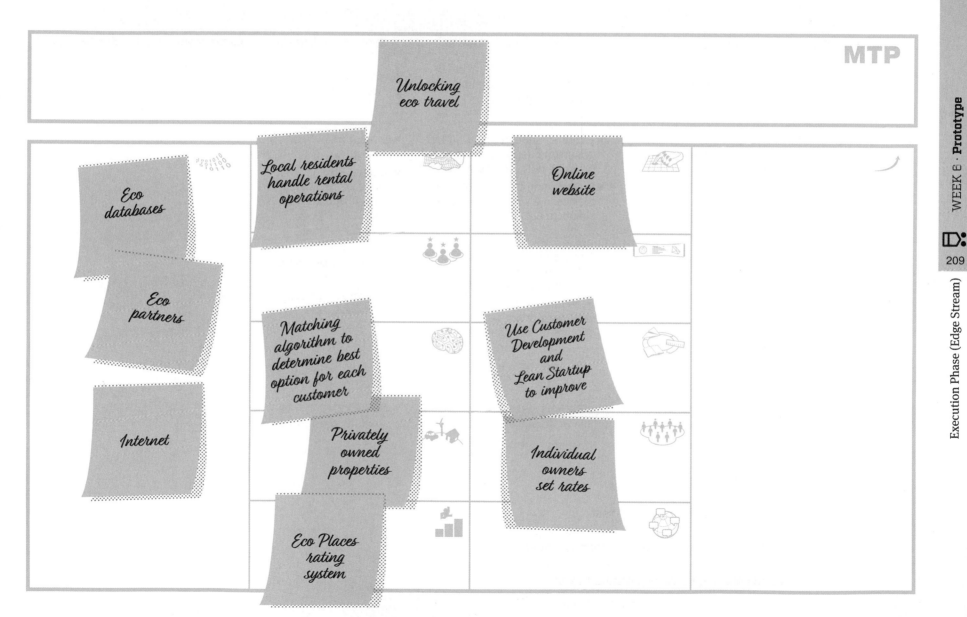

MTP

Unlocking eco travel

Eco databases

Local residents handle rental operations

Online website

Eco partners

Matching algorithm to determine best option for each customer

Use Customer Development and Lean Startup to improve

Internet

Privately owned properties

Individual owners set rates

Eco Places rating system

TEMPLATE for delivery

Eco Places

Template to identify and evaluate key hypotheses

ExO Initiative Name	Key Hypotheses	Experiment Description	Evaluation Criteria	Experiment Result	Key Learnings
		BUILD		MEASURE	LEARN
AirEco	The market is big enough.	Find statistics to determine if the number of potential clients is large enough.	We can sell 50 million nights per year.		
	Potential customers are willing to book a stay at a privately owned eco property.	▪ Landing page to test whether potential clients sign up; promote with Google AdWords. ▪ Presentation detailing the service to encourage potential clients to book a stay.	▪ At least 5% of visitors sign up. ▪ At least 25% of potential customers interviewed book a stay.		
	Potential owners really are willing to share their properties.	▪ Landing page to test whether potential owners sign up; promote with Google AdWords. ▪ Presentation detailing the service to encourage potential owners to rent their properties.	▪ At least 5% of visitors sign up. ▪ At least 25% of potential customers interviewed book a stay.		

Designing the MVP

FEATURE	IMPACT [VALUE]	COST [MONEY]	EFFORT [TIME]	PRIORITY
Sign-up landing pages for owners and travelers	2	2	2	6
Search engine for booking	2	1	0	3
Booking process through website	1	1	0	2
Presentation detailing service—potential property owners	2	2	2	6
Presentation detailing service—potential travelers	2	2	2	6

MVP Conclusions

After analyzing the different features and options for the MVP, we decided that rather than building a prototype of the entire platform—which would be time-consuming and expensive—we would launch a simple website designed to attract potential owners and customers.

We created two in-person presentations. The first introduced the AirEco platform to property owners, with a goal of having them sign a contract that would allow us to rent their properties to eco-minded vacationers. The second introduced the AirEco platform to potential customers and encouraged them to book a property for their next trip.

Suggestions for the week...

The perfect flow for this week:

Devote the next few days to building your MVP, which you will need next week.

| Sun | Mon | | Tue Wed Thu Fri | Sat |

Spend the first day outlining your business model, identifying the key hypotheses and designing your MVP.

Review progress with your ExO Coach on the fifth day.

Build something that you can use to test your value proposition with users.

For online channels such as landing pages, don't forget to implement some mechanism to gather feedback (e.g., contact forms) and data (e.g., stats engine).

Keep in mind that next week you will use whatever you build now to reach potential clients, elicit their feedback and close your first sales.

You will develop your MVP further next week, but it's important to get an initial version up and running now. If you want to produce an actual prototype but need two weeks to develop it, we recommend developing a landing page in the interim. You can at least gather data while getting the prototype ready for the experiments you'll be conducting in two weeks.

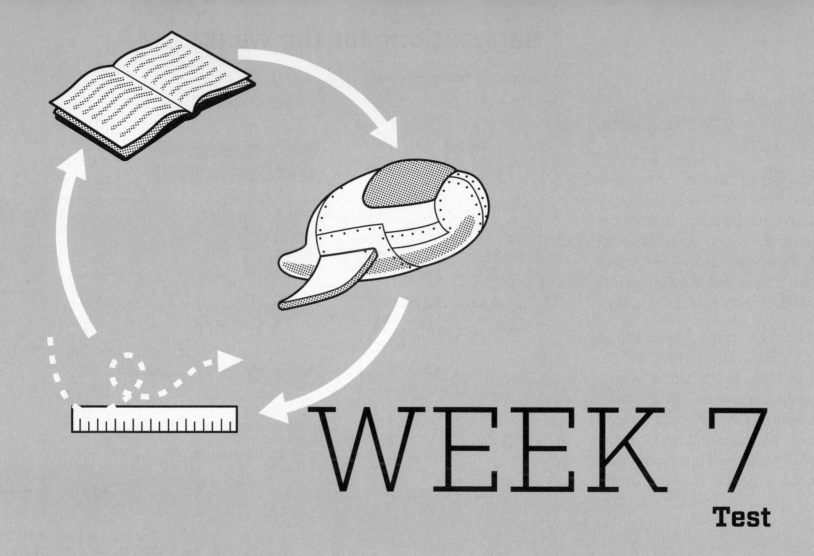

WEEK 7
Test

WHY THIS WEEK?

It's time for the truth!

Over the past week, you have been building prototypes of your MVPs, which will allow you to learn more about and improve your ExO Edge Initiatives.

This week's assignment provides experience exercising the Experimentation attribute at a deeper level by engaging early adopters with a concept they can respond to. The goal is to sell your MVPs to early adopters in order to validate that your value proposition for the market is the right one.

The experiment of building your MVP and selling to early adopters will help you evaluate the hypotheses related to the value proposition and the business model. This is what is called the product/market fit. In addition, you will also evaluate the hypotheses as they relate to the ExO attributes, which are key to building a truly Exponential Organization.

Getting your first client is one of the most exciting milestones for any new organization. Let's do it!

TASK 1 Find, reach and sell to early adopters

DESCRIPTION

An early adopter is an individual or business that uses a new product or technology before others, shares your vision and is willing to try your MVP even though it may not yet have been perfected.

Your task here is to define where to find early adopters for your MVPs and how to reach them in order to test the product and/or the sales process with them. This is considered yet another experiment, one that is focused on attaining product/market fit.

The technique used to find early adopters depends on the type of MVP you have developed:

If you created a landing page as your MVP, focus on online channels in one of three ways:

- Create online ads (e.g., using Google AdWords) and link them to your promotional sites.

- Promote the website with online communities populated by potential early adopters.

- Email the page links to potential early adopters you've identified.

If you've created a sales presentation, a set of wireframes, a video or a real prototype, focus on offline channels to reach early adopters:

- Promote your MVP to those people or organizations interviewed when you first tested the problem/solution hypotheses.

- Generate a new list of potential early adopters.

- Generate a list of communities that might be populated by MVP early adopters.

Finally, launch the different sales processes with early adopters and collect feedback. Remember that the real goal is not to sell but to learn.

TASK 1 Find, reach and sell to early adopters

Steve Blank's book *The Startup Owner's Manual* outlines how to find and sell to early adopters. Familiarize yourself with the section that covers the Customer Validation phase of the process.

In addition to a being great way to learn about selling to early adopters, Geoffrey Moore's *Crossing the Chasm* also addresses how to expand your target market.

The profile of the ideal early adopter is a person or organization that:

Shares your vision for the future.

Has the problem you defined some weeks ago.

Is trying to solve this problem in some way, although unsuccessfully thus far.

Is willing to pay to solve the problem.

Is honest and will provide valuable feedback.

To find early adopters, try to think as they do. This will help you identify new places to locate them.

Remember that your goal is to learn, so interact with your early adopters as much as possible.

- **For online channels** such as websites, after each user or buyer completes the process, send an email asking for feedback on how to improve your value proposition and pricing model.

- **For offline channels** including in-person meetings and phone calls, don't outsource the sales process. Handle it yourself after spending the week interacting with early adopters to learn as much as possible by testing your product with them and encouraging them to buy it.

TASK 2 Measure results and learn

After building your MVPs and the sales process you will have a lot of experience and data to use in evaluating your key hypotheses. Remember that the main goal is to learn about the ExO attributes and the business model (in particular the value proposition and revenue model).

After the sales process is completed, the next step is to dig into the data you've gathered.

TOOLS

Use the template to identify and evaluate the hypotheses you were working with last week and fill in the Measure and Learn columns.

ADVICE

Analyze the qualitative data as well as the quantitative data (metrics). At this early stage of the game, qualitative information is more important than quantitative.

TIP

Experimentation results often produce a lot of noise but digging into the data also presents learning opportunities. For example, after evaluating a solution, you might find that certain customer segments love your product or service, while others hate it. In fact, your results might indicate that people under 45 years of age love it and those over the age of 45 don't. The learning here? Focus the solution on the customer segment aged 45 and under.

TEMPLATE to identify and evaluate key hypotheses

Eco Places

		BUILD		MEASURE	LEARN
Exo initiative Name	Key Hypotheses	Experiment Description	Evaluation Criteria	Experiment Result	Key Learnings
AirEco	The market is big enough to launch this business.	Use statistics to determine if the number of potential clients is big enough.	We can sell 50 million nights per year.	The potential market is more than 80 million nights per year.	**Hypothesis Validated** There is an abundance of potential customers.
	Potential customers are willing to book a stay at a privately owned eco property.	■ Landing page to test whether potential clients sign up; promote with Google AdWords. ■ Presentation detailing the service to encourage potential clients to rent eco properties.	Potential customers are willing to book a stay at a privately owned eco property.	■ Results show that 7% of visitors signed up. ■ More than 35% of potential customers interviewed booked a stay, although some requested more information than was covered in the presentations.	**Hypothesis Validated** We learned that potential customers are demanding; property profiles that appear on the platform must be comprehensive.
	Potential owners are willing to share their properties.	■ Landing page to test whether potential owners sign up; promote with Google AdWords. ■ Presentation detailing the service for potential owners interested in renting their properties.	Potential owners are willing to share their properties.	■ Just 2% of visitors signed up. ■ Only 20% of owners interviewed were willing to rent their property to guests, but more than 40% indicated they'd be willing to rent their properties if they had the opportunity to screen potential guests.	**Hypothesis Invalidated** We learned that potential owners want background information on guests who will be renting their properties, so we need to offer a guest qualification process.

Suggestions for the week...

The perfect flow for this week:

Spend the first day defining how to reach out to early adopters. Then reach out to them as soon as possible!

Review results with your ExO Coach on the fifth day.

Sun	Mon	Tue Wed Thu Fri	Sat

The remainder of your time this week will be spent running early-adopter sales experiments. If you need more time to gather data, this step might spill into the beginning of the following week. Either way, you should have initial results by the end of the week.

The goal for the week is to compile enough data from the experiments to ensure valid results (and thus additional learning). What would be even better, of course, is to sell your idea during the process—an outcome that would be a great way to impress the panel at your final ExO Edge presentation. From nothing to real customers in less than 10 weeks...Let's do it!

Remember that early adopters are not simply your first clients. They are also special people and/or companies with a specific mindset.

To aid in your evaluation of the different types of hypotheses, you may need to reach out to external advisors who are specialists in your industry or in a specific technology or methodology.

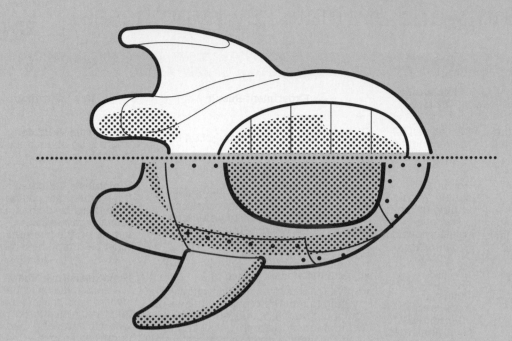

WEEK 8

Improve

WHY THIS WEEK?

Last week you should have learned a great deal about your business model and the ExO attributes by testing your MVPs with real clients. This week, you will continue to develop your MVPs by running experiments.

At some point during the week when you have enough data, it will be time to face reality and make the necessary changes to your ExO Edge Initiatives to maximize your opportunities for success.

Modify or even pivot your ExO Edge Initiatives to ensure they are well positioned for success.

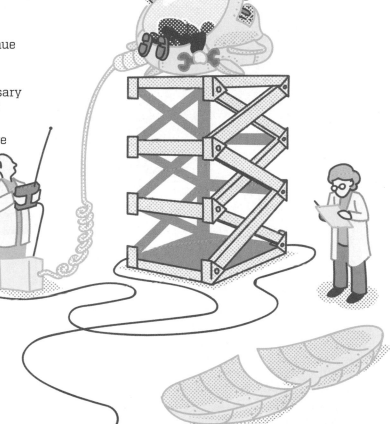

TASK 1 Further develop your ExO Edge Initiatives

DESCRIPTION

Just two weeks to build an MVP and encourage early adopters to buy your product or service may not seem like enough time. Despite the quick turnaround, however, it is possible.

Allot several days this week to running experiments and further developing and iterating your MVP based on what you've learned.

TOOLS

If you are still running experiments with early adopters, continue using the template to identify and evaluate the hypotheses you have been using over the last two weeks.

TIP

Insights gleaned from experiments with early adopters will provide you with new ideas and thus, potentially, new hypotheses. Keep the hypothesis definition and evaluation process dynamic. The idea is to use what you learn to redefine your experiments on an ongoing basis.

TIP

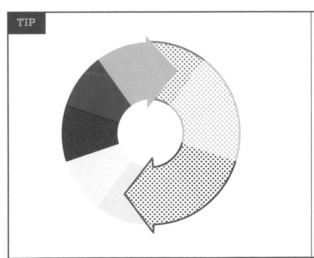

We recommend exploring Agile Development Methodologies (such as Scrum), which are basic techniques for developing and evolving an MVP. The main premise of these methodologies is to continually redefine features and development priorities for your product so that you can iterate it in a few days or weeks. Even if you don't use the techniques during the course of the ExO Sprint, it's a good idea to have a working knowledge of them for possible future use.

TASK 2 Pivot, iterate or proceed!

DESCRIPTION

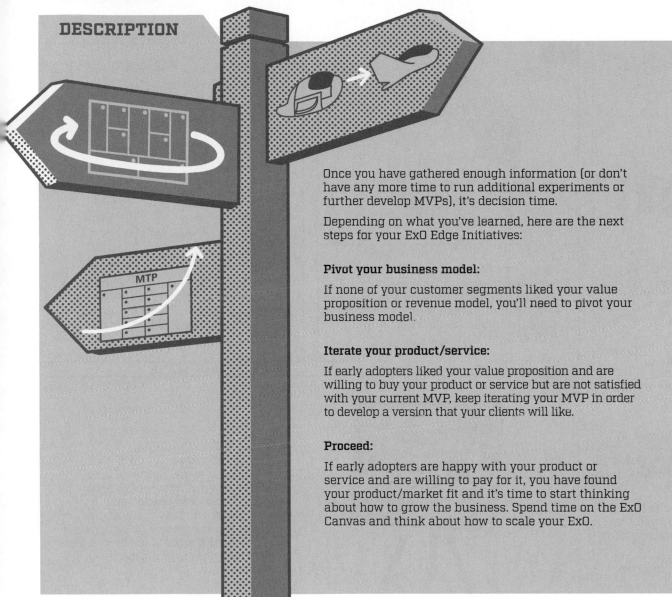

Once you have gathered enough information (or don't have any more time to run additional experiments or further develop MVPs), it's decision time.

Depending on what you've learned, here are the next steps for your ExO Edge Initiatives:

Pivot your business model:

If none of your customer segments liked your value proposition or revenue model, you'll need to pivot your business model.

Iterate your product/service:

If early adopters liked your value proposition and are willing to buy your product or service but are not satisfied with your current MVP, keep iterating your MVP in order to develop a version that your clients will like.

Proceed:

If early adopters are happy with your product or service and are willing to pay for it, you have found your product/market fit and it's time to start thinking about how to grow the business. Spend time on the ExO Canvas and think about how to scale your ExO.

TOOLS

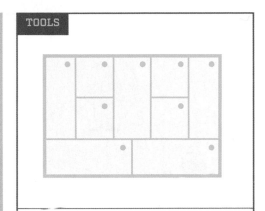

To pivot your business model, use the Business Model Canvas you worked on earlier in the ExO Sprint.

TASK 2   Pivot, iterate or proceed!

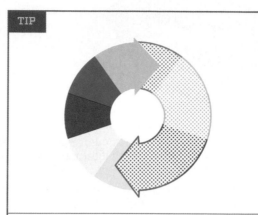

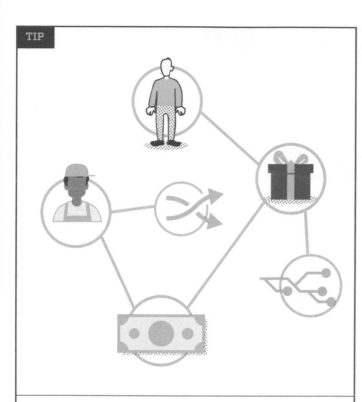

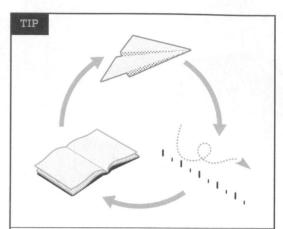

Iteration of your product or service may require updating your product backlog if you are using Agile Development Methodologies (unlikely given the time constraints of an ExO Sprint).

Carefully consider the feedback clients offer and re-prioritize your MVP's features as needed. Don't forget the Build-Measure-Learn loop, which is applicable to everything!

There are several types of pivots to consider.

- **Customer Segment pivot:** Your product or service may attract actual customers, just not the ones you anticipated. If so, adjust your target market.

- **Value Proposition pivot:** You may discover that your value proposition needs to charge, or even the way you deliver your product (perhaps entailing a pivot from a product to a service).

- **Revenue Model pivot:** You may need to change the pricing model.

- **Other pivots:** Channel pivot, Technology pivot, Key Partners pivot, etc.

Whether or not you pivot your business model or iterate your product or service, update your ExO Canvas as needed and consider what it would take to create a truly scalable business— i.e., what it would take to create an Exponential Organization.

TEMPLATE for delivery

ExO Canvas for AirEco

MTP

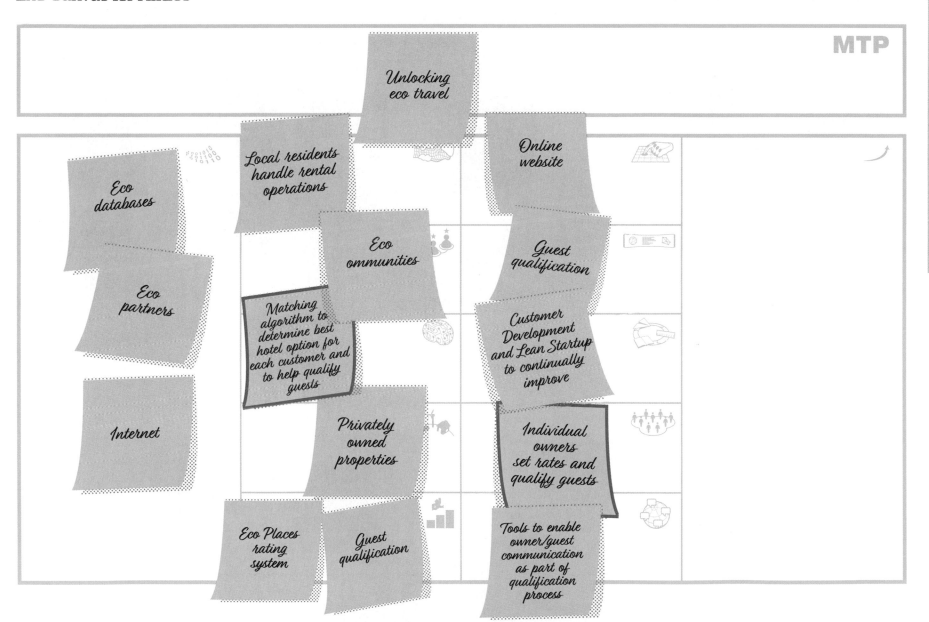

- Unlocking eco travel
- Eco databases
- Local residents handle rental operations
- Online website
- Eco partners
- Eco communities
- Guest qualification
- Matching algorithm to determine best hotel option for each customer and to help qualify guests
- Customer Development and Lean Startup to continually improve
- Internet
- Privately owned properties
- Individual owners set rates and qualify guests
- Eco Places rating system
- Guest qualification
- Tools to enable owner/guest communication as part of qualification process

TEMPLATE   for delivery

Business Model Canvas for AirEco

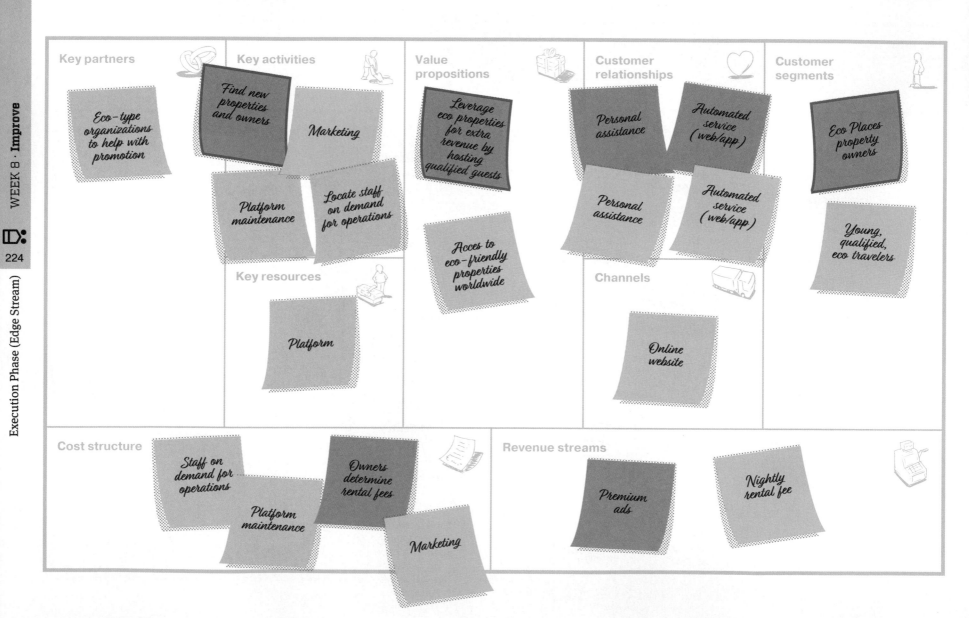

Key partners

Eco-type organizations to help with promotion

Key activities

Find new properties and owners

Marketing

Platform maintenance

Locate staff on demand for operations

Key resources

Platform

Value propositions

Leverage eco properties for extra revenue by hosting qualified guests

Acces to eco-friendly properties worldwide

Customer relationships

Personal assistance

Automated service (web/app)

Personal assistance

Automated service (web/app)

Channels

Online website

Customer segments

Eco Places property owners

Young, qualified, eco travelers

Cost structure

Staff on demand for operations

Platform maintenance

Owners determine rental fees

Marketing

Revenue streams

Premium ads

Nightly rental fee

Suggestions for the week...

The perfect flow for this week:

Spend the first two days gathering as much data as possible from early adopters and refining your MVP.

Share your progress with your ExO Coach on the fifth day and get ready to put together the final presentations for the Launch Session!

| Sun | Mon Tue | Wed Thu | Fri | Sat |

Devote the next two days to analyzing results and making any needed adjustments to the business model, the product or service, and the ExO Canvas.

Making changes to your ExO initiatives may prove challenging (it's not easy letting go of ideas you're attached to), but don't respond by initiating the corporate immune system! Instead, build the best ExO initiative possible based on what you're learning as you move through each stage of the ExO Sprint.

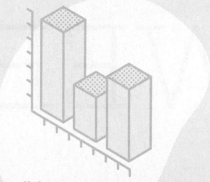

Keep all decisions data-based. Staying neutral often requires setting your ego aside and releasing any attachment to favored ideas or proposals.

Remember that within the ExO Sprint process everyone is equal and there is no room for corporate hierarchy. In short, decisions should never be based on corporate seniority.

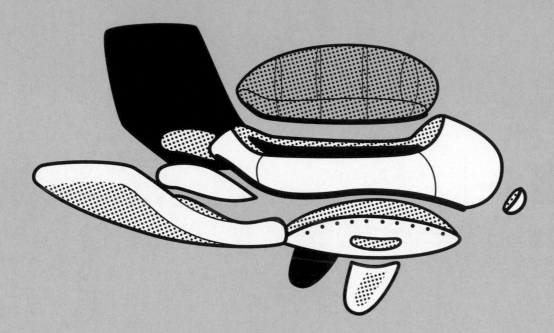

WEEK 9

Assemble

WHY THIS WEEK?

Time to prepare for the final presentation!

Next week you will present your best ideas to the leadership team. The goal is to elicit additional feedback and, most important, secure the funding needed to further develop the chosen ExO Edge Initiatives.

This week's assignment is to have your team assemble the components of your ExO Edge Initiative and create a comprehensive presentation showcasing the amazing work you've done throughout the ExO Sprint.

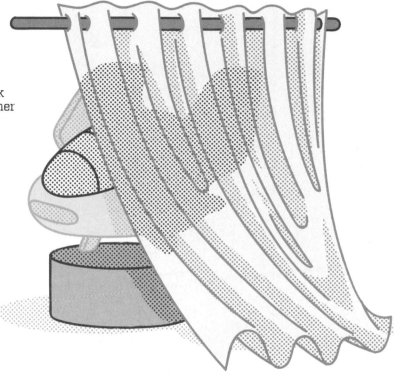

TASK 1

If possible, narrow the number of initiatives to be presented down to two

DESCRIPTION

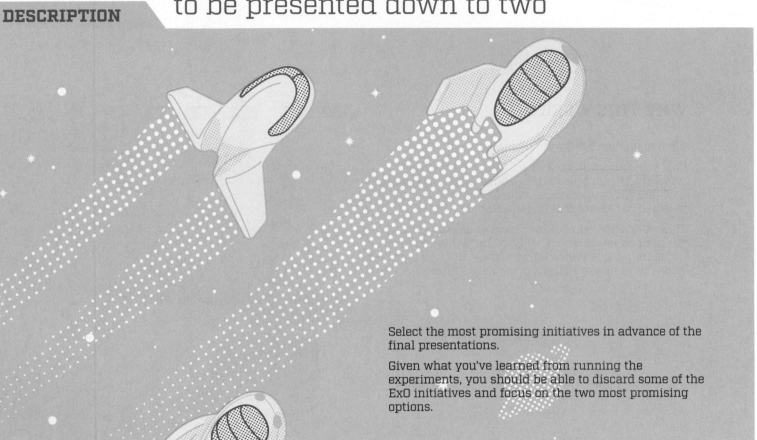

Select the most promising initiatives in advance of the final presentations.

Given what you've learned from running the experiments, you should be able to discard some of the ExO initiatives and focus on the two most promising options.

TASK 2

DESCRIPTION

Extend your ExO Edge Initiatives with key milestones and a budget

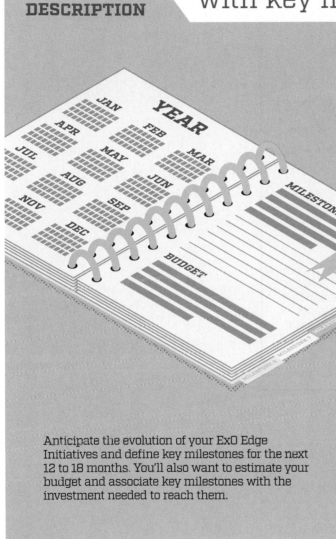

Anticipate the evolution of your ExO Edge Initiatives and define key milestones for the next 12 to 18 months. You'll also want to estimate your budget and associate key milestones with the investment needed to reach them.

TOOLS

Use the template in this section.

TIP

Key milestones may include:

- Finding the right team to execute the initiative

- Running further experiments to evaluate hypotheses

- Building an MVP and its revisions

- Securing early adopters and revenues

- Determining the ideal product/market fit—that sweet spot where client satisfaction is highest

- Pursuing partnerships where applicable

TIP

For estimating revenues, create a set of business parameters that take into account the innovation accounting metrics you defined (and experimented with) the previous week.

TASK 2   Extend your ExO Edge Initiatives with key milestones and a budget

TIP

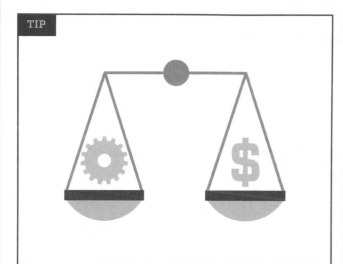

When it comes to estimating costs, be realistic about the resources and external help you will need to achieve your milestones. Milestones should align with easy-to-approve funding amounts.

TIP

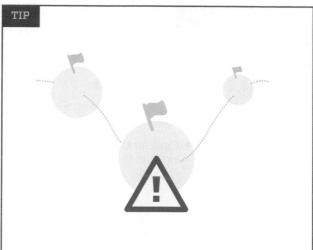

If your ExO Edge Initiative is heavily dependent on an emerging technology, your milestones may reflect the interim steps that will prepare your organization to adopt the technology when it matures.

TIP

Create a sequence of manageable milestones. For example, a milestone might test the concept with a small market segment. It could also test an individual component of the initiative.

TASK 3 Build a final presentation for the ExO Edge Initiatives

DESCRIPTION

To prepare the final presentations, you'll need to develop a deck for each of your ExO Edge Initiatives.

For this round, instead of using the short elevator pitch format, you will produce longer, more comprehensive presentations for each of the ExO initiatives.

TOOLS

Use the template in this section.

RESOURCE

A helpful book is Garr Reynolds' *Presentation Zen: Simple Ideas on Presentation Design and Delivery*.

TIP

Wherever possible, use pictures instead of text for your slides to avoid the scenario of people reading your slides rather than listening to what you have to say.

TASK 3   Build a final presentation for the ExO Edge Initiatives

Craft a story that makes a compelling case for each initiative, beginning with the problem space and including a clear definition of the value proposition. Is the concept easy to understand? Is its value easy to understand?

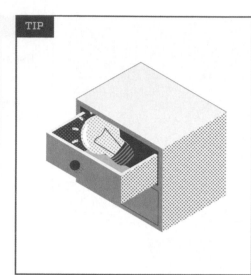

Don't worry if you end up killing one or more of your ExO initiatives. Although you should present at least two ExO Edge Initiatives at the Launch Session, you can always resurrect any of the initiatives you were working on prior to the Disruption Session. Be sure to develop any new additions as much as you can, following the process outlined in the previous weeks.

Keep in mind that you will have just 15 minutes to present each initiative.

Start practicing as soon as possible!

PRESENTATION

Each presentation should include the following slides/sections:

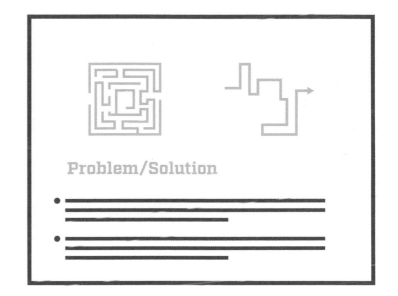

MTP

It's imperative to start each ExO Edge Initiative presentation with an MTP.

Note that you may have several ExO Edge Initiatives sharing the same MTP. If so, explain the MTP first, followed by each of the initiatives.

In general, use just one slide to introduce each MTP.

Problem/Solution

Introduce the problem before the solution.

Once the problem has been outlined, introduce the solution in an innovative way.

Present both the problem and the solution, either together or separately, using a single slide or set of slides.

PRESENTATION

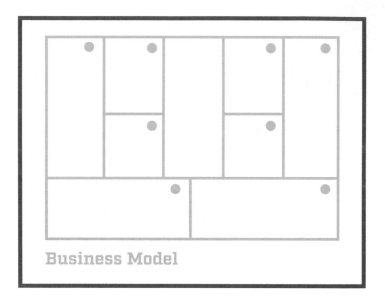

Storytelling

Business Model

Case Study

When communicating new ideas, it's helpful to use storytelling techniques.

One option is to invent a story and illustrate it with pictures and diagrams that explain the problem and how your solution solves it.

We recommend using case studies if you are presenting six or fewer initiatives. Count on five minutes to present each initiative.

Business Model

Be prepared to show not only how you will create value for users (this may already be clear from previous sections), but also how you plan to retain this value.

Show the Business Model Canvas on one slide or use a couple of slides to outline your business model's foundation.

PRESENTATION

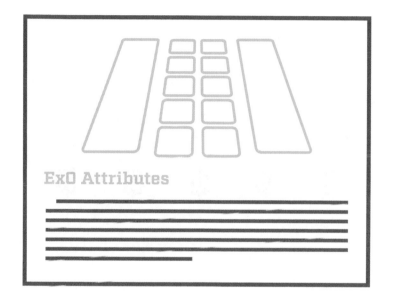

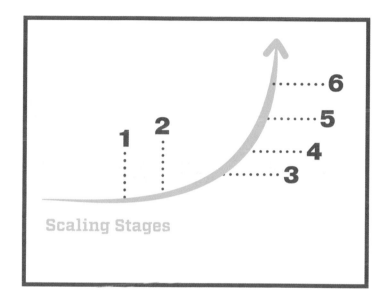

ExO Attributes

Since you are building new ExOs, you must show how you plan to reach abundance (using the SCALE attributes) and how you will manage that abundance (using the IDEAS attributes).

You may also want to present the ExO Canvas and explain something about each of the key ExO attributes as they are applied to the ExO Edge Initiative.

Scaling Stages

Using an exponential curve, show how the ExO Edge Initiative will, over time, have a global impact.

Include key points that address short-, mid- and long-term outlooks.

Maintain an exponential mindset!

PRESENTATION

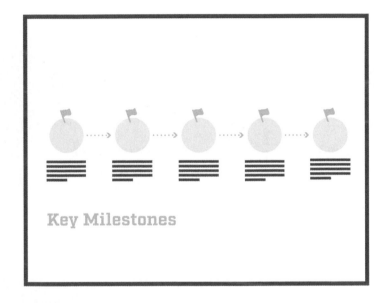

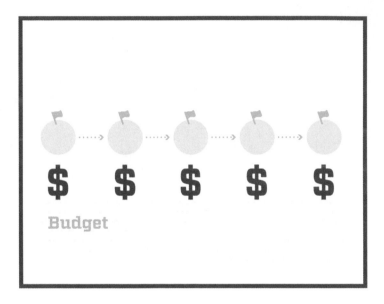

Key Milestones

Outline important milestones for the next few months.

Describe long-term milestones, applying exponential thinking and summarizing how you plan to achieve your MTP.

Budget

Estimate the budget needed to achieve the short-term milestones previously defined.

Suggestions for the week...

The perfect flow for this week:

Spend the first day building a milestone plan and budget.

Devote the fourth day to practicing the presentation. Run through your presentation several times to get comfortable with delivery and timing. Make sure you know exactly which team members will be presenting.

| Sun | Mon | Tue Wed | Thu | Fri | Sat |

Spend the next two days building the presentation for the following week.

On the fifth day, deliver the presentation to your ExO Coach for last-minute feedback and tips.

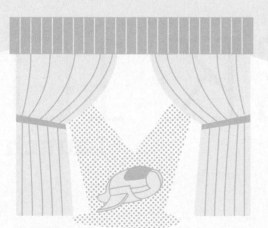

Be creative with your presentation format. For example, teams may want to augment their standard presentation with sound and video.

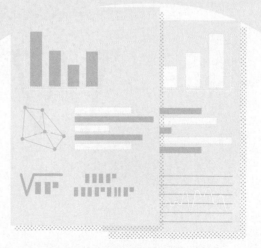

Include actual data from the experiments in the presentations. A great performance is a plus, but in the end it's only a nice deck. There is always more value in providing data and insights from actual clients (such as testimonials) to illustrate what you have learned.

WEEK 10
Launch

WHY THIS WEEK?

The big day is here!

This week you will present your ExO Edge Initiatives to the company's leadership team and selected advisors, who will then make a final decision about which initiatives to fund and develop.

The selection process is not the end—far from it, in fact. The development of your ExO Edge Initiatives marks the beginning of an industry revolution!

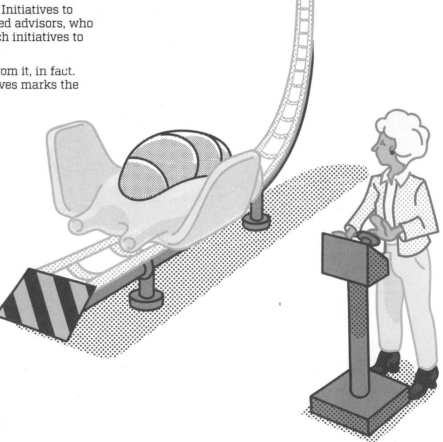

TASK 1 Prepare the scenario and logistics

Create the right environment and set up the logistics for the presentations.

Presentations can be done either in person or online. Much depends on where people are located and the size of your budget. If you present in person, consider decorating the space to create a unique atmosphere. If you conduct the presentations online, test the video conferencing system in advance.

TOOLS

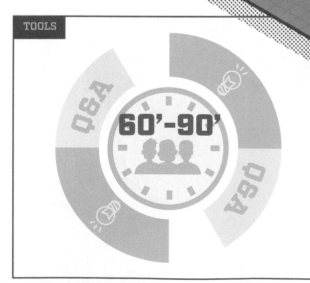

Follow an established agenda (we've included an outline below) for the presentation, which should take between 60 and 90 minutes depending on the number of ExO Edge Initiatives presented. Allot 15 minutes for each presentation, followed by a 10-minute Q&A session. Schedule a short break before the next event.

TIP

AGENDA

Time management is the key to presenting effectively. Communicate your agenda in advance, including the order of the presentations.

TASK 2 Presentations and discussion

DESCRIPTION

Teams will present their ideas to the leadership team and other relevant stakeholders. In contrast to the Disruption Session, this time the team will both receive feedback and answer questions.

The final presentation format is longer than that for the Disruption Session, which relied on the elevator pitch technique.

RESOURCES

Two books that can help you improve your presentations: *The Presentation Secrets of Steve Jobs: How to Be Insanely Great in Front of Any Audience* and *Talk Like Ted: The 9 Public-Speaking Secrets of the World's Top Minds*, both by Carmine Gallo.

TIP

We recommend a 10-minute Q&A session per initiative.

TASK 3 Final evaluation

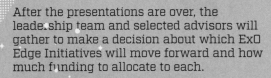

DESCRIPTION

After the presentations are over, the leadership team and selected advisors will gather to make a decision about which ExO Edge Initiatives will move forward and how much funding to allocate to each.

Remember that the initiatives must be evaluated from the point of view of *disruption*. The way the industry currently operates may not apply here, even when it comes to existing regulations. The leadership team must also be careful not to take on the role of the corporate immune system.

TOOLS

The leadership team should refer to the templates in this section, which will aid them in evaluating which initiatives to fund.

TIP

To help preempt an immune system reaction on the part of the leadership team members who are not participating in the ExO Sprint, we recommend that experts in disruption be included in the final presentation evaluations, just as during the earlier Disruption Session, held Week 5. Their independence from the organization (and its leadership), promotes honest and unbiased feedback.

TIP

Remember that old-school, traditional thinking doesn't apply here, so avoid input and recommendations that come from that mindset. This can prove challenging if you are an industry insider!

TASK 3 Final evaluation

TIP

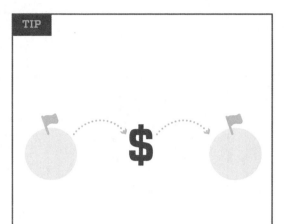

Keep in mind that the ExO Edge Initiatives are still in the early stages of development, which means they're likely to change in the coming months. For now, it's important to maintain a high-level perspective—focusing on the purpose and specific vision of the ExO Edge Initiatives—rather than zeroing in on the details.

TIP

The leadership team doesn't need to fund the chosen initiatives in full; it can follow a lean approach, allocating only enough funding to achieve the next key milestone.

TIP

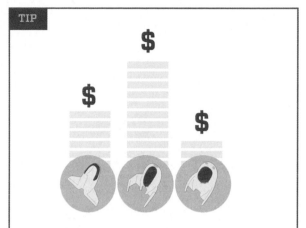

It's generally a good idea to determine the total amount of money you want to spend in the phase following the ExO Sprint. Split the sum among the different initiatives according to your expectations for each.

TIP

Choose external teams made up of one or more entrepreneurs to develop each ExO Edge Initiative further. ExO Sprint participants who worked on the initiatives should serve as external advisors. You'll find that many will be eager to jump into the new "ExO on the Edge"!

TASK 4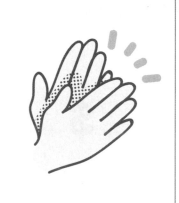

Announcements

DESCRIPTION

Informing ExO Sprint participants which ExO initiatives are being funded is key to keeping momentum going.

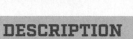

It's important to keep all ExO Sprint participants engaged, whether or not their initiatives are selected. Be sure to communicate your appreciation of a job well done. Everyone will have completed an incredible amount of work in a short period of time.

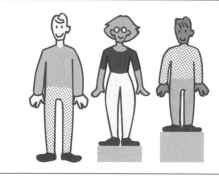

One way to keep everyone engaged and have them share in the outcome is to offer all ExO Sprint participants (and ExO Core teams, if applicable) equity in the ExO Edge Initiatives.

PRESENTATIONS AGENDA

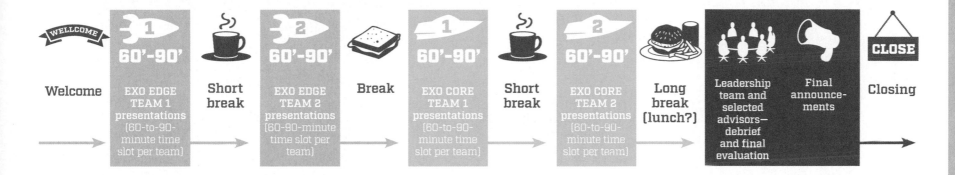

Welcome | EXO EDGE TEAM 1 presentations (60-to-90-minute time slot per team) | Short break | EXO EDGE TEAM 2 presentations (60-90-minute time slot per team) | Break | EXO CORE TEAM 1 presentations (60-to-90-minute time slot per team) | Short break | EXO CORE TEAM 2 presentations (60-to-90-minute time slot per team) | Long break (lunch?) | Leadership team and selected advisors—debrief and final evaluation | Final announcements | Closing

TEMPLATE for delivery

ExO Edge Initiative	Is It Aligned With ExO Sprint Scope?	Is It Disruptive?	Is It Scalable?	Is It Viable?	Selected?	Funding Allocated
AirEco	YES	YES	YES	YES	YES	$150K

Suggestions for the week...

FINAL TIPS

Practice as much as possible and keep working to improve your presentation.

When it's finally time to share your ExO initiatives with everyone, relax and enjoy the moment!

It's important to make an announcement about the selected initiatives and the funds allocated to each.

Pay attention to any personal transformation ExO Sprint participants may have experienced during the ExO Sprint. Some will be ready to jump into the ExO Edge Initiatives selected. Be open to supporting new career paths!

EXECUTION
CORE STREAM

Execution (**Core Stream**)

The Core Stream allows you to adapt your existing organization to external industry disruption by embracing the adoption of new technologies and organizational techniques—all while maintaining your current business model.

FEATURES

In addition to facilitating a comprehensive understanding of the existing organization and industry, the Core Stream also explores disruption coming from outside the industry. Your current organization has a working business model and existing legacy that you can't change from one day to the next, so even as you adapt it to external disruption—which can be viewed as either a threat or a great opportunity—you will preserve the basic foundation.

OPPORTUNITIES

- Make the organization more adaptable, flexible and agile in the face of external disruption.

- Improve the organization's value proposition.

- Increase efficiency.

- Increase sales.

- Diversify revenue streams.

- Increase impact related to the MTP.

CHALLENGES

- Learn about and evaluate all external elements—technologies and business models, for example—that might disrupt your industry.

- Create strategies to survive and thrive amidst accelerating disruption.

- Deal with the corporate immune system in advance to avoid having it throw up barriers to new strategies and projects.

- Embrace failure as part of the process. Keep experimenting and iterating ideas until you find the perfect fit with the market.

INPUTS

- The Core Stream applied to the entire organization or to a specific business unit (or units).

- A team of people able, willing and eager to spend the next 10 weeks creating new initiatives to adapt the organization to external industry disruption.

OUTPUTS

- An organization that is more flexible, agile and adaptable to external industry disruption.

- Generate exponential profits.

- Change the world for the better.

WEEK 1

Explore

WHY THIS WEEK?

The world changes every day. Exploring how change might affect your organization is an exciting learning experience—one that may even surprise you!

Many executives spend most of their time dealing with internal issues, never looking beyond what's happening within the organization. Don't be one of them!

The biggest threats and opportunities for your organization can be found in the emergence of new technologies and business models, as well as in changes to the environment beyond your industry as it stands today. All of these elements represent external disruption that may be relevant for the future of your organization over both the short- and long-term. So, let's find them!

This week's assignment sets the foundation for the Core Stream. It will help you gain a strategic overview of the most important technologies that may disrupt your industry either now or in the future. How is your industry already being reshaped? By looking "outside the building" you will gain an understanding of how your organization needs to be reshaped, not only to survive but to leverage existing opportunities.

TASK 1 Learn about exponential technologies

DESCRIPTION

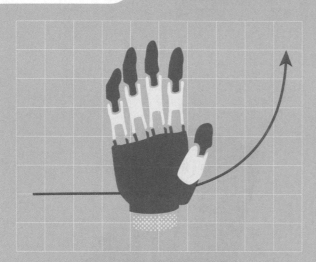

Most exponential technologies will impact your industry at some point, either directly or indirectly. While these technologies may disrupt the industry as it exists today, they will also bring new opportunities that can be leveraged.

Think about how some of these emerging/exponential technologies may impact or have already impacted your industry.

- Artificial intelligence
- Robotics
- 3D printing
- Virtual reality and augmented reality
- Biotechnology and bioinformatics

- Blockchain and Bitcoin
- Nanotechnology
- Drones
- The Internet of Things
- Quantum computing

Search the internet for terms and phrases such as "disruptive technologies for [X] industry," which should yield lots of great examples.

TOOLS

Use the template in this section.

RESOURCES

Explore tech-focused websites for articles on new technologies. Even if the articles aren't specific to your industry, you will find connections and potential applications. Helpful websites include:

- MIT Technology Review:

  www.technologyreview.com/

- Singularity University Hub:

  www.singularityhub.com

- Disruption Hub:

  www.disruptionhub.com/

- Wired:

  www.wired.com/

- Exponential View:

  www.exponentialview.com

- Futurism:

  www.futurism.com

TIP

Subscribe to the weekly newsletters these sites offer. They will keep you apprised of the latest developments in emerging technologies. A quick scan each week keeps you informed and enables you to research further when a particular topic catches your eye.

TIP

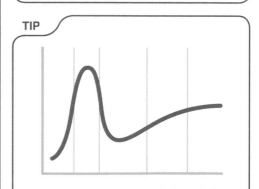

Check out the Gartner Hype Cycle for information on emerging technologies.

TASK 2   Learn about new business models that can disrupt your industry

DESCRIPTION

New business models and startups both within and beyond your industry may disrupt your existing business. Learn about these before it's too late to catch up.

Search the internet for terms and phrases such as "startups for [X] industry."

RESOURCES

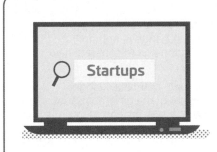

Visit startup-focused websites, where you will find articles about new ventures. Remember that you are not just looking for startups focused on your industry, but also for new business models that can be applied to your industry. Helpful websites include:

- TechCrunch:
  https://techcrunch.com/
- AngelList:
  https://angel.co/
- Gust:
  http://www.gust.com
- Entrepreneur:
  https://www.entrepreneur.com

TOOLS

Use the template in this section.

TIP

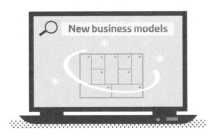

Search for new business models and companies that are solving the same market need that yours does. Sometimes the disruption comes from outside your industry, as new companies begin to solve customer needs in a completely novel way.

TIP

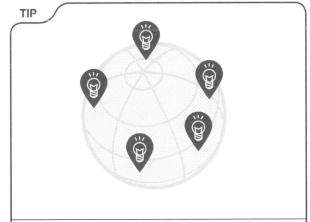

Countless startups are finding new ways to disrupt industries. Study them for inspiration on how to improve your own organization!

TIP

Ask the following questions in relation to your industry:

- What new and different ways of doing business are shaking things up?
- How are traditional businesses being bypassed as startups increasingly connect directly with consumers?

TASK 3

Find out about new changes in the context of your organization

DESCRIPTION

Changes in context can be either a threat or an opportunity for your business. Identify those changes—both to prepare the company for disruption and to generate new opportunities.

Facilitate the process of identifying potential changes contextually by brainstorming about the different issues that might affect your industry or organization:

Regulation:
New laws and policies

Clients:
New customer segments, trends, purchasing behaviors, user experience

Providers:
New suppliers, trends, operational models

Competitors:
New players, substitute products/services

Environment:
New events taking place in the physical or digital world that could affect your business

TOOLS

Use the template in this section.

TIP

Remember that exponential technologies generate abundance and new business models based on that abundance. To identify external disruption, note transitions from scarcity to abundance.

TASK 3 — Find out about new changes in the context of your organization

TIP

There is a lot of knowledge within your organization about how context is affecting your industry and business, so talk to people around you to gain insight.

TIP

Using traditional methods (e.g., Porter's Five Forces framework) will help you conduct a comprehensive analysis of how context changes are likely to affect your organization.

TIP

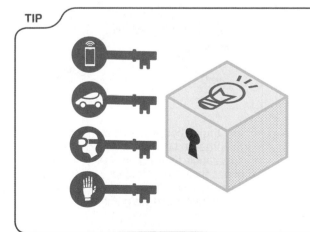

Some of these context changes may seem challenging, but you'll find that most have the potential to become great opportunities.

TASK 4

Describe your current organization's business model

DESCRIPTION

A business model is the way an organization creates, delivers and retains value. At this stage of the game, you are going to describe your current organization's business model, which will act as a framework for the ExO initiatives. Remember that the ExO Core Stream shouldn't change your current business model—it should instead adapt it to external industry disruption.

Use the Business Model Generation technique to describe your business model in a way that allows you to achieve a high-level overview.

TOOLS

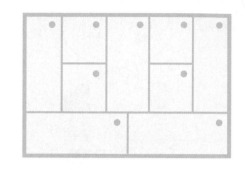

Use the Business Model Canvas template in this section.

RESOURCE

Alex Osterwalder's book *Business Model Generation* offers a guide to the Business Model Canvas.

RESOURCE

Go to the Align section and refer to the exercise for business model design. ➡ Pg. 136

TIP

Remember that you are describing how your current organization's business model works, not trying to redefine it.

TIP

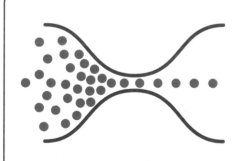

Identifying bottlenecks that make the organization less agile and more susceptible to disruption is key. In our experience, teams that take the time for such analysis are much better prepared for the upcoming assignments.

TEMPLATE for delivery

Exponential Technology	Risks	Opportunities	Timing
Name and/or description here...	How it can disrupt your industry...	How it can bring new business opportunities...	When this exponential technology might impact the industry...

Disruptive Business Model	Risks	Opportunities	Timing
Company name and/or description here...	How it can disrupt your industry...	How it can bring new business opportunities...	When this new business model might disrupt your industry...

Context changes	Risk	Opportunities
Description here...	How it would impact the industry...	How industry can benefit...

Exponential Technology	Risks	Opportunities	Timing
Name and/or description here...	How it can disrupt your industry...	How it can bring new business opportunities...	When this exponential technology might impact the industry...
Internet	Enables sharing economy and P2P business models.	Enables hotels to better reach clients and develop new business models.	Now
Artificial Intelligence & Robotics	Automate majority of hotel's operations and increase competition.	Help hotels better understand clients.	Within the next 2 years
Drones	Provide new ways of traveling.	Provide new ways of traveling.	Within the next 5 years
Virtual Reality	New technology could reduce desire to travel.	Leverage technology for hotels.	Within the next 2 years

Disruptive Business Model	Risks	Opportunities	Timing
Company name and/or description here...	How it can disrupt your industry...	How it can bring new business opportunities...	When this new business model might disrupt your industry...
Airbnb (sharing economy leverages assets)	Offers customers eco accommodations.	Launch a P2P sharing economy platform.	Now
Uber (on demand staff)	Allows competitors to be more responsive to market needs.	Implement the Community attribute.	Now
Cratejoy (subscription business model)	Lose market share as consumers gravitate to hotels participating in subscription services.	Launch a subscription business model.	Now

TEMPLATE for delivery

Context changes	Risk	Opportunities
Description here...	How it would impact the industry...	How industry can benefit...
New players based on sharing economy.	Sharing economy platforms are a huge threat to traditional players.	Integrate traditional offering on sharing economy platforms or launch new businesses based on this approach.
Travelers want efficiency and personalization.	Established businesses that don't evolve may become obsolete.	Personalize products/services.
Travelers need hourly based stays.	Industry not adapted for this need.	Launch new product/services based on hourly stays.

TEMPLATE

Eco Places

Business Model Canvas for Eco Places (Parent Organization)

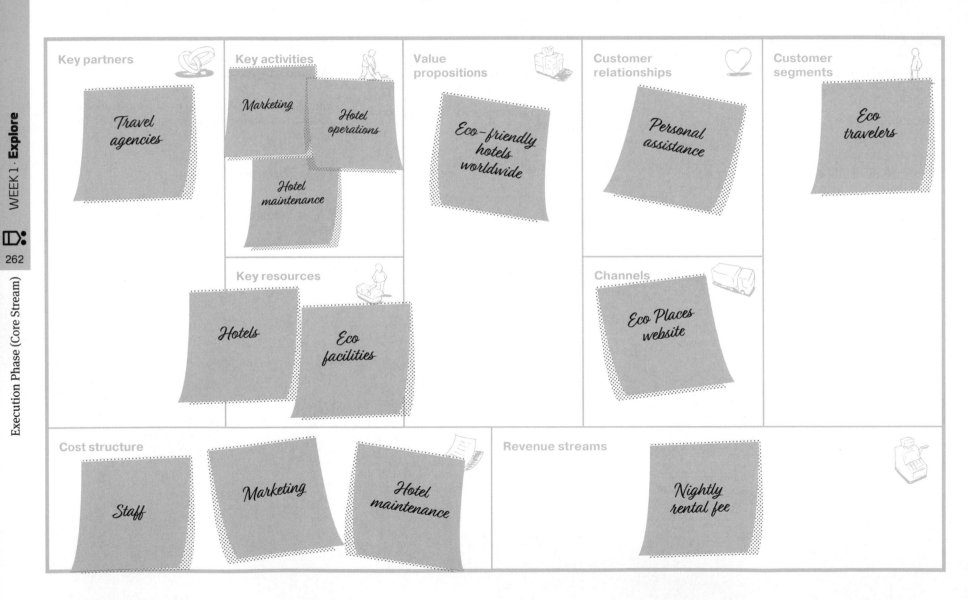

Key partners

Travel agencies

Key activities

Marketing

Hotel operations

Hotel maintenance

Value propositions

Eco-friendly hotels worldwide

Customer relationships

Personal assistance

Customer segments

Eco travelers

Key resources

Hotels

Eco facilities

Channels

Eco Places website

Cost structure

Staff

Marketing

Hotel maintenance

Revenue streams

Nightly rental fee

Recommendations for the week...

The perfect flow for this week:

Spend the first four days on research.

Review results with your ExO Coach on the fifth day.

Sun	Mon	Tue	Wed	Thu	Fri	Sat

By the end of the week, you should have a good understanding of your organization and the risks it faces. You should also be assessing external technologies and business trends that can be leveraged for growth.

Talk to people within your organization to gain new insights.

Step outside your comfort and knowledge zones and explore unknown areas.

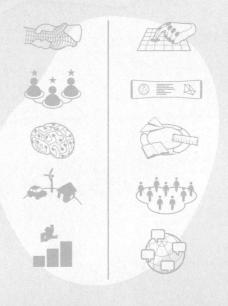

In addition to this week's tasks, you may also want to explore the ExO attributes on a deeper level. Make sure you have read the previous section of this book, and then research companies to understand how they are applying ExO attributes.

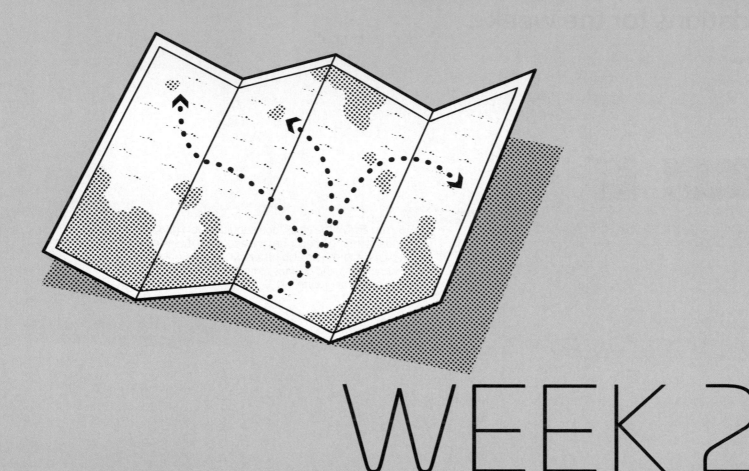

WEEK 2
Ideate

WHY THIS WEEK?

You have at your fingertips the opportunity to (re)invent your organization and make the world a better place.

Every industry sees occasional disruption. However, the frequency of that disruption is accelerating as exponential technologies impact both business models and the environment in general.

As Thomas Edison said, "To have a great idea, have a lot of them." This week you will generate as many ExO Core Initiative ideas as possible in order to ensure success.

Adapt your current organization to external industry disruption to protect it from the threats disruption poses and to take advantage of the great opportunities continually emerging from that disruption.

TASK 1

Define a (Massive) Transformative Purpose for the organization

DESCRIPTION

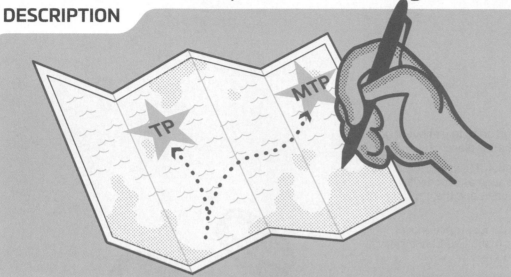

Exponential Organizations have a vision and a mission. They also have a purpose. In order to adapt your organization to the current environment, you must define your purpose. If your organization already has a global market or aims to have one, you will need to define a Massive Transformative Purpose (MTP). If your organization is or aims to be focused on a local market only, you will define a Transformative Purpose (TP).

Running an ideation session using techniques such as brainstorming, "what-ifs" and visual thinking will help.

RESOURCES

Review the MTP section to refresh your understanding of how to implement a good MTP for your organization. ⤷ **Pg. 40**

TIP

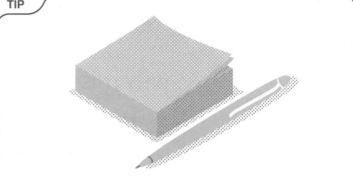

A set of sticky notes and a pen are all you need for a brainstorming session.

TIP

Remember that you are in the generation phase of the ExO Sprint. The more ideas you come up with for MTPs and TPs, the better. (For simplicity's sake, from here on out we'll refer just to MTPs; TPs are implied where applicable.) At the end of this week, we recommend picking a single MTP as the foundation for the upcoming assignments, keeping in mind that you will be able to modify it in the future.

TASK 2

Define multiple External Disruption/Internal Reaction pairs for your MTP

DESCRIPTION

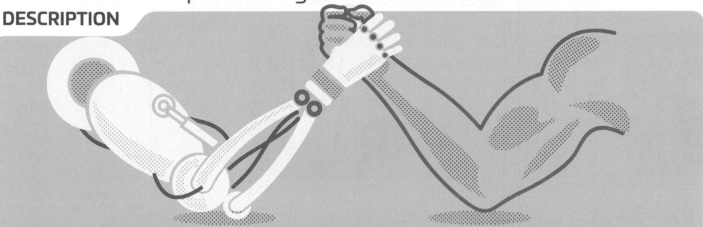

The first step is to think about any external disruptions that are relevant to your organization and its purpose. You'll also want to think about internal reactions you can create to adapt to or to take advantage of external disruption. To that end, you will define a set of external disruption/internal reaction pairs within the domain of the purpose outlined in the previous step. Note that each disruption/reaction pair is an ExO Core Initiative.

Based on the internal reactions you define, you'll need to consider the different types of ExO Core Initiatives, which are dependent on those reactions:

Pure Core

An ExO Core Initiative that is specific to the existing organization and cannot be replicated and sold to other organizations. For example: a digital transformation project that is unique to an individual organization; using AI-based technology to automate all processes.

Edge Core

An ExO Core Initiative that is first implemented in your organization and then replicated and sold elsewhere. For example: Amazon Web Services, today a successful subsidiary of the parent company.

Blue Core

An ExO Core Initiative based on launching a product or service to capture an untapped demographic (known as Blue Ocean Strategy). For example: Nintendo Wii discovered a new and lucrative market in older consumers.

TOOLS

Use the template in this section.

TASK 2   Define multiple External Disruption/Internal Reaction pairs for your MTP

RESOURCES

To identify external disruptions, review the exponential technologies, business models and context changes addressed in Week 1. ➡ **Pg. 254**

RESOURCES

For internal reactions inspiration, review the exponential technologies identified Week 1. In addition, revisit the 10 ExO attributes. ➡ **Pg. 254**

RESOURCE

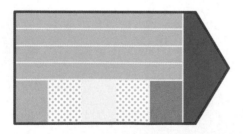

To stimulate internal reaction ideas for Pure Core Initiatives and Edge Core Initiatives, draw the Porter's Value Chain for your organization and think about where you can make improvements.

RESOURCE

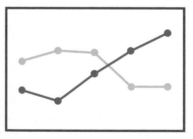

For more internal reaction inspiration when it comes to Blue Core Initiatives, review the Blue Ocean Strategy Canvas found in the Align section and refer to the exercise included there.

TIP

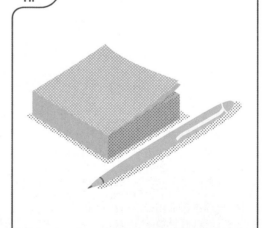

A set of sticky notes and a pen are all you need for a brainstorming session.

TASK 2

Define multiple External Disruption/Internal Reaction pairs for your MTP

TIP

Running an ideation session and using brainstorming and storytelling techniques can help define the external disruption. For the internal response, use the "what-if" technique.

TIP

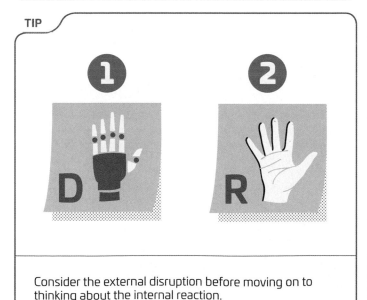

Consider the external disruption before moving on to thinking about the internal reaction.

TIP

Remember that the goal isn't to change your organization's existing business model. In fact, all ExO Core Initiatives should fit into the Business Model Canvas you completed last week. Small improvements are always a plus but try to avoid making any major changes.

TIP

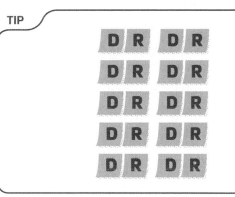

Remember that the minimum number of disruption/reaction pairs you should define is 10, but feel free to come up with more. Also note that an external disruption may have more than one internal reaction, meaning you might have more than one pair per external disruption.

TIP

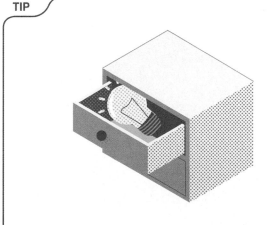

Use this week to determine if any of the ideas your team has come up with existed previously in the organization. You'll want to be careful to avoid using the ExO Sprint as a vehicle to advance existing projects. If you do choose to advance a pre-existing idea, the executive leadership team needs to be on board. The idea must also meet all ExO criteria. There may be an opportunity to improve the idea, so start with a blank slate and make the idea exponential!

TEMPLATE for delivery

Eco Places

MTP	ExO Core Initiative Name	External Disruption	Internal Reaction
Personalized eco experience for everyone	Smart Eco	Decreased margins due to growth of sharing economy; travelers want more efficiency and personalization.	Automate as many processes as possible using AI; robots replace some staff members.
	Short eco stays	Travelers want option of booking on an hourly basis.	Update hotel pricing and technology systems to allow hourly bookings.
	Personal room	New virtual reality (VR) technologies could reduce desire to travel.	Equip hotel with VR technologies that enable those not staying at the property to travel virtually and "meet" with hotel guests.

Recommendations for the week...

The perfect flow for this week:

Spend the first two days of the week defining MTPs.

Review results with your ExO Coach on the fifth day.

| Sun | Mon | Tue | | Wed | Thu | | Fri | | Sat |

Over the next two days, consider disruption/reaction pairs for the previously defined MTPs.

The minimum number of disruption/reaction pairs for this week is 10 but the idea is to create as many as you can. We have seen some teams generate more than 30!

The goal of the Core Stream is to adapt the current organization to industry disruption. Ideas you come up with at this stage should apply either to the whole organization or to a specific business unit. Maintain this focus as you ideate.

The more ideas you generate, the better! (At this point, each ExO Core Initiative includes an MTP/TP and a disruption/reaction pair.) You will present a minimum of four initiatives during the Disruption Session, so it's better to work on as many as possible now, since some may not survive the experimentation stage coming up next week.

We know that it can be hard to develop and manage so many ExO initiatives. If you need to skip certain elements, it's fine. At this stage, it's better to generate a lot of ideas even if they have yet to be fleshed out than to be left with only a small number of initiatives, no matter how meticulously detailed.

WEEK 3
Share

WHY THIS WEEK?

Experimentation is crucial to any innovative project.

By definition, any innovative idea under consideration is a hypothesis (or a set of hypotheses), which means it (or they) will need to be tested prior to development. The first set of hypotheses to evaluate should be the external disruption/ internal reaction pairs defined last week.

Of the 10 ExO attributes that the ExO framework defines, Experimentation is the one that must always be included.

This week you will focus on running experiments to evaluate your hypotheses. There is no better place to start than by asking the people involved in the ExO Core Initiatives what they think about them.

TASK 1 Define key hypotheses and run experiments

DESCRIPTION

The innovative ideas previously defined are a set of hypotheses that now need to be evaluated to determine whether or not they are true. You won't have time to evaluate all of them, however, so limit your focus to those hypotheses that will enable your ExO initiative to succeed.

The goal is to adapt the current organization to external industry disruption by implementing ExO attributes and using exponential technologies. Before doing so, however, you'll need to evaluate whether the external disruption under consideration is a true threat and/or opportunity. You'll also need to evaluate whether the defined internal reaction is feasible and fits the market.

Identify the key hypotheses and define experiments for each. Your approach will vary depending on the type of ExO Core Initiative.

 Blue Core Initiatives

These are new products and services to test with the market (using real customers). The best thing to do with such initiatives is to run a version of Steve Blank's Customer Development technique: ask people if they have the specific problem you're addressing and whether or not they like the product or service under consideration (product/solution fit). Here are the steps to follow:

- **Identify which hypotheses to evaluate at this stage:** Most will focus on whether or not your clients/users have the problem you think they do, and whether they like your proposed product or service. You can also consider other hypotheses, such as whether it's technically feasible to build your product or service.

- **Design an experiment to evaluate the hypotheses:** In general, you'll want to design an interview for gathering actual data about the previously defined hypotheses. Each experiment will include evaluation criteria to aid in validating or invalidating each hypothesis.

Pure Core and Edge Core Initiatives

These are usually internal projects designed to help an organization become more agile, adaptable and efficient. Begin by evaluating whether or not the external disruptions identified are realistic. You will also need to consult the stakeholders who will ultimately approve and use the internal solutions defined. In order to do that, follow these steps:

- **Identify the key hypotheses:** These are the ones that are critical for the success of your ExO Core Initiative. Most will concern whether or not the external disruption identified is a real threat or opportunity. The key hypotheses for ExO Core Initiatives, however, are usually those related to internal reactions. Ensure that they are both accepted within the organization and technically feasible.

- **Design an experiment to evaluate the hypotheses:** Conduct further research on external disruption hypotheses to determine whether they are valid and consult with key people. For internal disruption hypotheses, interview internal stakeholders and/or users of the project under consideration. You may also need to talk to technology providers and experts about the feasibility of the solution.

TASK 1 Define key hypotheses and run experiments

TOOLS

Use the template in this section.

RESOURCE

Go to the Align section and refer to the exercise dedicated to designing experiments. ➡ **Pg. 140**

RESOURCES

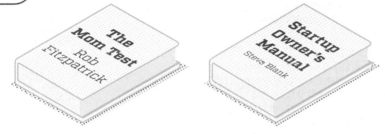

For the experiments focused on information gathering, consult Rob Fitzpatrick's book *The Mom Test*. Steve Blank's *The Startup Owner's Manual* outlines how to conduct interviews with potential customers, which is particularly helpful when researching Blue Core Initiatives.

TIP

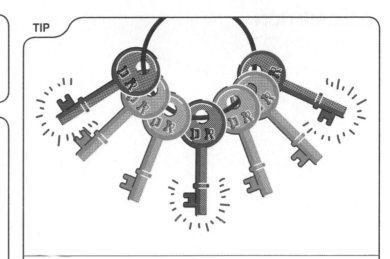

Prioritizing experiments is important, since you may have so many hypotheses to evaluate that you won't have time to run them all.

TIP

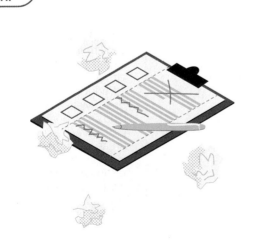

Think through the design of your experiments before beginning them. Results should allow you to evaluate the external disruptions and better define the right internal reaction, not just answer the question, "Is this a good idea?" How you construct the interview questions is very important. Issues to consider in advance: How can you ask questions creatively? How will the results allow you to improve the initiative? Clearly define what will determine the success of an experiment, including what thresholds need to be met.

TIP

Ask for honest feedback. Invalidating a hypothesis is not bad; in fact, it's an important part of the innovation process. Either outcome results in great learning and progress.

TASK 2 — Run experiments to evaluate your ExO initiatives

DESCRIPTION

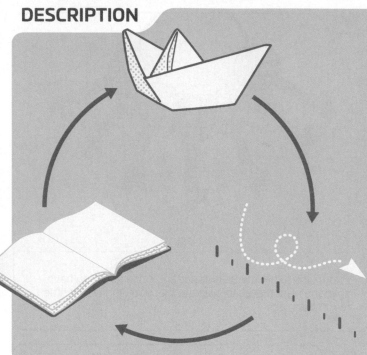

The next step is to run the experiments you have defined. In addition to conducting further research on external disruptions, you'll also interview users/potential clients (to evaluate disruptions/reactions) and/or tech people (to evaluate product feasibility). Reach out now to arrange calls and meetings. Your goal with these interviews is to gather actual data.

After running the experiments, it's important to spend sufficient time analyzing the results. You will evaluate all hypotheses, improve the ExO initiatives based on what you've learned and make a final evaluation of the improved ExO initiatives.

The Build-Measure-Learn loop provides a set of useful guidelines for running ongoing experiments and will help you learn as much as possible (your primary goal at this juncture).

TOOLS

Use the template in this section.

RESOURCE

Eric Ries' *The Lean Startup* introduces the Build-Measure-Learn loop and is a great reference for how to run these processes.

TIP

Your number one asset at this point is actual data, since the goal of the Build-Measure-Learn loop is to base all your decisions on solid data and not on opinions or intuition.

TIP

Ask for honest feedback. Invalidating a hypothesis is not bad, it's part of the innovation process. Remember: the main goal is to learn!

TIP

A great way to implement the Experimentation attribute is by introducing the Build-Measure-Learn loop as an ongoing process within your organization. Ongoing identification and testing of hypotheses will increase learning and move you in the right direction.

TEMPLATE for delivery

Define and run experiments

ExO Initiative Name	BUILD		MEASURE		LEARN
	Key Hypotheses	Experiment Description	Evaluation Criteria	Experiment Result	Key Learnings
Smart Eco	Eco travelers desire increased efficiency and personalization.	Interview 10 eco travelers using the Customer Development interview template.	At least 60% of potential clients should validate hypothesis.	90% of potential clients validated hypothesis.	**Hypothesis Validated** Clients would like to personalize room features (e.g., room temperature, specific requests).
	Eco travelers like the idea of robots supplementing human staff.	Interview 10 eco travelers using the Customer Development interview template.	At least 60% of potential clients should validate hypothesis.	Only 20% of potential clients validated hypothesis.	**Hypothesis Invalidated** Eco travelers like the idea of robots but only for specific services.

Suggestions for the week...

The perfect flow for this week:

Use the first day to identify hypotheses, define experiments, arrange interviews and build surveys.

Use the fourth day to gather results and determine key learnings.

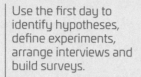

| Sun | Mon | Tue Wed | Thu | Fri | Sat |

Over the next two days, perform experiments (conducting interviews or sending surveys).

Use the fifth day to review results with your ExO Coach.

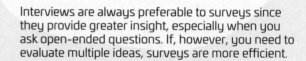

Interviews are always preferable to surveys since they provide greater insight, especially when you ask open-ended questions. If, however, you need to evaluate multiple ideas, surveys are more efficient.

The idea is to run experiments for all external disruption/internal reaction pairs defined. If you have one or two disruption/reaction pairs per team member, we recommend assigning one or two initiatives per team member to run experiments. If you have more than two initiatives per team member, consider running a much bigger but more superficial experiment by sending surveys to potential clients instead of conducting direct interviews.

To evaluate different types of hypotheses, reach out to external advisors who are specialists in your industry or in a specific technology or methodology.

Remember that getting out and talking to customers and colleagues is the only way to turn your hypotheses into facts.

Different ExO Core Initiatives may share the same group of people to be interviewed. In that case, ask the group about the different ExO Core Initiatives at the same time.

WEEK 4
Select

WHY THIS WEEK?

It's time to select your top ExO Core Initiatives and take them to the next level.

Next week you will present your ExO initiatives at the Disruption Session and receive feedback that will help you improve your projects.

This week's assignment is to work on the presentations for the upcoming Disruption Session, which entails a five-minute pitch for each of four initiatives. You will present your project to the company's leadership team, the other members of the ExO Sprint and a select panel of ExO Disruptors.

TASK 1

Select the four most promising ideas

DESCRIPTION

The first task is to pick the top four ideas to present at the Disruption Session. To narrow your options, evaluate each initiative according to the previous week's results (experiments and key learnings) and the following criteria:

- **The external disruption you're focusing on:** Is it global? Was it validated during the previous experiment?

- **The internal reaction you're considering building:** Once completed, will it help the organization adapt to—or take advantage of—external industry disruption? Is it feasible to build? If not, will exponentials make it feasible to build sometime in the future? Was it validated during the experiment phase?

TIP

All decisions should be data-based, so select projects with strong evidence to support them.

TIP

All remaining ExO initiatives should be filed away for possible development in the future.

TASK 1   Select the four most promising ideas

TIP

TIP

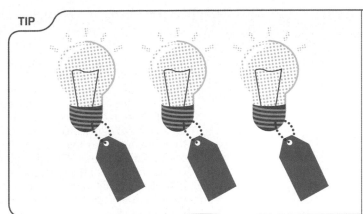

Give each initiative a compelling title that makes it easy to understand, along with a one-line description.

TIP

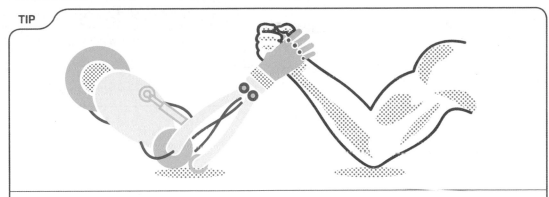

To test how well your initiative enables the organization to adapt to external industry disruption, ask the following: Will this initiative help us face external threats or take advantage of industry disruption?

If some ideas don't rate as ExO Core Initiatives but qualify as ExO Edge Initiatives, it's possible they can be repositioned. Instead of building a particular ExO Edge Initiative, consider defining a new ExO Core Initiative that would react to the ExO Edge idea under consideration (and which may be already happening in the world). For example, if you are a hotel chain considering building a new online platform offering hotel rooms (an ExO Edge Initiative), the idea could be transformed into a ExO Core Initiative by focusing on building the APIs that the hotel chain would need in order to connect with the original ExO Edge Initiative's platform.

TASK 2 Design the ExO Canvas

DESCRIPTION

In order to ensure your organization will be set up to adopt the ExO model—and thus adapt to external disruption based on the abundance being generated in your industry—the ExO Canvas will prompt you to think about how to leverage each of the 10 ExO attributes. Design an ExO Canvas for each of the disruption/reaction pairs defined in the previous step. Each represents a different ExO Core Initiative.

Run a brainstorming session using the blocks in the ExO Canvas as steps for the ideation process.

TOOLS

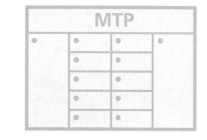

Use the ExO Canvas template.

TIP

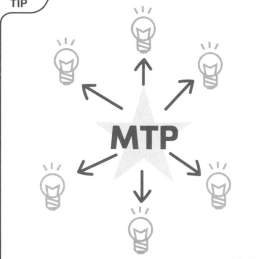

Remember to include the MTP in the ExO Canvas of each of the ExO initiatives. All ExO Core Initiatives should share the MTP you defined for the organization.

RESOURCE

Review the ExO Canvas section on defining each of the ExO attributes.
⮕ Pg. 76

TIP

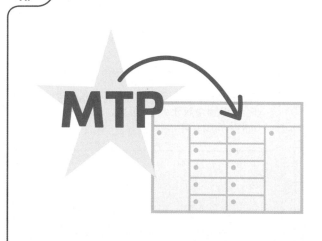

Remember to include the MTP/TP in your ExO Canvas.

TASK 3

Create an extended elevator pitch for each ExO Core Initiative

DESCRIPTION

Create a five-minute pitch and supporting presentation for each of the ExO initiatives to be presented.

At this stage of the process (idea-stage ExO initiatives), we recommend composing an elevator pitch—a summary of each idea that could conceivably be delivered during a standard elevator ride. An elevator pitch is usually delivered in 60 to 90 seconds, but in this case, you're going to a write a five-minute version.

The elevator pitch should include the following items:

MTP

Explain why your organization exists, demonstrating how the specific ExO Core Initiative will help it achieve the MTP.

External Disruption

Describe the external disruption that triggered the ExO Core Initiative.

Internal Reaction

Present the internal reaction, focusing on how you will address the external disruption, the value it will provide and how it will make the organization more adaptable and even scalable.

ExO Attributes

Discuss the ExO attributes you will use the most, identifying those that will help the organization reach abundance and those that will help manage that abundance.

TASK 3 Create an extended elevator pitch for each ExO Core Initiative

RESOURCES

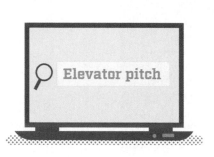

There are thousands of great websites dedicated to describing how to prepare and deliver elevator pitches.

RESOURCE

For an ExO Blue Core Initiative (focused on a product/service), check out the Pitch Canvas, an online brainstorming tool that helps entrepreneurs visualize an entire pitch on one page.

TIP

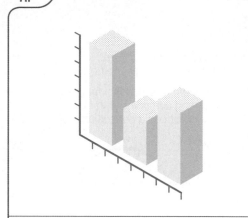

Include actual data from the experiments. Cool ideas are valuable but validated ones are even better.

TIP

Storytelling is a great way to present an elevator pitch.

TIP

Get your pitch down on paper so you can practice it repeatedly.

TIP

Time management is important, so create a pitch you can deliver in five minutes without having to rush.

TASK 4

Create a presentation to support the pitch

DESCRIPTION

You may want to create slides to accompany your extended elevator pitch.

If you opt for a presentation, keep it simple, using only a few inspiring and informative images and graphs.

TOOLS

Use the presentation template in this section.

RESOURCE

A good book to help you prepare is Garr Reynolds' *Presentation Zen: Simple Ideas on Presentation Design and Delivery,* which describes using simplicity and storytelling to reach an audience.

TIP

Include some context about the organization, since external disruptors who don't know much about your organization may attend next week's session.

TIP

Whenever possible, use pictures instead of text for your slides. You want people to listen to what you have to say rather than be distracted by reading your slides.

TIP

Using the ExO Canvas to design your ExO initiative is helpful. However, you don't need to share it during the presentation. Instead, explain the individual pieces using other, more visual and creative means.

TASK 5   Practice your pitch!

DESCRIPTION

You will be presenting a large number of ideas, so each pitch should be concise and to the point. The more you practice, the better you will do.

Practice, practice, practice!

RESOURCES

Your pitch, your voice and your passion.

RESOURCES

External feedback is great at this point, so share your presentation with your team and anyone else you can.

TIP

Time management is important, so practice as much as possible.

TIP

A relaxed and natural delivery is key, so again, practice as much as possible.

TEMPLATE

ExO Canvas for Smart Eco

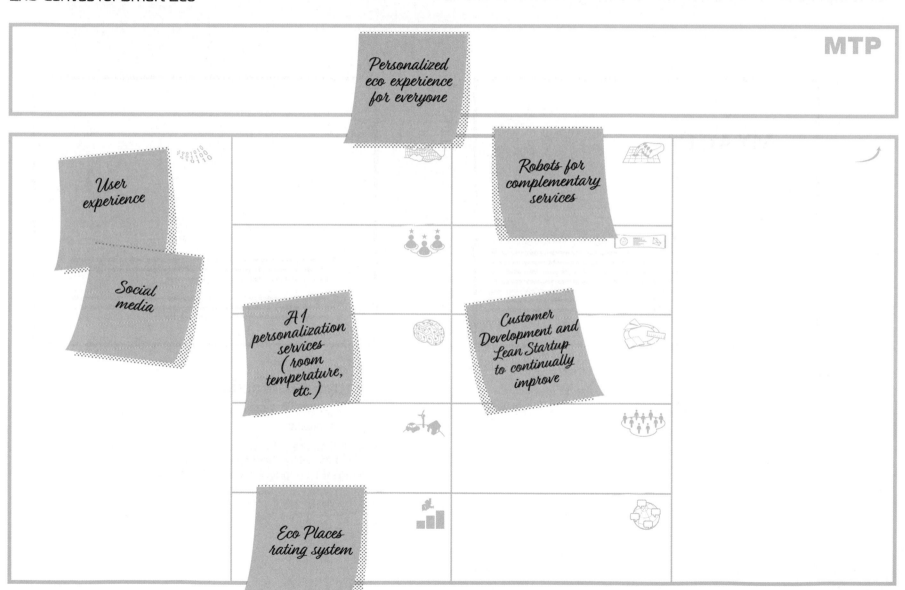

MTP

Personalized eco experience for everyone

Robots for complementary services

User experience

Social media

A1 personalization services (room temperature, etc.)

Customer Development and Lean Startup to continually improve

Eco Places rating system

PRESENTATION

Your template should include the following slides or sections:

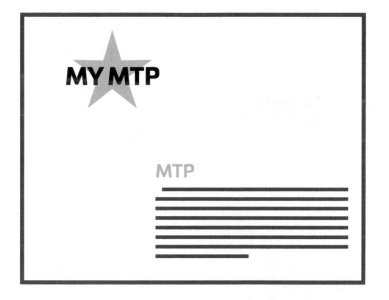

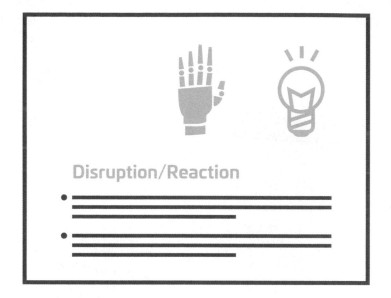

MTP

It's imperative that you begin the presentation with the MTP/TP.

Note that all ExO Core Initiatives will share the same MTP.

In general, use just one slide to introduce the MTP.

Disruption/Reaction

Discuss the external disruption, which is the main driver of the ExO Core Initiative.

Once the nature of the disruption is clear, introduce the internal reaction that will either prevent the fallout from the disruption or leverage the opportunities it can bring.

Suggestions for the week...

The perfect flow for this week:

Spend the first day prioritizing and selecting the ideas you will present and assign people (or groups) to build each of the presentations.

On the fifth day, present the pitch to your ExO Coach for feedback. Continue iterating and practicing the presentation in advance of the Disruption Session.

| Sun | Mon | Tue Wed | | Thu | Fri | Sat |

The next two days should be devoted to building the presentations.

Spend the fourth day practicing the presentation with the team, using internal feedback to improve it. We recommend looking ahead to next week's assignment, where you will find pitch techniques.

Include actual data from the experiments. A great performance is always a plus, but in the end, it's only a nice deck. There is always much more value in providing data and insights (e.g., testimonials) from clients, stakeholders and users to illustrate what you have learned.

Running further experiments is always a good idea if you have the time. The more data you have, the better—especially in the case of any ExO initiatives that were developed the previous week—in the event that some hypotheses were invalidated. You now have the opportunity to run more experiments on the new ExO initiatives (which are actually new hypotheses).

ExO Attributes

ExO Attributes

Show how you will reach abundance (using the SCALE attributes) and how you will manage that abundance (using the IDEAS attributes).

You may want to include the ExO Canvas and explain how each of the key ExO attributes applies to the ExO Core Initiative.

WEEK 5
Disrupt

WHY THIS WEEK?

It's time to disrupt your company before someone else beats you to it!

This week's assignment provides an opportunity to present your most promising ExO initiatives to a group of disruptors, who will then provide feedback on how to improve them.

Remember: failure is part of the process. If some ExO initiatives are rejected post-presentation, don't take it personally. It's better to fail fast and cheap now than to fail later after having invested a lot of time and money.

Based on the feedback you receive, you may end up killing some of your ExO Core Initiatives. On the flip side, you may create new ones that will complement your portfolio. Always keep your eyes and ears open for new opportunities!

TASK 1   Prepare the scenario and logistics

DESCRIPTION

Create the right environment for the presentations.

You can deliver the presentations either in person or online, depending on everyone's location and the parameters of your budget. If the Disruption Session is held in person, consider decorating the space to create a unique atmosphere. If you conduct it online, test the video conferencing system in advance. Note that if the ExO Sprint is running both an ExO Edge Stream and ExO Core Stream, the Disruption Session will include teams for each.

TIP

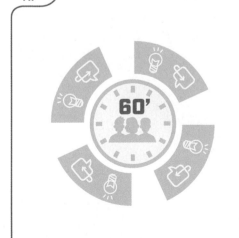

Follow an established agenda for each presentation, allowing 60 minutes for each team to present all four of its ExO initiatives, with a short break between each. Present each of the four ExO initiatives within five minutes, followed by five minutes of feedback.

TIP

AGENDA

Time management is the key to presenting effectively. Communicate your agenda in advance, including the order of the presentations.

TASK 2 Present!

DESCRIPTION

The big moment has arrived! It's time to present your ExO Core Initiatives for feedback.

Each team will have 60 minutes to present its ExO initiatives and receive feedback. The presentations will be given to the company's leadership team, the other ExO teams and a group of ExO Disruptors made up of three to five people from outside the organization who have specific experience in your industry or of innovation in general.

TIP

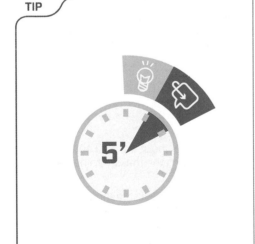

After each presentation, the audience will offer five minutes of feedback. We recommend limiting this part of the session to feedback only, with no questions allowed. At this stage, the goal is not to sell the initiatives but to learn.

TIP

Record all presentations for later review.

TASK 3 Gather feedback

DESCRIPTION

Take note of all feedback received from your peers and the disruptors. Everything you hear is valuable. Keep in mind that this set of presentations, combined with the feedback you receive, is yet another aspect of the experiments you've been running, and is included to improve your ExO initiatives.

Classify the feedback into different categories, one of which may include new hypotheses. Also remember to gather feedback about potential ExO initiatives.

RESOURCES

It is particularly important for ExO Core team participants to listen to the ExO Edge presentations, since the external disruptions they address must be taken into account when building ExO Core Initiatives. The idea is to make the organization's ecosystem compatible with itself.

TIP

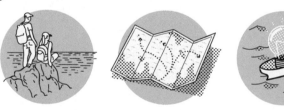

You will likely receive two types of feedback:

- **A focus on the ExO framework:** ExO Disruptors knowledgeable about the ExO approach are well equipped to offer advice on moving forward so as to gain the maximum benefit from the ExO process.

- **A focus on content:** Feedback relates to the ideas themselves and will sometimes include opinions about the problem you are working to solve or the solution you are trying to create. In that case, such feedback doesn't need to affect your approach; it can simply provide additional data points for evaluating your hypotheses.

TASK 4 Debrief with the leadership team

DESCRIPTION

You will have a debrief meeting with the management team to determine which of the ExO Core Initiatives is aligned with the general direction the leadership team wants to go. The management team also has the option of picking one of the MTPs presented—or even defining a new one.

TIP

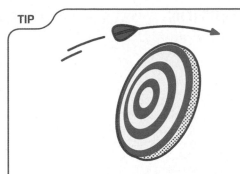

Remember that although you may have come up with amazing initiatives, some may ultimately fall outside the scope of what the company's leadership team has defined for the ExO Sprint.

TIP

We recommend that the ExO Head Coach meet with the leadership team separately to facilitate the decision-making process.

TIP

The leadership team may be inclined to select the ExO initiatives it wants to see move forward, but we suggest the group limit itself to recommendations (to avoid acting as the corporate immune system) and leave the ExO Sprint teams to make their own decisions. That said, be prepared for the possibility that the leadership team may make the final call.

TIP

Even though the organization doesn't yet have a defined MTP, it's possible that it has already been working with an unofficial version. In that case, pick the MTP that aligns most closely with the organization's identity.

TIP

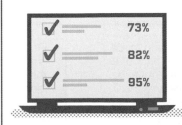

We recommend providing the leadership team with actual data when it comes to feedback. For example, providing ExO Disruptors with an online survey to complete during the in-person presentations ensures further comments and feedback are captured for later review at the leadership debrief meeting.

TASK 5

Narrow the number of initiatives down to three

DESCRIPTION

It's time to select the most promising initiatives and take them to the next level. Digest the feedback received in the Disruption Session and during the meeting with the leadership team and pick the top three ExO initiatives (or those the management team chose).

TIP

The leadership team may have already made a decision about which initiatives to back or to kill. If so, accept the decision and try not to be too disappointed if more ExO initiatives than anticipated are scratched off the list. Rejection and failure are part of the process; don't take it personally. Just keep being awesome!

TIP

Picking the top three initiatives is not just a matter of choosing the ones that received the best feedback. There may be other reasons: alignment with the selected MTP, something strategic or a gut feeling.

TIP

Remember you can also create new ExO Core Initiatives based on the feedback received during the Disruption Session or in response to ExO Edge Initiatives presented by other teams. The goal is simply to have three ExO Core Initiatives by the end of the week.

TASK 6

Improve the selected initiatives based on the feedback received

DESCRIPTION

Review the work you've done on the ExO Core Initiatives so far and refine them after taking all feedback into account. If you have any new ExO Core Initiatives, draft as many of the main elements (MTP, disruption/reaction pair and ExO Canvas) as you can and use the following weeks to catch up.

In the event that the leadership team has already selected a definitive MTP for the organization, you will need to update and align your ExO Core Initiatives in response.

TIP

Follow the previous weeks' assignment descriptions to refine your initiatives.

TIP

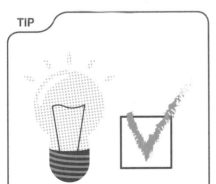

The goal with the Core Stream is to make the company more adaptable to the external environment. Do your ideas qualify?

TIP

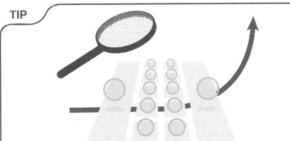

The Disruption Session can highlight where participants need to do further work to fully understand the ExO model and concepts. Take time this week to address any gaps in understanding. For example, does everyone on the team have a good grasp of the ExO attributes? Do they understand what it means for an initiative to be scalable? Do they see where their MTPs can be improved? Revisiting some of the initial concepts might have greater impact now that the team has experience applying them.

TIP

At this point in the ExO Sprint, we recommend splitting the team into subgroups and assigning each subgroup one or two initiatives. For example, if there are six team members, you can split the team into three groups of two team members and assign an ExO Core Initiative to each. No matter how you organize the groups, it's important that all team members offer feedback on all initiatives, regardless of their level of involvement.

PRESENTATIONS AGENDA

 Eco Places

 Welcome

 ExO Edge Team 1 presentations (60-minute time slot per team)

 Short break

 ExO Edge Team 2 presentations (60-minute time slot per team)

 Break

 ExO Core Team 1 presentations (60-minute time slot per team)

 Short break

 ExO Core Team 2 presentations (60-minute time slot per team)

 Closing and next steps

 ExO Sprint Leader meets with the organization's leadership team

Feedback Form		Alignment With Leadership Objectives?
	General Feedback	
Smart Hotel	Leadership team liked this business objective!	Yes
MTP	Leadership team chose this MTP for the organization.	
External Disruption	Leadership team and ExO Disruptors agree that the concept will be disruptive to the industry.	
Internal Reaction	ExO Disruptors suggested improvements to the business model (e.g., storing customer data as a resource).	
ExO Attributes	ExO Disruptors suggested improvements to the ExO attributes (e.g., build a smartphone app featuring an intelligent assistant to complement personalization services and robot assistance).	
(Initiative Name Here)		
MTP		
External Disruption		
Internal Reaction		
ExO Attributes		
ExO Edge Initiatives that Led to New ExO Core Initiatives	AirEco will increase competition in the marketplace as a result of decreased staffing needs and margins. An internal reaction to this ExO Edge Initiative could be to launch an ExO Core Initiative to provide hotel staff services to AirEco. This would allow AirEco to offer guest services using professional hotel staff. It also creates an opportunity for the existing organization.	
Other Feedback (General, Other Projects, etc.)		
Final MTP/TP for the Organization	Personalized eco experiences for everyone.	

Suggestions for the week...
FINAL TIPS

The perfect flow for this week:

If the presentations are given in person, prepare the setting and take care of logistics.

| Sun | Mon | Tue | Wed Thu Fri | Sat |

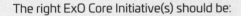

Schedule the presentations during the latter half of the week so that teams will have enough time to improve their pitches based on feedback received the previous week.

The right ExO Core Initiative(s) should be:

Adaptable

You are applying the ExO framework to make your existing organization more adaptable to external industry disruption; all initiatives should aim for this objective.

Scalable

Since you will define a Massive Transformative Purpose (or at least a Transformative Purpose), you may need to increase the existing organization's reach. If so, evaluate whether the ExO Core Initiatives will help scale the impact.

Designate one team member in charge of writing down all feedback. It can be a different team member for each initiative. Just make sure all feedback is captured.

After the presentations, discuss your initiatives with the attendees (the management team, members of other ExO Sprint teams and the ExO Disruptors) and request additional feedback.

As always, remember that failure is a part of the process, so try not to get upset about any negative feedback you receive. It's better to know sooner rather than later that you may need to change, hold off on or even kill one or more of your initiatives.

If some (or even all) of your ExO initiatives are rejected following the Disruption Session, don't take it personally! This is just part of the process.

We have worked with teams whose ExO initiatives were all killed off during the Disruption Session but by the end of the ExO Sprint their new or improved initiatives were the most highly rated. Consider this session a learning exercise and an opportunity to improve your initiatives and process.

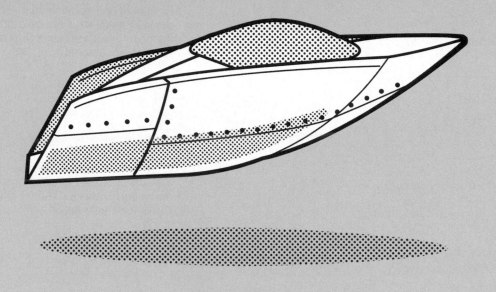

WEEK 6
Prototype

WHY THIS WEEK?

It's time to take your ExO initiatives to the next level!

This week's assignment is to formally define the assumptions underlying your ideas and prepare to test them further.

Start by defining your ExO Core Initiative in greater detail so that you can identify the key hypotheses to test.

Next on the agenda is to begin building a Minimum Viable Product (MVP) that facilitates learning more about your ExO Core Initiative and how to improve it.

Are you worried you won't be able to accomplish all this in only one week? You can!

TASK 1

Further define your ExO Core Initiatives

DESCRIPTION

During the previous weeks, you have identified external disruptions and defined internal reactions that will help adapt your organization to the external environment. You should also have defined which ExO attributes to implement.

It's now time to think more deeply about the implementation details of the ExO Core Initiatives in order to identify key hypotheses and test them as soon as possible.

Since you may have different types of ExO Core Initiatives (internal projects designed to increase the flexibility or efficiency of the organization, new products or services, etc.), each will need to be further defined. Regardless of how you define your initiatives, be sure to address the following issues:

USERS/CLIENTS	STAKEHOLDERS	SOLUTION	ECONOMICS
Who will use or buy the solution you are defining? What are their pain points and needs? What value will your solution deliver?	Who within the organization will approve and fund your ExO initiative? What is the value it offers stakeholders?	What will your ExO Core Initiative look like once completed? What will be the user's experience of it? What will you need to implement it?	What will it cost to implement the initiative? How will your organization benefit? What is the return on investment?

TOOLS

There are several tools that will help further define your initiatives:

  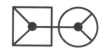 

| Empathy Map | Customer Journey Map | Value Proposition Canvas | Blue Ocean Strategy Canvas | Your own method |

TASK 1   Further define your ExO Core Initiatives

RESOURCE

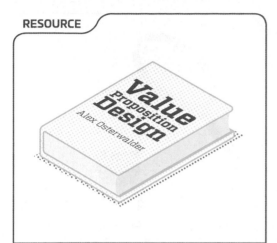

Value Proposition Design, by Alex Osterwalder, will help with the Value Proposition Canvas.

RESOURCE

Blue Ocean Strategy, by Renée Mauborgne and W. Chan Kim, will help with the Blue Ocean Strategy Canvas.

RESOURCES

You can find plenty of online information about how use the Empathy Map, Customer Journey Maps and other tools.

TIP

For Pure Core Initiatives and Edge Core Initiatives, use the tool that best fits the project you are considering. For example, if you are thinking of developing an AI-based decision-support system for your staff, consider using an Empathy Map. if you are thinking about how to improve or automate the processes of your organization, you may want to base your use case on a process map.

TIP

For Blue Core Initiatives, use an Empathy Map or Value Proposition Canvas to better understand your customer. Use a Blue Ocean Strategy Canvas to define the innovative product or service.

TASK 1

Further define your ExO Core Initiatives

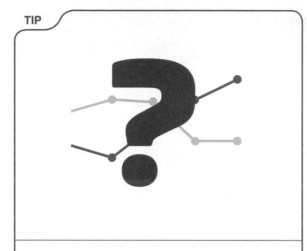

If none of the suggested tools work for your ExO Core Initiative, invent or modify one on your own.

Research the economics of the initiative. This might entail calculating the cost of the ExO initiative and the return on investment (high accuracy is not necessary at this stage), or the pricing model of your product/service and its profitability.

When building ExO Core Initiatives, we generally recommend using external technology providers and not building the technology in-house (there's no need to re-invent the wheel). For an Edge Core Initiative that might become a new ExO Edge Initiative in the future, we recommend using external technology providers for a first internal prototype and then looking into building the technology yourself once your "ExO on the Edge" has been launched.

When your ExO Core Initiatives have been defined in greater detail, consider reviewing and improving their ExO Canvases as well.

TASK 2

Frame your ExO Core Initiatives within your organization's business model

DESCRIPTION

To analyze the scope and impact your ExO Core Initiatives would have within your existing organization, include the different elements the ExO Core Initiative would contribute to your current business model (all without changing its foundation).

When updating the Business Model Canvas, add new sticky notes as needed to see how the original business model is being impacted by including the ExO Core Initiative.

TIP

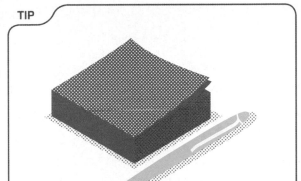

Use different color sticky notes so it will be easier to identify how the organization's business model has been improved.

TIP

Remember that an ExO Core Initiative doesn't change an organization's business model; it improves it. If the initiative in question alters the way your company does business, the idea is a potential ExO Edge Initiative.

TASK 3

Identify the key hypotheses you want to evaluate with your MVP

DESCRIPTION

Eric Ries, who launched the Lean Startup movement, defines an MVP as "a version of a new product which allows a team to collect the maximum amount of validated learning about customers with the least effort." In terms of an ExO project, the idea is to use the MVP concept to build something that will help you learn about your initiatives. Before designing and building your MVP, however, consider the outcome—i.e., think about what you want to learn as a result of building and testing it.

The next step is to identify the key hypotheses to evaluate—those that are critical for the success of your ExO Core Initiatives. At this stage, most of the hypotheses will be found in the ExO Canvas, the Business Model Canvas and based on what you learned from further defining your ExO Core Initiatives (the previous task):

- **ExO Attributes:** whether the different ExO attributes you have defined are the right ones, or even if it's realistic to implement them.

- **Value Proposition:** whether your clients, users and stakeholders like your value proposition.

- **Feasibility of project implementation:** whether your implementation will actually work in the way you think it will, especially if it's based on new technologies.

- **Investment:** whether it will prove a worthwhile investment.

TOOLS

Use the template in this section to identify and evaluate hypotheses. At this stage you only need to fill in the Build column (or columns), including the key hypotheses you're evaluating and the experiment design details. The table's Measure and Learn columns will be fleshed out in the coming weeks.

TIP

Each ExO Core Initiative is different, so think about the critical factors that will make your business a success. These are the key hypotheses to evaluate.

TIP

To define the success criteria of the sales experiment (especially for ExO Blue Core Initiatives), define meaningful metrics for the process. The right metrics are usually expressed as a percentage that reflects the conversion rate of potential customers from one phase to another. Example: percentage of potential clients who buy the product. This is known as Innovation Accounting.

TASK 4   Define your Minimum Viable Product (MVP)

DESCRIPTION

You don't need to implement your ExO Core Initiative to start testing and learning about it. There is no need to waste time and money building something that no one might want to use or pay for. Instead, experiment with an MVP.

Before developing that MVP, determine the minimum set of features it should have at the outset. To do so, follow these steps (note that some will have already been addressed in previous tasks):

1 Define the user flow and processes of your ExO Core Initiative according to the external disruption detected and the internal reaction defined.

2 List all necessary features that your ExO Core Initiative must have to react to the external disruption.

3 Weigh each feature using the ICE approach. ICE is an acronym for the three primary factors to consider when setting priorities: Impact (in terms of value for the user), Cost (in terms of money) and Effort (in terms of time). Award each factor a value between 0 and 2, with 2 representing the highest value (greatest impact, lowest cost and least effort), and 0 the lowest value (least impact, highest cost and greatest effort).

4 Prioritize the features according to their total ICE value. The features with the highest ICE scores should be included at the top your MVP list.

5 Analyze the results and define how the first version of the MVP might look according to:

- The key hypotheses you need to evaluate. Remember that the primary goal of this MVP is to learn, so take these hypotheses into account before defining your next experiment, which is to build your MVP.

- ICE prioritization of features. For this first version of the MVP, you will likely need to add or delete features. Some may be required for technical reasons, while others could take too long to develop and thus should be removed for now.

RESOURCE

Eric Ries' book *The Lean Startup* is a good source for learning about MVPs and the foundation underlying the concept.

TIP

Remember that your goal here is not to see your ExO initiative implemented perfectly but to develop a product that allows you to learn. To that end, include learning-oriented features and add-ons that will result in further feedback.

TASK 5 Build your MVP!

DESCRIPTION

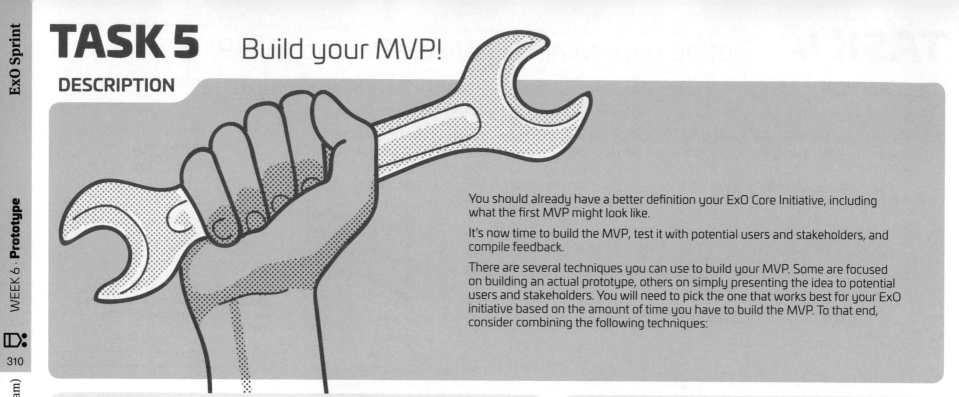

You should already have a better definition your ExO Core Initiative, including what the first MVP might look like.

It's now time to build the MVP, test it with potential users and stakeholders, and compile feedback.

There are several techniques you can use to build your MVP. Some are focused on building an actual prototype, others on simply presenting the idea to potential users and stakeholders. You will need to pick the one that works best for your ExO initiative based on the amount of time you have to build the MVP. To that end, consider combining the following techniques:

Landing Page

Develop a landing page that shows and describes your MVP. (This applies mainly to Blue Core Initiatives and other initiatives based on launching a new product or service, where the goal is to evaluate a value proposition with potential clients.) You can also describe the complete version of the product or service, although we recommend focusing the landing page on the key features of the MVP. In addition to describing your product or service (either the MVP or a complete version), encourage clients to pre-order. Another option is to run an A/B test, which consists of building two different versions of the landing page—each with a different value proposition—and see which visitors prefer.

RESOURCES

Visit www.launchrock.com and www.landerapp.com for help creating a landing page.

HOW MUCH YOU WILL LEARN

A bit: how clients like the value proposition of your product/service and its price based on the number of pre-orders the website receives and the actual data you gather.

Video

Create a video that shows and promotes your MVP. Again, this technique is useful when evaluating the value proposition for clients and internal supporters.

RESOURCES

Use a professional video creation service or online tools such as www.animoto.com or www.goanimate.com.

HOW MUCH YOU WILL LEARN

A bit more: how users and stakeholders like the value proposition of your ExO Core Initiative based on their reactions after watching the video. Encouraging clients to pre-order can result in data about the price and revenue model.

TASK 5 Build your MVP!

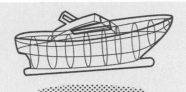

Wireframes

Build a set of wireframes or digital designs that will help illustrate for clients what your product will look like. This technique is useful when evaluating the value proposition for clients and internal supporters.

RESOURCES

Use any rapid prototyping tool like www.invisionapp.com, www.justinmind.com or even PowerPoint.

HOW MUCH YOU WILL LEARN

Even more: how the users like the value proposition of your ExO Core Initiative and its details based on their reactions and interactions with the wireframes. Encouraging clients to pre-order can also provide data about the price and revenue model.

Working prototype

Build a prototype that includes only the key features you want to learn more about. This is actually the real MVP, and in many cases it's possible to build it in just a few days. Remember, it doesn't have to be perfect; it just needs to be something that will help you learn over a several-day period.

HOW MUCH YOU WILL LEARN

A lot: how easy or hard it is to build and deliver the actual ExO Core Initiative; how users, clients and stakeholders like the value proposition; and what the user experience is like based on interactions with the prototype. Encouraging clients to pre-order can also provide data about the price and revenue model.

REFERENCE

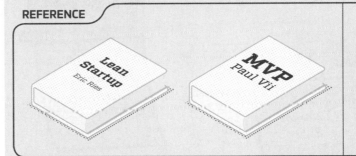

The Lean Startup offers great ideas on how to build MVPs in just a few days. Another good book is *MVP*, by Paul Vii, which provides tips for creating an MVP using Agile Development Methodologies.

TIP

Compiling a list of prioritized features and the number of hours that each will take to develop will tell you whether or not it is possible to have a prototype ready within the next week.

TEMPLATE for delivery

Business Model Canvas For Eco Places (Parent organization)

Eco Places

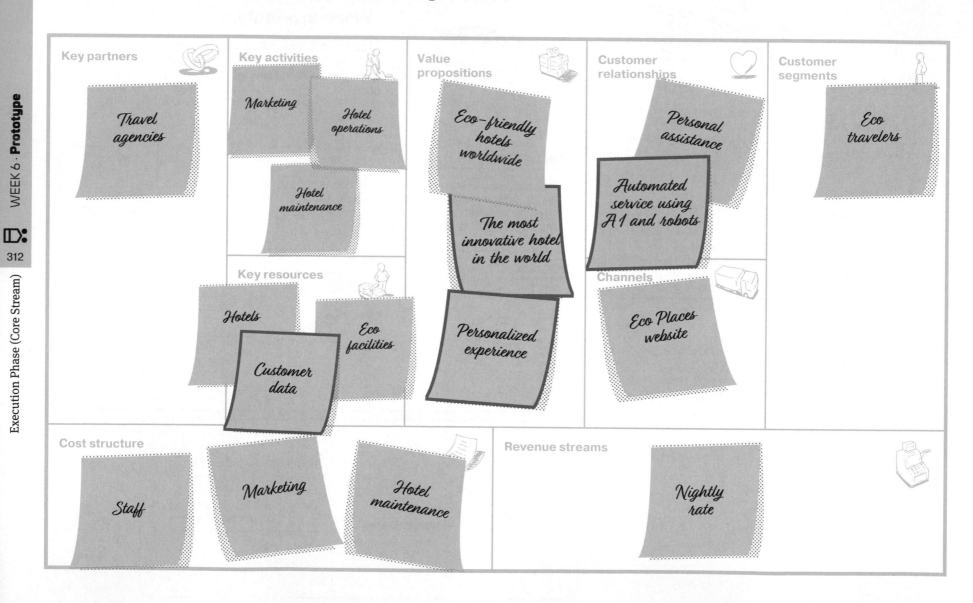

Key partners

Travel agencies

Key activities

Marketing

Hotel operations

Hotel maintenance

Key resources

Hotels

Eco facilities

Customer data

Value propositions

Eco-friendly hotels worldwide

The most innovative hotel in the world

Personalized experience

Customer relationships

Personal assistance

Automated service using AI and robots

Channels

Eco Places website

Customer segments

Eco travelers

Cost structure

Staff

Marketing

Hotel maintenance

Revenue streams

Nightly rate

TEMPLATE for delivery

ExO Canvas for Smart Eco

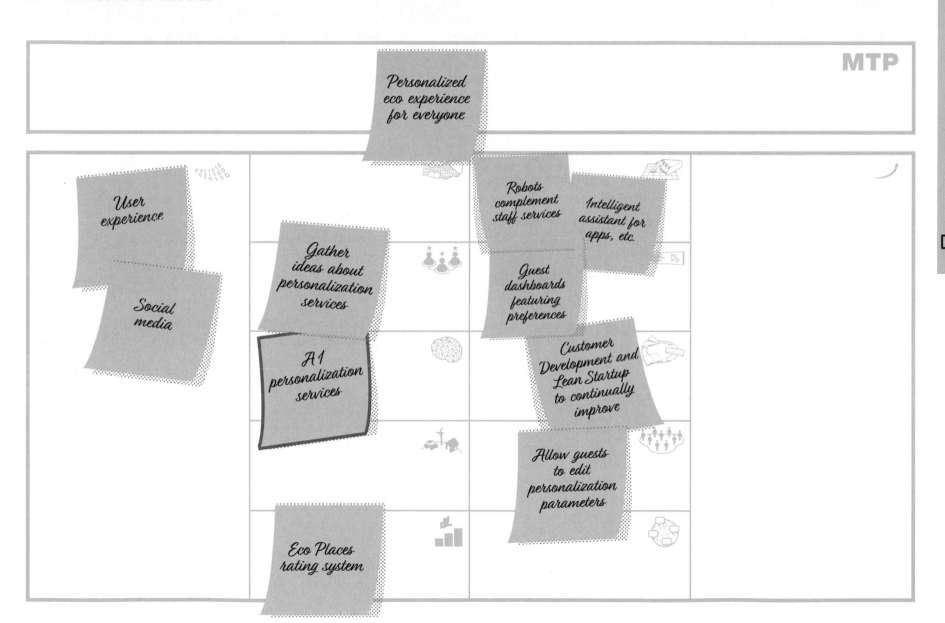

MTP

Personalized eco experience for everyone

User experience

Social media

Gather ideas about personalization services

AI personalization services

Eco Places rating system

Robots complement staff services

Intelligent assistant for apps, etc.

Guest dashboards featuring preferences

Customer Development and Lean Startup to continually improve

Allow guests to edit personalization parameters

TEMPLATE for delivery

Eco Places

Template to identify and evaluate key hypotheses

ExO Initiative Name	BUILD			MEASURE	LEARN
	Key Hypotheses	Experiment Description	Evaluation Criteria	Experiment Result	Key Learnings
Smart Eco	Customers are willing to book a room in a hotel with AI-based personalization services, assistants and robots.	A/B testing with two landing pages (one with current offering and another with Smart Eco initiative) to determine which receives more bookings.	At least 60% of visitors prefer the AI-based approach.		
	Building AI-based services, assistants and robots is feasible.	Talk to AI companies to evaluate whether it's possible to build AI-based personalization services.	Find AI providers able to build AI-based personalization services.		
	AI-based services provide value.	Build a prototype to test hypothesis.	More than 60% of customers should be happy with the experience.		

Designing the MVP

FEATURE	IMPACT (VALUE)	COST (MONEY)	EFFORT (TIME)	PRIORITY
Landing page	1	2	2	5
First prototype of AI-based personalization service for controlling room temperature	1	1	1	3
First prototype of AI-based assistant	2	0	0	2
First prototype of AI-based robot	2	0	0	2
Simulation of AI-based assistant backed by a human	2	2	1	5

Conclusions about the MVP

After analyzing the different features and options, we decided to design a simple online landing page offering two versions of the MVP. Next up: conduct A/B testing to determine whether customers preferred our value proposition over the existing one.

In the end, we opted to build a simulation of the AI-based assistant that features a smartphone-based app with a simple, human-backed interface. The goal: to ascertain what kinds of interactions customers like best and embed those interactions within the final, automated version of the app.

Suggestions for the week...

The perfect flow for this week:

Devote the next few days to building the MVP, which you will need next week.

 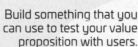

| Sun | Mon | Tue Wed Thu Fri | Sat |

Spend the first day outlining your business model, identifying key hypotheses and designing the MVP.

Review progress with your ExO Coach on the fifth day.

Build something that you can use to test your value proposition with users.

For online channels such as landing pages, don't forget to implement some mechanism to gather feedback (e.g., contact forms) and data (e.g., stats engine).

Keep in mind that next week you will use whatever you build now to reach potential users, clients and stakeholders and learn from them.

You will develop your MVP further next week, but it's important to get an initial version up and running now. If you want to produce an actual prototype but need two weeks to develop it, we recommend developing another kind of MVP in the interim, such as a presentation. You can at least gather data while getting the prototype ready for the experiments you'll be conducting in two weeks.

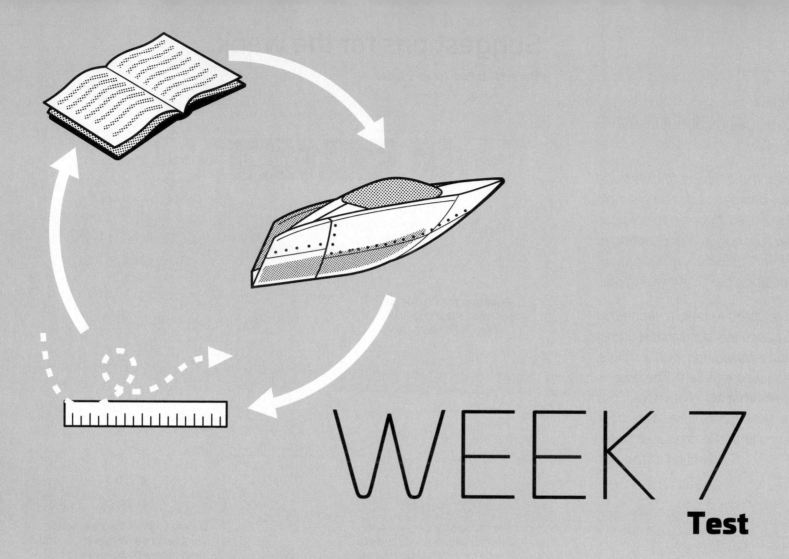

WEEK 7
Test

WHY THIS WEEK?

It's time for the truth!

Over the past week, you have been building initial versions of your MVPs, which will allow you to learn more about and improve your ExO Core Initiatives.

This week's assignment provides experience exercising the Experimentation attribute at a deeper level. The goal is to test your MVPs so that you can determine if your value proposition is the right one.

Using Experimentation to build and test your MVP enables you to evaluate the key hypotheses to determine whether the ExO Core Initiative you are developing will help adapt your organization to external disruption.

If any of your ExO Core Initiatives entail developing a new product or service, you may be able to attract clients. Getting your first client is one of the most exciting milestones for any new organization, so let's do it!

TASK 1

Find your Early Adopters!

DESCRIPTION

An early adopter is an individual or business that uses a new product or technology before others, shares your vision and is willing to try your MVP even though it may not yet have been perfected. Your job here is to define how to find early adopters and get their buy-in for your ExO Core Initiatives.

The technique used to find early adopters depends on the type of ExO Core Initiative and MVP you have developed:

 For Blue Core Initiatives (new product or service):

If you created a landing page MVP, focus on online channels in one of three ways:

- Create online ads (e.g., using Google AdWords) and link them to your promotional sites.
- Promote the website with online communities populated by potential early adopters.
- Email the page links to potential early adopters you've identified.

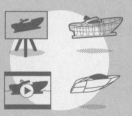

If you've created a sales presentation, a set of wireframes, a video or a real prototype, focus on offline channels to reach early adopters:

- Promote your MVP to those people or organizations interviewed when you first tested the problem/solution hypotheses.
- Generate a new list of potential early adopters.
- Generate a list of communities that might be populated by MVP early adopters.

For Pure Core Initiatives and Edge Core Initiatives:

Regardless of the type of MVP, you need to identify a variety of early adopters:

Stakeholders

Decision-makers within your organization who will approve and fund your ExO Core Initiative

Internal users

Employees who will use and benefit from your ExO Core Initiative

External clients/users

Potential clients who will use and benefit from your ExO Core Initiative

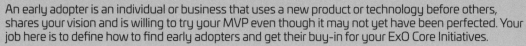

TASK 1 Find your Early Adopters!

RESOURCE

For Blue Core Initiatives: Steve Blank's book *The Startup Owner's Manual* outlines how to find and sell to early adopters. Familiarize yourself with the section of the book that covers the Customer Validation phase of the process.

RESOURCE

Another book for Blue Core Initiatives: In addition to a great way to learn about selling to early adopters, Geoffrey Moore's *Crossing the Chasm* addresses how to expand your target market in the future.

TIP

When it comes to ExO Core Initiatives, there are two groups of early adopters:

External Clients

(Your ExO Core Initiative improves an existing product or service; alternatively, your initiative entails creating a new product or service)

Share the vision you have about the future

Have the problem you defined some weeks ago

Are trying to solve this problem in some way, although not yet successfully

Are paying to solve the problem

Are honest and will provide valuable feedback

Internal Supporters

(Your ExO Core Initiative improves an existing organization and you have internal approval and/or usage)

Acknowledge the external disruption you are trying to manage

May already be reacting to this external disruption in some way, although not yet successfully

May be investing (or willing to invest) resources to manage this external disruption

Are honest enough to provide valuable feedback

TASK 1   Find your Early Adopters!

To find early adopters, try to think as they do. This will help you identify new places to locate them.

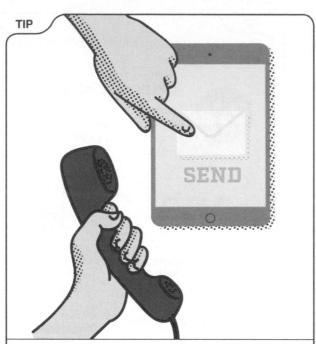

Remember that your goal is to learn, so interact with your early adopters as much as possible.

- **For online channels** such as websites, after a user or buyer completes the process, send an email asking for feedback on how to improve your value proposition, pricing model, etc.

- **For offline channels** including in-person meetings and phone calls, don't outsource the sales process. Handle it yourself after spending the week interacting with early adopters to learn as much as possible by testing your product with them and encouraging them to buy it.

TASK 2
Measure results and learn

DESCRIPTION

After building and testing your MVPs, you will have a lot of experience and data to use in evaluating your key hypotheses.

ExO Core Initiatives shouldn't be implemented across the organization as a whole, at least not at first. In addition to finding early adopters, you'll also need to determine exactly where in the organization to begin the implementation process.

Once the sales process is complete, the next step is to dig into the data you've gathered.

TOOLS

Use the template to identify and evaluate the hypotheses you were working with last week and fill in the Measure and Learn columns.

TIP

Remember to analyze the qualitative data as well as the quantitative data (metrics). At this early stage of the game, qualitative information is more important than quantitative.

TIP

Experimentation results often produce a lot of noise but digging into the data also presents learning opportunities. For example, after evaluating a new product or service, you might find that certain customer segments love your product or service, while others hate it. In fact, your results might indicate that people under 45 years of age love it and those over the age of 45 don't. The learning here? Focus the product or service on the customer segment aged 45 and under.

TEMPLATE for delivery

Template to identify and evaluate key hypotheses

ExO Initiative Name	BUILD			MEASURE	LEARN
	Key Hypotheses	Experiment Description	Evaluation Criteria	Experiment Result	Key Learnings
Smart Eco	Customers are willing to book a room in a hotel with AI-based personalization services, assistants and robots.	A/B testing with two landing pages (one with current offering and another with the Smart Eco initiative) to determine which receives more bookings.	At least 60% of visitors prefer AI-based approach.	Landing page featuring the AI-based approach resulted in 50% more sign-ups.	**Hypothesis Validated**
	Building AI-based services, assistants and robots is feasible.	Talk to AI companies to evaluate whether it's possible to build AI-based personalization services.	Find AI providers able to build AI-based personalization services.	Unable to find an AI provider to meet all our requirements. Most requirements, however, can be met with some restrictions. For example, due to technical limitations, AI providers recommend limiting use of robots to room delivery for now. They also note that technical capabilities will significantly improve over the next couple of years.	**Hypothesis Partially Validated** We learned that we can't develop everything we want, but if we limit robot functionality to room delivery for now we can launch a first version that can be improved over the next couple of years.
	AI-based services provide value.	Build a prototype to test hypothesis.	More than 60% of customers will be happy with their AI experience.	As many as 80% of customers love AI-based personalization services.	**Hypothesis Validated** We found that customers most frequently request that meals be delivered to their rooms. They love that the intelligent assistant remembers their preferences, especially when they arrive at a new hotel within the chain.

Suggestions for the week...

The perfect flow for this week:

Spend the first day defining how to reach out to early adopters. Then reach out to them as soon as possible!

Review results with your ExO Coach on the fifth day.

| Sun | Mon | | Tue Wed Thu Fri | | Sat |

The remainder of your time this week will be spent running early-adopter sales experiments. If you need more time to gather data, this step might spill into the beginning of the following week. Either way, by the end of the week you should have initial results to review with the ExO Coach.

The goal for the week is to compile enough data from the experiments to ensure valid results (and thus additional learning). What would be even better, of course, is if you are able to sell your idea during the process, an outcome that would impress the panel at your final ExO Core Initiative presentation. From nothing to real customers in less than 10 weeks...Let's do it!

Remember that early adopters are not just first clients or internal supporters. They are also special people and/or companies with a specific mindset.

To aid in your evaluation of different types of hypotheses, you may need to reach out to external advisors who are specialists in your industry or in a specific technology or methodology.

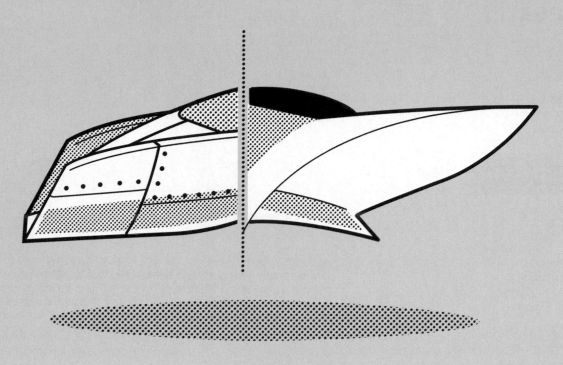

WEEK 8
Improve

WHY THIS WEEK?

Last week you should have learned a great deal about your ExO Core Initiatives as a result of testing your MVPs. This week, you will continue to develop your MVPs by running experiments.

At some point during the week, when you have enough data, it will be time to face reality and make the necessary changes to your ExO Core Initiatives to maximize your opportunities for success.

Refine your ExO Core Initiatives!

TASK 1   Further develop your ExO Core Initiatives

DESCRIPTION

Just two weeks to build and test an MVP may not seem like enough time. Despite the quick turnaround, however, it is possible.

Allot several days this week to run experiments and iterate your MVP based on what you've learned.

If you are still running experiments with early adopters, continue using the template to identify and evaluate the hypotheses you have been using over the last two weeks.

TIP

Insights gleaned from the experiments with early adopters will provide you with new ideas and thus, potentially, new hypotheses. Keep the hypothesis definition and evaluation process dynamic. The idea is to use what you learn to redefine your experiments on an ongoing basis.

TIP

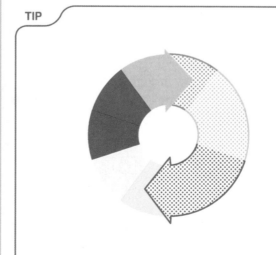

We recommend exploring Agile Development Methodologies (such as Scrum), which are basic techniques for developing and evolving an MVP. The main premise of these methodologies is to continually redefine features and development priorities for your product so that you can iterate it in a few days or weeks. Even if you don't use the techniques during the course of the ExO Sprint, it's a good idea to have a working knowledge of them for possible future use.

TASK 2

Improve and proceed!

DESCRIPTION

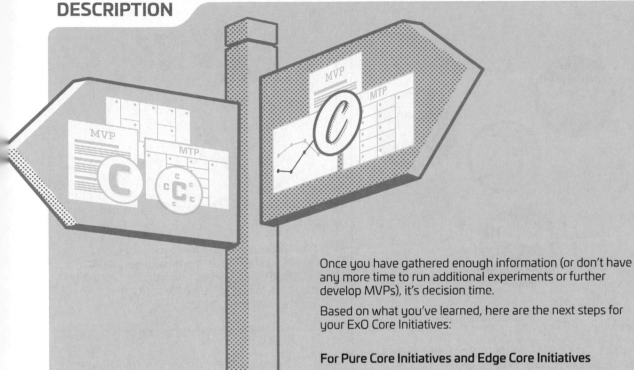

Once you have gathered enough information (or don't have any more time to run additional experiments or further develop MVPs), it's decision time.

Based on what you've learned, here are the next steps for your ExO Core Initiatives:

For Pure Core Initiatives and Edge Core Initiatives

Update the previous elements defined—the ExO Canvas, the MVP's requirements and any other element or canvas used—and look for ways to further improve the ExO initiative so that it best fits the needs of users and stakeholders.

For Blue Core Initiatives

Update the previous elements defined—ExO Canvas, Blue Ocean Strategy Canvas, the MPV's requirements and any other element or canvas used—and look for ways to further to improve the product or service in a way that fits the needs of customers. You should also finesse the pricing model to maximize the likelihood that customers will be willing to pay for that product or service.

TOOLS

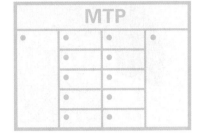

To edit your business model, use the Business Model Canvas you worked on earlier in the ExO Sprint. ➡ Pg. 135

TASK 2   Improve and proceed!

TOOLS

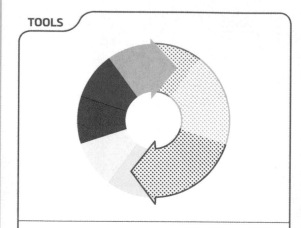

Iteration of your product or service may require updating your product backlog if you are using Agile Development Methodologies (unlikely given the time constraints of an ExO Sprint).

TIP

For Blue Core Initiatives, there are several ways to iterate your product or service:

- **Customer needs:** You may discover a new need, one whose solution looks more promising than that currently under consideration.

- **Features:** You may find that the set of features you defined for your product needs to change.

- **Pricing:** You may need to modify the pricing structure for your product or service.

TIP

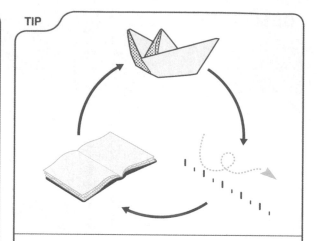

Carefully consider the feedback your clients, users and stakeholders offer and re-prioritize your MVP's features as needed. Don't forget the Build-Measure-Learn loop, which is applicable to everything!

TEMPLATE for delivery

ExO Canvas for Smart Eco

Eco Places

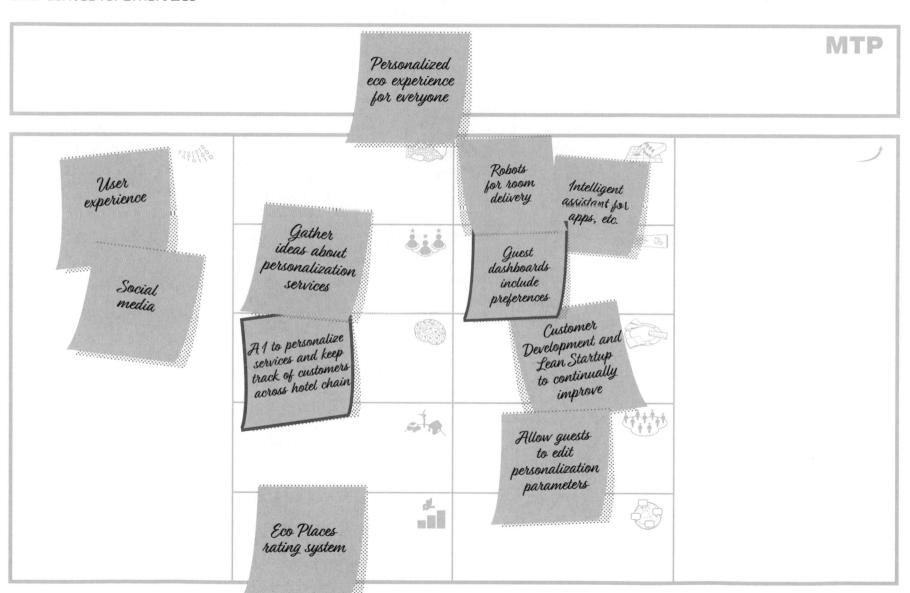

MTP

Personalized eco experience for everyone

User experience

Social media

Gather ideas about personalization services

AI to personalize services and keep track of customers across hotel chain

Eco Places rating system

Robots for room delivery

Guest dashboards include preferences

Intelligent assistant for apps, etc.

Customer Development and Lean Startup to continually improve

Allow guests to edit personalization parameters

TEMPLATE for delivery

Business Model Canvas For Eco Places (Parent Organization)

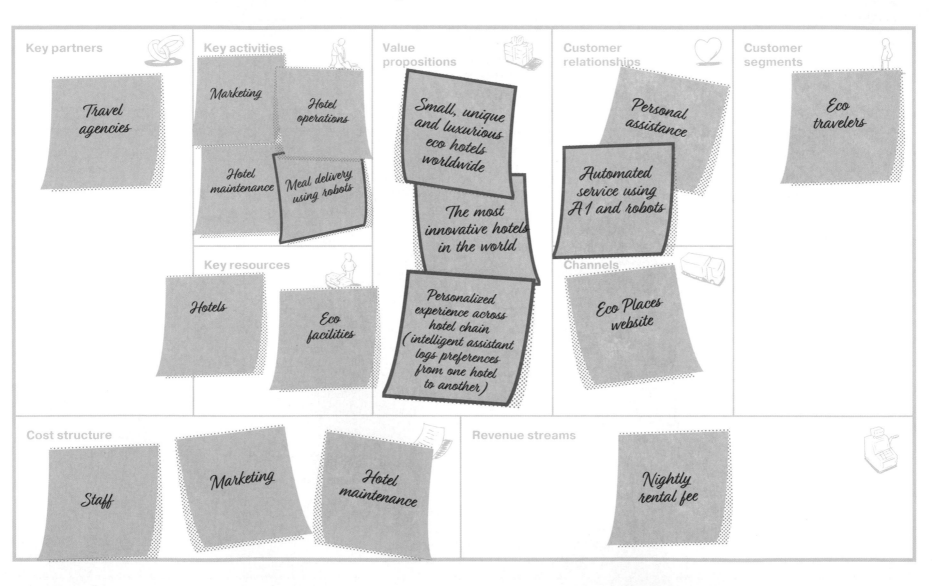

Key partners

Travel agencies

Key activities

Marketing

Hotel operations

Hotel maintenance

Meal delivery using robots

Key resources

Hotels

Eco facilities

Value propositions

Small, unique and luxurious eco hotels worldwide

The most innovative hotels in the world

Personalized experience across hotel chain (intelligent assistant logs preferences from one hotel to another)

Customer relationships

Personal assistance

Automated service using AI and robots

Channels

Eco Places website

Customer segments

Eco travelers

Cost structure

Staff

Marketing

Hotel maintenance

Revenue streams

Nightly rental fee

Suggestions for the week...

The perfect flow for this week:

Spend the first two days gathering as much data as possible from early adopters and refining your MVP.

Share your progress with your ExO Coach on the fifth day and get ready to begin putting together the final presentations for the Launch Session.

| Sun | Mon Tue | Wed Thu | Fri | Sat |

Devote the next two days to analyzing results and further refining the ExO Core Initiatives.

Making changes to your ExO initiatives may prove challenging (it's not easy letting go of ideas you're attached to), but don't respond by initiating the corporate immune system! Instead, build the best ExO initiative possible.

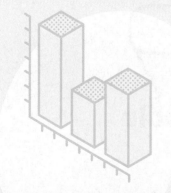

Keep all decisions data-based. Staying neutral often requires setting your ego aside and releasing any attachment to favored ideas or proposals.

In order to evaluate different types of hypotheses, you may need to reach out to external advisors who are specialists in your industry or in a specific technology or methodology.

Remember that within the ExO Sprint process everyone is equal and there is no room for corporate hierarchy. In short, decisions should never be based on corporate seniority.

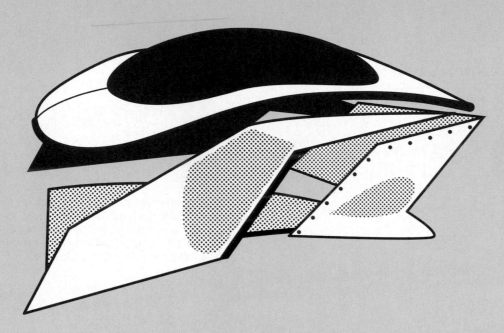

WEEK 9

Assemble

WHY THIS WEEK?

Time to prepare for the final presentation!

Next week you will present your best ideas to the leadership team. The goal is to elicit additional feedback and, most important, secure the funding needed to further develop the chosen ExO Core Initiatives.

This week is dedicated to creating a comprehensive presentation to showcase the awesome work you've done throughout the ExO Sprint.

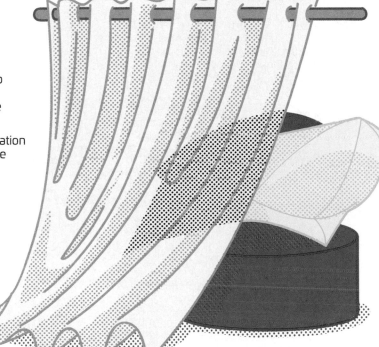

TASK 1

Narrow the number of initiatives down to two

DESCRIPTION

Select the most promising initiatives in advance of the final presentations.

Given what you've learned from running the experiments, you should be able to discard some of the ExO initiatives and focus on the two most promising options.

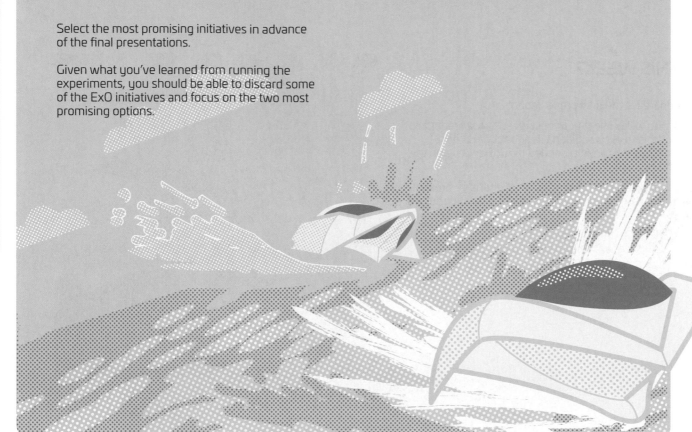

TASK 2

Extend your ExO Core Initiatives with key milestones and a budget

DESCRIPTION

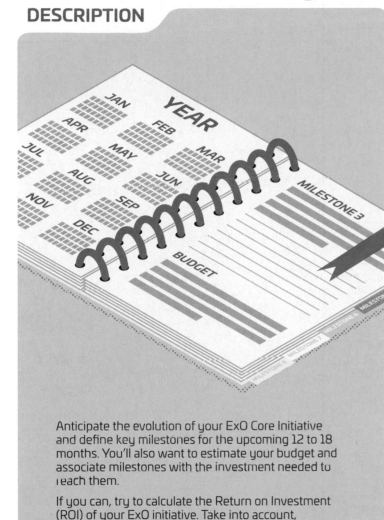

Anticipate the evolution of your ExO Core Initiative and define key milestones for the upcoming 12 to 18 months. You'll also want to estimate your budget and associate milestones with the investment needed to reach them.

If you can, try to calculate the Return on Investment (ROI) of your ExO initiative. Take into account, however, that is very difficult to accurately calculate ROI for innovative projects, so whenever you present these numbers be sure to emphasize that they are preliminary.

TIP

Key milestones may include:

- Finding the right area of the company to implement the initiative

- Finding the right team to execute the initiative

- Running further experiments to evaluate the hypotheses

- Building an MVP and its revisions

- Securing early adopters, internal funding and external revenues

- Pursuing partnership relationships where applicable

TIP

For estimating revenues, create a set of business parameters that take into account the innovation accounting metrics you defined and experimented with the previous week.

TASK 2   Extend your ExO Core Initiatives with key milestones and a budget

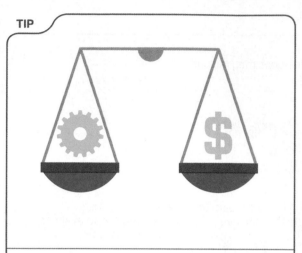

When it comes to estimating costs, be realistic about the resources and external help you will need to achieve your milestones. Milestones should align with easy-to-approve funding amounts.

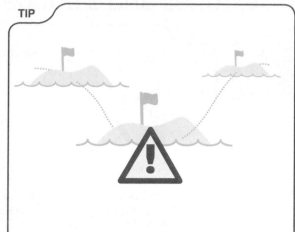

If your ExO Core Initiative is heavily dependent on an emerging technology, your milestones may reflect the interim steps that will prepare your organization to adopt the technology as it matures.

Create a sequence of manageable milestones. For example, a milestone might test the concept with a small market segment. It could also test an individual component of the initiative.

TASK 3

Build a final presentation for the ExO Core Initiatives

DESCRIPTION

To prepare for next week's final presentations, you'll need to develop a deck for each of your ExO Core Initiatives.

For this round, instead of using the short elevator pitch format, you will produce longer, more comprehensive presentations for each of the ExO initiatives. Follow the outline in the templates found later in this section.

TOOLS

Use the presentation template in this section.

RESOURCE

A helpful book is Garr Reynolds' *Presentation Zen: Simple Ideas on Presentation Design and Delivery.*

TIP

Whenever possible, use pictures instead of text for your slides. You want people to listen to what you have to say rather than be distracted reading your slides.

TASK 3

Build a final presentation for the ExO Core Initiatives

TIP

Craft a story that makes a compelling case for the initiative, beginning with the problem space and including a clear definition of the initiative's value proposition. Is the concept easy to understand? Is its value obvious?

TIP

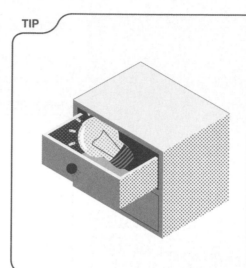

Don't worry if you end up killing one or more of your initiatives. Although you should present at least two ExO Core Initiatives at the Launch Session, you can always resurrect any of the initiatives you were working on prior to the Disruption Session. Be sure to develop any new additions as much as you can, following the process outlined over the previous weeks.

TIP

Keep in mind that you will have just 15 minutes to present each initiative.

TIP

Start practicing as soon as possible!

PRESENTATION

Each presentation should include the following slides/sections:

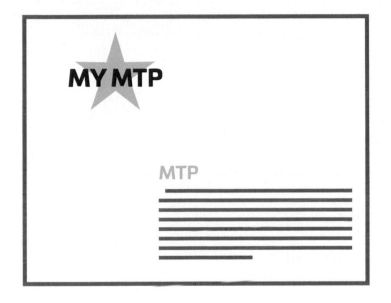

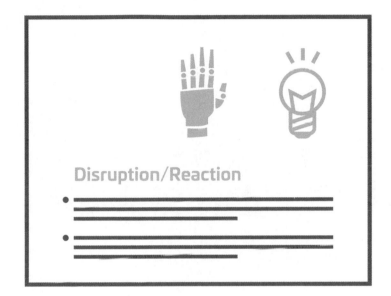

MTP

In order to frame the ExO Core Initiative, it's imperative to begin each presentation with an MTP.

In general, use just one slide to introduce the MTP.

Disruption/Reaction

It's also important to explain the external disruption, which is the main driver of the ExO Core Initiative. If the disruption comes from an ExO Edge Initiative, don't forget to mention that.

Once the external disruption is made clear, introduce the internal reaction that will either enable you to avoid the threat coming from external disruption or leverage the opportunities that threat can bring.

PRESENTATION

Storytelling

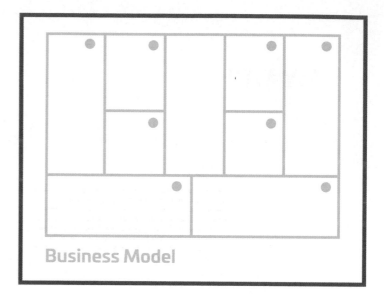

Business Model

Case Study

When communicating new ideas, it's helpful to use storytelling techniques.

One option is to invent a story and illustrate it with pictures and diagrams that explain the problem and how your solution solves it.

We recommend using case studies if you are presenting six or fewer initiatives. Count on five minutes to present each initiative.

Business Model

It's a good idea to show how your ExO Core Initiative fits within your organization's current business model.

You'll want to illustrate how you are improving and adapting your business model to external industry disruption (as opposed to changing it).

PRESENTATION

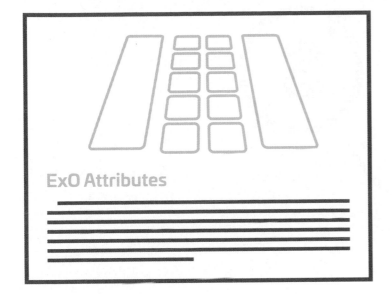

ExO Attributes

Since you are both adapting the organization to external industry disruption and connecting it to external abundance, it is important to illustrate how you plan to reach that abundance (using the SCALE attributes) and how you will manage it (using the IDEAS attributes).

Present the ExO Canvas and explain how the ExO attributes apply to the ExO Core Initiative.

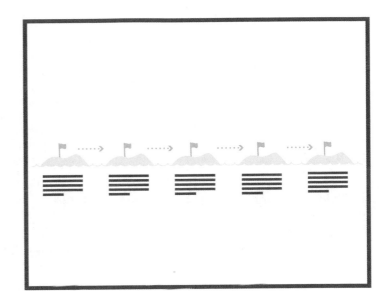

Key Milestones

Outline important milestones for the next few months.

You'll also need to describe long-term milestones, applying exponential thinking and summarizing how you plan to achieve your MTP.

PRESENTATION

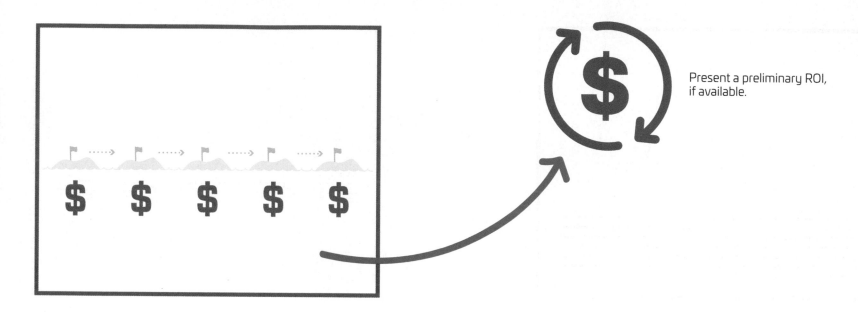

Present a preliminary ROI, if available.

Budget

Estimate the budget needed to achieve short-term milestones.

Suggestions for the week...

The perfect flow for this week:

Spend the first day refining the ExO initiatives based on feedback received the previous week.

Devote the fourth day to practicing the presentation. Run through the presentation several times to get comfortable with delivery and timing. Make sure you know which team members will be presenting.

| Sun | Mon | Tue Wed | Thu | Fri | Sat |

Use the next two days to build the milestone plan, budget and presentation.

On the fifth day, deliver the presentation to your ExO Coach for last-minute feedback and tips in advance of the big day.

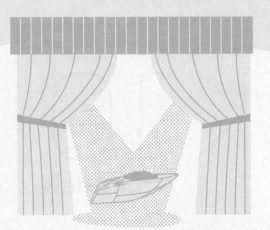

Be creative with your presentation format. For example, teams may want to augment their standard presentation with sound and video.

Include actual data from the executed experiments in the presentations. A great performance is a plus, but in the end it's only a nice deck. There is always more value in providing data and insights (such as testimonials) from actual clients to illustrate what you've learned.

WEEK 10
Launch

WHY THIS WEEK?

The big day is here!

This week you will present your ExO Core Initiatives to the company's leadership team and selected advisors, who will then make a final decision about which initiatives to fund and further develop.

The selection process is not the end—far from it, in fact. The development of your ExO Core Initiatives marks the beginning of your organization's transformation process!

TASK 1 Prepare the setting and logistics

DESCRIPTION

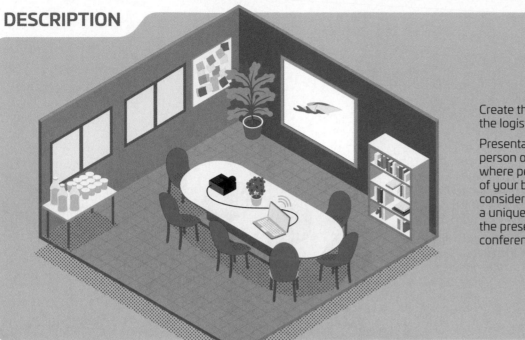

Create the right environment and set up the logistics for the presentations.

Presentations can be done either in person or online. Much depends on where people are located and the size of your budget. If you present in person, consider decorating the space to create a unique atmosphere. If you conduct the presentations online, test the video conferencing system in advance.

TIP

Follow an established agenda for the presentation (we've included an outline below), which should take between 60 and 90 minutes depending on the number of ExO Core Initiatives presented. Allot 15 minutes for each presentation, followed by a 10-minute Q&A session. Schedule a short break before the next event.

TIP

AGENDA

Time management is the key to presenting effectively. Communicate your agenda in advance, including the order of the presentations.

TASK 2

Presentations and discussion

DESCRIPTION

Teams will present their ideas to the leadership team and other relevant stakeholders. In contrast to the Disruption Session presentations, this time around the team will both receive feedback and answer questions.

The final presentation format is longer than that for the Disruption Session, which relied on the elevator pitch technique.

TIP

Two books that can help you improve your presentations are *The Presentation Secrets of Steve Jobs: How to Be Insanely Great in Front of Any Audience* and *Talk Like Ted: The 9 Public-Speaking Secrets of the World's Top Minds*, both by Carmine Gallo.

TIP

We recommend a 10-minute Q&A session per initiative.

TASK 3 Final evaluation

DESCRIPTION

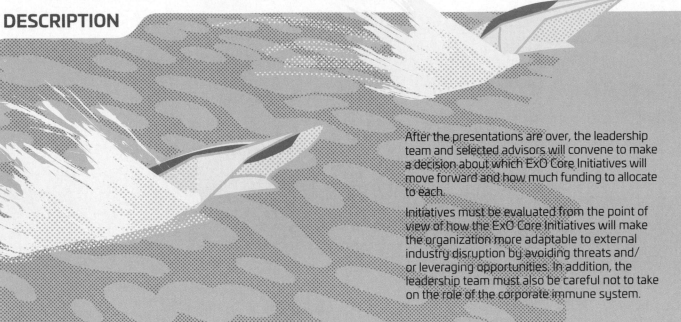

After the presentations are over, the leadership team and selected advisors will convene to make a decision about which ExO Core Initiatives will move forward and how much funding to allocate to each.

Initiatives must be evaluated from the point of view of how the ExO Core Initiatives will make the organization more adaptable to external industry disruption by avoiding threats and/or leveraging opportunities. In addition, the leadership team must also be careful not to take on the role of the corporate immune system.

TOOLS

The templates in this section will aid the leadership team in evaluating which initiatives to fund.

TIP

To help preempt an immune system reaction on the part of those members of the leadership team who are not participating in the ExO Sprint, we once again recommend that ExO Disruptors be included in the final presentation evaluations, just as during the earlier Disruption Session, held Week 5. Their independence from the organization (and its leadership) promotes honest, unbiased feedback.

TIP

Remember that old-school, traditional thinking may not work here, so avoid input and recommendations that come from that mindset. This can prove challenging if you are an industry insider!

TASK 3   Final evaluation

Keep in mind that these are still early stage initiatives, and much can change in the coming months. For now, it's important to maintain a high-level perspective—focusing on the purpose and goal of the ExO Core Initiatives—rather than zeroing in on the details.

The leadership team doesn't need to fund the chosen initiatives in full; it can follow a lean approach, allocating only enough funding to achieve the next milestone.

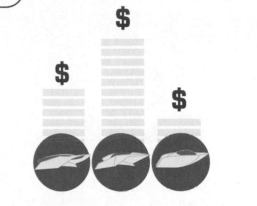

It's generally a good idea to determine the total amount of money you want to spend in the phase immediately following the ExO Sprint. Split the sum among the different initiatives according to your expectations for each.

Choose the teams that will oversee further development of the ExO Core Initiatives. Teams should include some of the ExO Sprint participants who developed the initiatives.

TASK 4 Announcements

DESCRIPTION

Informing the ExO Sprint participants which ExO initiatives have been chosen for funding and further development is key to keeping the momentum going.

TIP

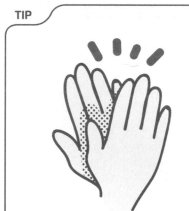

It's important to keep all ExO Sprint participants engaged, whether or not their initiatives are selected. Be sure to communicate your appreciation of a job well done. Everyone will have completed an incredible amount of work in a short period of time!

TIP

One way to keep everyone engaged and have them share in the outcome is to offer all ExO Sprint participants (including ExO Edge team members, if applicable) a percentage of the future profits generated from the ExO Core Initiatives.

PRESENTATIONS AGENDA

Final day presentations agenda template

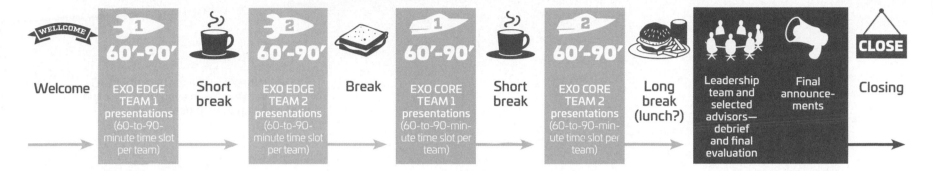

Welcome	EXO EDGE TEAM 1 presentations (60-to-90-minute time slot per team)	Short break	EXO EDGE TEAM 2 presentations (60-to-90-minute time slot per team)	Break	EXO CORE TEAM 1 presentations (60-to-90-minute time slot per team)	Short break

EXO CORE TEAM 2 presentations (60-to-90-minute time slot per team) · Long break (lunch?) · Leadership team and selected advisors—debrief and final evaluation · Final announcements · Closing

TEMPLATE for delivery

ExO Edge Initiative	Is Initiative Aligned With ExO Sprint Scope?	Does Initiative Adapt Existing Organization to Industry Disruption?	Does Initiative Make Existing Organization More Scalable?	Is Initiative Viable?	Selected?	Funding Allocated
Smart Eco	YES	YES	YES	YES	YES	$150K

Suggestions for the week...

FINAL TIPS

When it's time to share your ExO initiatives with everyone, relax and enjoy the moment.

Practice as much as possible and keep working to improve your presentation.

It's important to make an announcement about the selected initiatives, the funds allocated to each and who will develop them further.

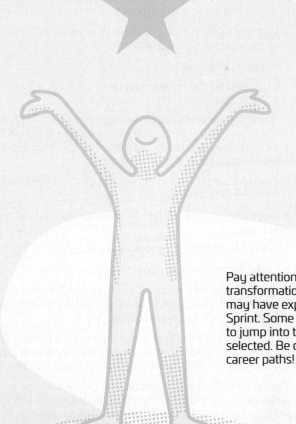

Pay attention to any personal transformation ExO Sprint participants may have experienced during the ExO Sprint. Some of them will be ready to jump into the ExO Core Initiatives selected. Be open to supporting new career paths!

Follow-Up Phase

Congratulations! You have now completed an ExO Sprint!

In addition to creating an organization—or set of organizations—primed to become exponential, your team has gone through a personal transformation process. As a result, they have:

- Learned new methods of working together across organizational boundaries.

- Acted as entrepreneurs.

- Experienced the productivity that real-time virtual collaboration and communication offers.

- Become "comfortable being uncomfortable" in presenting ideas to. The leadership team in a far less polished form than they have likely been accustomed to (the leadership team has also experienced the value of this format.)

- Been "forced" into a lean mindset by the pace and intensity of the weekly assignments.

- Seen the value of the fast iteration of ideas based on early feedback.

- Witnessed the disruption process in action.

- Come to understand that learning lies in "failure."

- Gained experience across a range of business innovation models and practices—including the ExO model—which they can now carry into their daily work.

All participants in the ExO Sprint should now possess an exponential mindset that will ensure the innovation process continues to move forward throughout the organization.

The fact that your team ideated and developed the ExO initiatives helps maintain the company's DNA, since all were created by employees with shared DNA (organizationally, at least). This makes all resulting ExO initiatives compatible with your team and organization.

Depending on the goal you set at the beginning, you will have one of the following outcomes:

If you are a leading organization aiming to both reinvent an industry and transform your organization for an external industry disruption, the outcome of the ExO Sprint has been a set of ExO Edge Initiatives and a set of ExO Core Initiatives. While the ExO Edge Initiatives should result in next-generation organizations structured to lead your industry (and perhaps even others), the ExO Core Initiatives will help your organization adapt to external industry disruption—including the disruption posed by the new ExO Edge Initiatives.

If you are an established organization wanting to adapt to external industry disruption, the outcome of the ExO Sprint has been a set of ExO Core Initiatives. By successfully implementing these ExO Core Initiatives, your organization has the ability to remain relevant in a rapidly changing world for many years to come.

If you are an entrepreneur or company builder wanting to develop one or more Exponential Organizations in order to transform a specific industry, the outcome of the ExO Sprint has been one or more ExO Edge Initiatives. Developing these ExO Edge Initiatives offers the opportunity to both accomplish your goals and become the Next Big Thing in your industry.

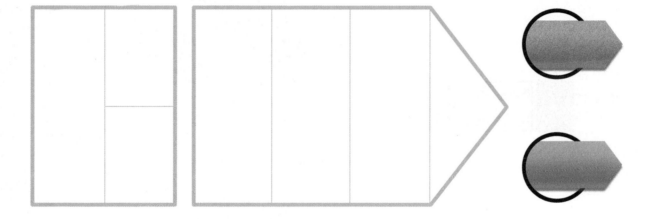

The circle diagram provides a template that can be used to position a resulting set of ExO initiatives to summarize the ExO Sprint outcome.

If you ran the ExO Edge Stream, the outcome is one or more organizations primed to lead the industry.

If you ran the entire ExO Sprint, the outcome is more than a set of independent ExO initiatives. It represents a new ecosystem in which your organization has not only adapted to industry disruption but also to the ExO Edge Initiatives created.

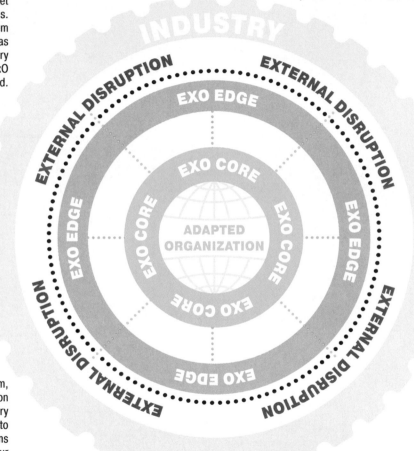

If you ran the ExO Core Stream, the outcome is an organization adapted to external industry disruption—one that is ready to connect to other ecosystems that may be created within your industry.

As you can see, the ExO Sprint outcome represents not only the transformation of an existing organization, but one that may also contribute to the transformation of an entire industry!

The next section offers practical advice for further developing your ExO initiatives and taking them to the next level.

• • • • • Ecosystem

· · · · · · · Main organization adapted to its own ecosystem

· · · · · · · Main organization adapted to external industry disruption

YOUR EXO SPRINT OUTCOME

Draw the outcome of your own ExO Sprint

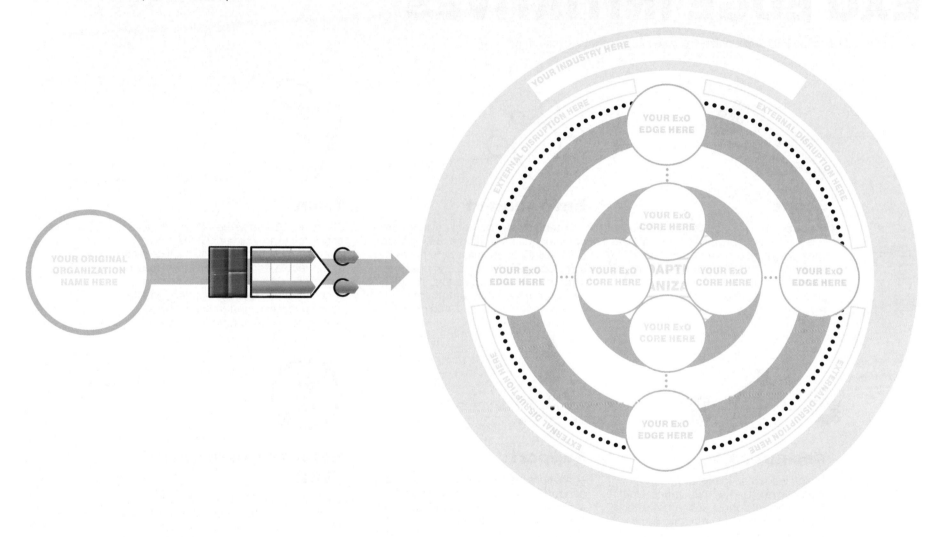

Follow-Up Phase

IMPLEMENTING
EXO EDGE INITIATIVES

To successfully develop ExO Edge Initiatives, take into account the following:

Scope

Focus on the MVP and iterate until you achieve the right product/market fit. You'll know you're there when a significant percentage of your customers are happy. Next, turn your attention to growth and boosting marketing and sales.

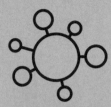

Environment

You need to find the right environment or elements (innovation ecosystem) to take an ExO Edge Initiative to the next step. Company builders and business incubators can help with this. You also need access to key collaborators— entrepreneurs, investors and partners.

Team

Chose a CEO and gather a team. It's a good idea to source your CEO from an external innovation ecosystem, since most of the people working within an established organization are focused on execution-based methodologies rather than search-based ones. Also remember to allocate vesting equity to the founding team.

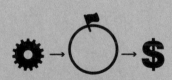

Resources

Assign resources to the ExO Edge Initiative linked to key milestones. Update the allocation of those resources after achieving milestones and applying important learnings. Looking for external funding for a second investment round is also a good idea, since in addition to providing money, external investors can validate your ExO.

Support

Make sure the ExO initiative has the full support of the company's leadership team before you get started. Each ExO team must be free to operate without interference, with the CEO of any new organization making all decisions. This is essential to prevent the corporate immune system from attacking the new company.

Return on Investment (ROI)

Don't assign an ROI to early stage ExOs, which are essentially startups. In fact, you won't be able to assign an ROI until you find the right business model and achieve a clear product/market fit.

IMPLEMENTING EXO CORE INITIATIVES

To successfully implement ExO Core Initiatives within the main organization, take into account the following:

Scope

Your first step is to implement a pilot project within a specific area or business unit of the organization. Next, scale it, applying key learnings from the pilot.

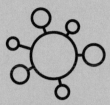

Environment

Grow the ExO Core Initiatives within the organization. Start with your designated "sandbox" (the pilot project) and gradually branch out across the organization.

Team

Assign a leader—someone who participated in the ExO Sprint—to oversee the team in charge of implementing the initiatives. (Team members don't necessarily need to have participated in the ExO Sprint.)

Resources

Assign resources to the ExO Edge Initiative linked to key milestones. Update the allocation of those resources after achieving milestones and applying what you've learned.

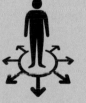

Support

Make sure the ExO initiative has the full support of the company's leadership team before you get started.

Return on Investment (ROI)

Assign and track the ROI but keep your expectations flexible. Remember that innovative projects include many hypotheses, so it's difficult to set a realistic ROI—at least until after you've run the pilot phase.

EXPONENTIAL TRANSFORMATION!

Running an ExO Sprint provides exponential results by transforming your organization so that it is able to keep up with external industry disruption and leverage exponential technologies.

But you can go even further! Here are some things you can do to both create an Exponential Organization and exponentially *transform* it for global impact.

Apply technology:

The only way to scale something is by applying technology to access and manage abundance.

ExO Lever is a global transformation ecosystem that provides online access to an abundance of certified ExO staff on demand (ExO Coaches, ExO Advisors, etc.) and other key resources for running an ExO Sprint and other ExO services. The ExO Lever platform also enables and encourages ongoing feedback among participants, including the organization's leaders and middle management.

Repeat!

Whether or not you ran your ExO Sprint with external help (the support of ExO Coaches and other ExO-related roles), having completed this first one, you are now in an excellent position to run further ExO Sprints on your own.

All ExO Sprint participants now have solid experience with the ExO model and other related innovation methodologies (Customer Development, Design Thinking, Lean Startup). You also have a team of people with the necessary knowledge and mindset to run or facilitate future ExO Sprints. It's still a good idea to call on external ExO Coaches as needed, but chances are you'll require much less of their time.

Companies periodically run ExO Sprints not only to define new initiatives, but also to encourage evolution, update skill sets and deepen employee knowledge of the company's culture and commitment to evolve.

Having incorporated the ExO process within their DNA, your own team is best equipped to manage and lead future ExO Sprints.

Schedule your next ExO Sprint now!

ExO Sprint Case Studies

INTERprotección

📍 Mexico City ⏳ 10 weeks 👥 36 participants

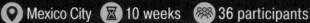

364

INTERprotección

INTERprotección is a Mexican group of companies specializing in insurance brokerage, reinsurance and surety of the highest quality. As an insurance broker, INTERprotección negotiates the best possible terms and conditions with insurers, providing cost effective solutions to clients. With over 5,000 institutional clients in Latin America, the company has a global presence and is widely recognized.

Prior to running the ExO Sprint, INTERprotección was aware of industry disruption happening not only in insurance but also across other industries. As a result of that awareness, it chose to become a disrupter rather than allow itself to be disrupted. The company also realized that new technologies and business models would enable it to reach exponential growth beyond its current market by, for example, launching new B2C disruptive business models.

Preparation

The company's ExO Sprint goal was to transform the organization, the industry and related industries, so all ExO initiatives were focused on the insurance industry and adjacent industries.

INTERprotección's ExO Sprint was one of the first ever executed, so the approach in terms of the number and type of ExO teams differed from what we recommend today. In fact, the ExO Sprint presented in this book is the result of lessons learned—and improvements made—after executing several ExO Sprints with early adopters such as INTERprotección.

Execution

INTERprotección's ExO Sprint began in March 2016 and ran for a total of 11 weeks (one week for the Awake Session and Align Session at the outset, plus 10 weeks for the ExO Sprint weekly assignments).

The project was led by INTERproteccion CEO Paqui Casanueva, who also played a role as an ExO Sprint participant. His participation was a powerful motivator to his team and helped drive a mindset change.

Six teams were created: Two focused on the main business (ExO Core); two focused on creating new businesses (ExO Edge), gaining inspiration from new technologies; and two focused on creating new businesses (ExO Edge), gaining inspiration from new business models in other industries. Each of the teams had an ExO Coach, with Francisco Palao acting as the Head Coach overseeing and supporting all ExO Coaches on the methodology.

The main challenge was managing and coordinating six ExO teams, which turned out to be too many. A particular issue was that the schedule for the ExO Disruption Session and later Launch Session was tight; there was little time for each team to present its ExO initiatives. Nonetheless, the ExO teams

EXO COACHES

HEAD COACH
Francisco Palao

COACHES

Kent Langley   *Joel Dietz*

Lars Lin   *Daniel Marcos*
Villebæk

Diego Soroa   *Rene de Paula*

managed to deliver a great outcome. INTERprotección was a true early adopter of the ExO Sprint methodology, and the learnings there significantly contributed to the improvement of the ExO Sprint process for future projects.

Outcomes

The ExO Sprint resulted in six ExO initiatives (two ExO Core Initiatives and four ExO Edge Initiatives), as well as an innovation lab that was designed during the course of the ExO Sprint. All ExO initiatives presented were selected for further development and received a total of $2.5 million in funding.

Overall, INTERproteccion learned how to transform the organization by keeping incremental innovation within the organization and allocating disruptive innovation outside the main organization. The company also learned that not only is it important to generate a lot of ExO Initiatives (content) but also to either design an innovation lab (a container) or find an external company builder to further develop the ExO initiatives once the ExO Sprint is completed.

INTERproteccion also figured out what the insurance industry will look like as a result of the disruption currently underway and launched ExO initiatives that will allow it to keep (and solidify) its leadership position. In short, INTERproteccion adopted a "learn-by-doing" approach to transformation.

Finally, the INTERproteccion ExO Sprint resulted in a mental shift throughout the organization, transforming those with an immune-system-response mindset into ExO-minded innovators.

Follow-Up

The impact of the ExO Sprint was huge on multiple levels. Some of the ExO Edge Initiatives generated thousands of dollars in revenues within a few days of their market launch. The newly formed innovation lab is developing the ExO Edge Initiatives and investing in external projects. Finally, the company mindset was transformed and most of the ExO Sprint participants were either promoted or given new responsibilities as a result of the intensive professional growth they experienced during the ExO Sprint.

PROJECT SPONSOR
Francisco Casanueva
CEO, INTERprotección

We were in the perfect place to be disrupted but didn't know where to begin. The ExO Sprint was the answer. It was our best investment for moving forward. It shook the organization and completely transformed our culture, breaking down boundaries and opening a whole new world of innovation.

Our entire mindset has shifted. It prompted us to make the best of ourselves. All our competitors are wondering what happened.

DEWA

هيئة كهرباء ومياه دبي
Dubai Electricity & Water Authority

DEWA

📍 Dubai ⏳ 10 weeks 👥 20 participants

Dubai Electricity & Water Authority (DEWA) has been the utility company of the Emirate of Dubai since 1992, managing electricity, water and district cooling needs. We currently employ 12,000 people across seven lines of business serving B2B and B2C customers (covering commercial, residential and industrial markets). With annual revenues of about US$6 billion and earnings of US$1.8 billion, we're considered a role model in the Gulf Region. The United Arab Emirates, represented by DEWA, ranked first worldwide for ease of getting electricity, as per the World Bank's 2018 Doing Business Report.

Preparation

In 2016, aware of the profound industry transformations forthcoming on a global and local scale, we decided to redefine our innovation strategy to remain relevant and, even more, to take a leading position in the future by creating and seizing new opportunities. To this purpose, we took the ExO framework as a reference and went a step further to engage ExO Works to propel our transformation.

Our primary goal was to shift from operating as a conventional utility to a digitized, innovation-driven one. The scope involved any and all aspects of the business, including energy, utilities, finance, service and government.

We were eager to test the ExO Sprint methodology in-house. DEWA was being encouraged by the Dubai government to try out new approaches to spark innovation, and a methodology like the ExO Sprint was a perfect channel for this. All divisions of DEWA were involved. The intention was to transform the industry and the organization.

Execution

We embarked on this phenomenal journey as soon as we could: the ExO Sprint kicked off in Dubai December 5, 2016, and ran to March 12, 2017.

TEAM

HEAD COACH
Michelle Lapierre

CORE COACHES

Augusto Fazioli   *Emilie Sydney-Smith*

EDGE COACHES

Lars Lin Villebæk   *Michal Monit*

DEWA

We had wanted to expedite the pre-Sprint process and jump in prior to engagement of the full leadership team and final selection of participant teams. We learned, however, that this preparation is critical for the success of the Sprint. When we next do another engagement of this type, we will also choose a time of the year where most of the employees who need to be engaged in the ExO Sprint will have fewer competing demands on their time.

Outcomes

The ExO Sprint was a unique opportunity for our different divisions to collaborate closely on a common purpose and experience the richness that this brings. It also helped to uncover untapped talent within the organization and open up opportunities for experimentation.

The teams developed seven initiatives that together represented a new business ecosystem for the company. The projects were developed based on transformative business models combined with exponential technologies such as blockchain, artificial intelligence, water out of air and energy storage.

We achieved amazing results on multiple levels:

- **Strategic:** DEWA was the first organization in the region to learn the ExO methodology. We became an early adopter and received a boost in the right direction of innovation.

- **Cultural:** The ExO Sprint introduced effective collaboration, helped in overcoming cultural barriers and offered a new approach to developing ideas and solutions.

- **Personal:** The ExO Sprint introduced our employees to new resources (internal and external), and participants gained a new understanding of where and how they could implement emerging technologies.

- **Ideas:** Some of the ExO Sprint initiatives were taken on by our R&D department, including the initiative to transform air into water; others were presented to the Dubai 10X program for disruptive innovation launched by the Government of Dubai.

Follow-Up

DEWA continues to work with concepts similar to the ones developed during the ExO Sprint through the investments in startups it carries out as part of the Dubai Government Accelerators' program and its comprehensive Research and Development Program.

Our employees gained a heightened awareness of innovative resources and technology, and the culture became collaborative—clear evidence of a shift in mindset.

A goal for the organization was to test a completely new approach for creating value along with a new velocity for decision-making. In the end, not only did we achieve this, but we also experienced significant positive benefits such as increased team collaboration and instituting experimentation and agile exploration of new technologies and trends into all facets of our work.

PROJECT SPONSOR
Marwan Bin Haider
EVP Innovation and The Future, DEWA

"The ExO methodology offers a path to convert great ideas into viable business opportunities."

Stanley Black & Decker

Stanley Black & Decker

📍 North America and Europe   ⧖ 10 weeks

👥 30 participants

Stanley Black & Decker is the world's largest tools and storage company, the second largest electronic security company and a leader in engineered fastening. Stanley Black & Decker is headquartered in the greater Hartford city of New Britain, Connecticut.

The company has annual revenues of more than US$12 billion and approximately 58,000 employees across the globe. Its brands are sold in more than 175 countries in all of the world's major markets. Stanley Black & Decker draws a broad demographic of customers due to its large B2C and B2B product offering, and total revenues have grown an average of 20% over the last 10 years.

Preparation

Over the past couple of years, Stanley Black & Decker has initiated efforts to double revenues in the next half-decade through organic growth and acquisitions. To achieve this growth, the company must be open to new business models, adopt new technologies and pursue new businesses with high opportunities for growth. With the ExO Sprint we saw a unique opportunity to experience how to ideate, test and, importantly, launch initiatives with exponential potential.

We wanted to generate a deep transformation of our organization quickly. We chose to run four ExO Sprints, each in a different business unit, to achieve company-wide impact. Concurrently, we selected existing internal projects to accelerate with ExO Incubation Partners and established an internal incubation unit, our Exponential Learning Unit (ELU), to orchestrate the work of generating new exponential businesses.

Our first ExO Sprint was focused on our Security business unit, which is in an industry seeing rapid commoditization of services. Our objectives were to address external disruptions and create new, fast-growing businesses.

Execution

The ExO Sprint for the Security business took place in our North American and European offices over the course of 10 weeks, from the Awake session on August 24, 2017, to the final presentations on December 12, 2017.

EXO COACHES

HEAD COACH
Luciana Ledesma

CORE COACHES

Laurent Boinot   Ralf Bamert

EDGE COACHES

KristinaMaria Troiano   Eduardo Labarca
Gutierrez

It was a challenge to unlearn some of our organizational practices—how we typically do things—in order to learn new alternatives. For example, this was evident when the teams had to validate their hypotheses. There was a natural tendency to want to engage third parties to do this, rather than "getting out of the building" to do it ourselves. The Sprint was valuable in bringing more agile ways of working to life.

One of the greatest challenges for participants was having the availability to commit the required time to the ExO Sprint. Learning to juggle day-to-day business responsibilities while creating new structural value for the organization was a bumpy road, but we recognized it as a crucial exercise required by any organization that wants to remain relevant in this era of disruption.

Overcoming the implicit tension between meeting quarterly numbers and going into uncharted waters with the ExO Sprint was achieved with strong support by our leadership, who demonstrated courage in their willingness to try new approaches and gave unwavering support to participants throughout the process.

Outcomes

Outstanding results were achieved over the course of the ExO Sprint. Many of the teams came to the final presentation with demos. Seven of the eight initiatives presented at the final session were funded on the spot and approved for next steps.

The ExO Sprint created the opportunity to tap into new markets, solve some of our current challenges, and discover new technologies and applications. Furthermore, it catalyzed a profound mindset shift not only for participants, but also for outside employees who were attracted by the process and amazed by the results.

Along the way, we learned that:

- We have significant in-house talent. Without the opportunity to commit time to create structural value for the company in an orchestrated way through an agile process, this talent would have remained untapped or beyond reach.

- The process of creation may initially seem overwhelming but by gaining confidence through persistence and practice, it becomes an empowering experience.

- Opportunities to create value are ubiquitous.

The process and results of the ExO Sprint confirmed to leadership the need for transformation and the need for a new way to seize opportunities and achieve growth.

Follow-Up

The impact of the ExO initiatives is tremendous: new businesses are being launched, the Core initiatives are making our company 10x more efficient in some areas, and startup acquisitions are being explored that are expected to accelerate the development of some of the ExO Edge Initiatives.

From the ExO Sprint, we gained the benefit of being able to identify, structure and rapidly validate exponential opportunities for growth and adaptability. We instilled a profound mindset shift from a single-speed operating model focused only on meeting quarterly goals, to a dual-speed operating model focused simultaneously on meeting quarterly goals while creating value by leveraging the abundance of a hyper-connected and tech-powered world.

We are now underway with our next two ExO Sprints for other business divisions.

PROJECT SPONSOR
Jaime Ramirez
SVP and President Global Emerging Markets, Stanley Black & Decker

"We are using the ExO Sprint to transform our entire organization."

HP Inc.

HP Large Format Printing

📍 Barcelona, Spain ⏳ 10 weeks

👥 28 participants

The ExO Sprint for the Large Format Design Printing Business of HP Inc. took place in Barcelona, Spain, over the course of 10 weeks. The Awake session was held September 7, 2017, and the final presentations were delivered December 14, 2017.

The Large Format Design Printing Business of HP is the indisputable leader in the Large Format (LF) industry, far ahead of our closest competitor. HP has been the leader in LF Design for more than 25 years! We service a broad universe of customers: technical design (architects, designers, construction, utilities, engineers); production (repro houses, copy shops, CRDs); indoor and outdoor graphics production; and graphic design and professional photo. HP is constantly innovating to reinvent itself and create new businesses such as 3D and Latex.

Preparation

Our ExO Sprint lasted 10 weeks, with a one-week break before Week 1 and a two-week break prior to its completion. The goal was to build on the success of the LF Design business in a way that nobody would expect by adopting a new methodology for innovation that harnesses the power of exponential technologies, provides new vectors of discovery and growth, and accelerates our capacity to always be innovating.

The scope of work was defined to focus on the Large Format Design segment with two main intents: transform the LF printing industry and make the current organization more flexible and adaptive. We recognized that many industries could be transformed by applying the core competences of the LF Design division, such as pharma, cosmetics, printing, communications and construction.

HP decided to start with Large Format Design Printing because our Project Sponsor was recognized as a visionary within the company when it comes to innovation and the application of new methodologies.

Execution

We made four customizations to the standard ExO Sprint:

1 Edge teams were open to the possibility of disrupting other industries by building on the existing core competencies of the current business.

2 We created an "uncontaminated" team (i.e., participants with less than six months with the company) made up of millennials.

3 We brought external ExO Advisors to the closing session.

4 We conducted an extra feedback loop during Week 9, allowing teams to really adopt the Experimentation attribute as a fundamental change to the way they usually work.

As could be expected, challenges during our ExO Sprint were mainly related to having participants get used to changing their usual ways of working, keeping up with the weekly deliverable schedule and bringing in new, external perspectives.

We found that the "soft skills" of coaching (empathy, encouragement, reframing, etc.) were valuable in supporting participants through their new experiences. We also grappled with low bandwidth, which we addressed by bringing additional participants to the teams.

EXO COACHES

HEAD COACH
Corina Almagro

EXO SPRINT ADVISOR
Francisco Palao

CORE COACHES

Soledad
Llorente

Tony Manley

EDGE COACHES

Diego Soroa

Michal Monit

Outcomes

At the close of the ExO Sprint, eight initiatives (names withheld) were presented, along with specific next steps:

Initiative 1

- 3 Engineers to be assigned within a month
- 1 Product Manager to be assigned within a month
- Technical Sponsor named

Initiative 2

- $50K assigned to move forward
- Technical Sponsor named

Initiative 3

- $20K assigned to move forward
- 1 Subject Expert to be assigned within a month
- 50% Product Manager and 50% Customer Experience role to be assigned within a month
- Technical Sponsor named

Initiative 4

- $50K assigned to move forward
- Team assigned, with 25% commitment

Initiative 5

- Find external company builder/entrepreneur; challenge to be launched within a month
- Decision expected within a quarter

Initiative 6

- Feature for new products in existing line
- 30% of Customer Experience role and 30% of R&D

Initiative 7

- Merge with existing product

Initiative 8

- Present to a different business division within a week

Follow-Up

The results were extraordinary. On the organizational front, the following transformations took place:

- Cultural shift to becoming more agile in execution; we moved away from the idea of perfection in favor of going FAST.
- Cultural shift towards customer insights; we initiated a culture of experimentation (customer development, fast prototyping).
- Opened our business to the outside. For example, external ExO Advisors were engaged to do periodic (once or twice monthly) checks on the progress of the projects.
- Incorporation of the word "disruption" in strategic conversations where it had been formerly taboo.
- Developed deep knowledge of disruptive technologies and ExO attributes.
- Created new opportunities and ideas to explore; ExO ideas were integrated into our current innovation processes.

Other business units have now followed our lead and are running self-provisioned ExO Sprints supported by some of our ExO Sprint participants, who are serving as internal facilitators.

PROJECT SPONSOR
Guayente Sanmartin
General Manager, HP Large Format Design Business, HP Inc.

"The most important thing I see is a shift in the culture."

Grupo Cuerva

📍 Granada, Spain ⌛ 10 weeks 👥 24 participants

Our ExO Sprint took place in Granada, Spain, over the course of 10 weeks beginning in October 2017.

Grupo Cuerva has been active in the electricity sector for over 75 years and oversees the generation, distribution and sale of electric power. It is also involved in the establishment and maintenance of electricity installations.

In addition, the company features a disruptive innovation "Lab on the Edge" called Turning Tables. It was launched a couple of years ago with a vision of incubating next-generation businesses for the energy industry.

Grupo Cuerva employs approximately 80 people, and some 30 percent of the company—representing all areas of the organization—was involved in the ExO Sprint.

Preparation

The energy industry is being exposed to many changes that will ultimately transform it completely—so much so that we're assuming that electricity will be free in a decade! Given this tectonic shift in the industry, our main goal was to transform our company into an innovation-centric organization. Our intent was to transform not only the industry but the company as well. To that end, the Edge Stream was designed to work on any sector whether or not it was in an adjacent market.

Execution

The project was led by our CEO, Ignacio Cuerva, who provided us with a draft of this book and which we used as a guide with great success.

Our ExO Sprint was structured into four teams, two Core and two Edge, each comprised of five people. Paqui Rubio was the ExO Coach for both Core teams as well as a team member on one of the Edge teams. Alfredo Rivela (CEO of Turning Tables) acted as the ExO Coach for both Edge teams, and Francisco Palao, co-author of this book, acted as Head Coach in support of both ExO Coaches whenever they had any questions about the methodology.

EXO COACHES

HEAD COACH
Francisco Palao

EDGE COACH
Alfredo Rivela

CORE COACH
Paqui Rubio

Outcomes

Ten initiatives were presented at the Launch Session: five from the Core teams and five from the Edge teams. Eight initiatives were selected by Cuerva's leadership team and received funding for their next stages. The ExO Core Initiatives are being coordinated internally by the Innovation Department, and Turning Tables, Grupo Cuerva's innovation lab, is developing the ExO Edge Initiatives.

While it's too early to report on results of the recently launched initiatives, it's clear that the mindset of the organization as a whole has completely shifted, and that those who participated in the ExO Sprint feel empowered to try new things in their goal of leading the way to industry transformation.

Follow-Up

Two of our ExO Edge Initiatives are most likely to result in two new companies, while the other two will become part of the Disruptive Innovation Lab ecosystem previously launched by Turning Tables in its role as an implementation partner.

Our ExO Core Initiatives are predominantly focused on digital transformation and include designing new roles (e.g., a data scientist) and making the company more adaptable to clean energy disruption.

The biggest challenge of the ExO Sprint was the level of dedication required and ensuring that executive management was at all times aware that employees needed to dedicate over 50% of their time to the project. However, strong support from the CEO of the company and a high level of passion among the participants working on the ExO Sprint made the whole project a great experience for everyone, especially given the outstanding results.

In particular, the ExO Sprint participants value their new mindset around experimentation and early exposure to customers, and they are currently applying this new way of thinking and doing to their daily basis tasks.

With a third of our employees engaged in the project, the ExO Sprint was a massive commitment, one that translated into a tremendous shift in terms of our company's culture and in defining what is possible. Many of our staff have now come to adopt a transformational mindset, and our new "normal" involves creating and testing new hypotheses on a daily basis.

PROJECT SPONSOR
Ignacio Cuerva
CEO, Grupo Cuerva

"Our company now knows what to do in order to transform the organization for the next industry disruption, and we have a team of people ready and eager to do it."

Annexes

ExO Workshop

The ExO Workshop is a one-day event designed to help participants understand the ExO framework and gain experience using it. It can be run for one organization or as an event featuring participants from different firms. Companies then have the option of running the complete ExO Sprint to achieve real transformation.

What you will achieve with an ExO Workshop

- Inspire participants with the power of exponential technologies and organizational transformation.
- Awareness within the organization about the need for transformation.
- Learn about the ExO model and its attributes.
- Understand how the ExO Sprint process can transform an organization.
- Recognize the difference between innovation and disruption and how to achieve both.

What you won't achieve with an ExO Workshop

- Behavioral changes. The ExO Sprint takes place over a 10-week period and results in a new mindset. You won't see the same shifts in behavior with an ExO Workshop, but it will excite participants and provide and understanding of why the ExO approach works.
- ExO initiatives ready to be implemented. While an ExO Workshop often results in great ideas, it won't prepare the organization to implement them. (Even if the organization were to try, it would fail, creating frustration and discontent.) In fact, ideas are not even the most important ingredient of the transformation process. More important, at least initially, is understanding how to block the corporate immune system response—which kicks into gear at the first sign of change—and preparing the organization for the internal process of transformation should the company leadership decide to take the next step and conduct an ExO Sprint.

Who should attend

- **Leadership Team**: Since the primary goal of the ExO Workshop is to create awareness within an organization about the need for transformation and how the ExO framework can help, it's imperative for the leadership team to be in the room. The CEO and other executive team members (including the CIO, CTO and even CFO) serve as the first line of defense against the corporate immune system.
- **Middle Management**: You may also want to invite middle management employees to learn about the ExO framework (especially if the ExO Workshop is run for only a single company). Their presence, however, is not mandatory as it is for an ExO Sprint (since middle managers are the ones who execute the ExO initiatives that grow out of an ExO Sprint).

Content

The one-day workshop—or even half-day workshop, although we generally recommend the longer version—explores the Exponential Organization model and provides participants with an opportunity to experiment with key concepts of the ExO framework.

Exponential Technologies Session

Similar to the Awake Session of the ExO Sprint, the first phase of the ExO Workshop introduces cutting-edge exponential technologies and their implications for every industry.

Case Study Example

To provide participants with context, we examine a case study for all exercises, exploring the company's business model and other relevant information.

Exponential Technologies Exercise

Participants brainstorm about which technologies might impact the case study's industry. Each team comes up with at least three technologies that could threaten the industry in question, taking into consideration the different risks and opportunities each poses to the particular case study.

Exponential Organizations Session

Introduction to the ExO framework, a model that will enable your organization to keep up with industry disruption and take advantage of the abundance generated by exponential technologies.

Exponential Organizations Exercise

Participants think about how to apply the ExO attributes to the case study in order to help the company connect with and manage abundance.

ExO Implementation Session

Outlines how to implement the ExO framework using the 10-week ExO Sprint and describes the difference between ExO Core Initiatives and ExO Edge Initiatives.

ExO Core/Edge Exercise

Participants consider different ExO Core Initiatives and ExO Edge Initiatives for the case study.

Debrief and Next Steps

Following a summary of the workshop, participants identify their main takeaways and determine next steps.

The ExO Workshop offers a perfect environment for taking awareness of exponential transformation to the next level!

Preparation

- Choose participants for an ExO Workshop carefully. It's a good idea to have the CEO and as many leadership team members in the room as possible (from one company or all of them, depending on the workshop makeup), since they will be the ones to follow up with an ExO Sprint after the workshop, and thus enable transformation. Including middle management from throughout the organization is also advised.

- Participants are grouped into teams. The number of teams affects the dynamics of the workshop, since all teams will present their results after each exercise. We recommend four to six teams, each comprised of four to eight people. (The total number of participants should range from 16 to 48 people.)

- To create a welcoming and inspiring environment, look for a spacious venue featuring natural light and even live plants. You'll also need a stage for the presenters and one large round table per team.

Execution

- **Staff:** The ExO Workshop is run by an ExO Trainer, who is knowledgeable about the ExO framework and has experience facilitating workshops. If you'd like additional support for your teams as they work through the exercises, another person to oversee the process is also an option.

- **Flow:** The ExO Workshop features sessions dedicated to key concepts, followed by practical exercises that allow participants to put those concepts into action. Sessions include enough time for all teams to present their results, for the ExO Trainer to provide feedback and for a Q&A period.

Follow-Up

An ExO Workshop helps attendees understand how the ExO framework can help their organization successfully undergo a transformation process. Running an ExO Sprint is a natural next step that will help participants manage the corporate immune system and build internal capabilities to achieve successful transformation.

Good Practices

- Choose a different company than your own as a case study for the ExO Workshop. Using your own organization as a case study encourages participants to believe that the ExO initiatives they come up with during the exercises are ready to be implemented. (They won't be.)

- Look for a B2C business model when picking a case study. Consumer-oriented businesses are well known and thus easier to understand when it comes to applying the ExO framework. It's also a good idea to select a company that everyone can easily relate to, such as a retailer, airline, car company or bank.

- Encourage experimentation and learning. The ExO Workshop allows participants to experiment with the ExO framework, which offers a learn-by-doing approach. As such, participants should understand that the goal with the workshop exercises is not to produce a polished outcome; instead, it is to practice key elements of the ExO framework.

Tips for ExO Sprint Roles

Experience is always the best teacher, which is why we've interviewed hundreds of people who have gone through the ExO Sprint experience to gather the following advice. As you know by now, the ExO Sprint is a powerful methodology that transforms organizations. Here are some tips that will help take your company's transformation to the next level!

**ExO Sprint
Sponsor**

ExO Sprint Sponsor

- The ExO Sprint Sponsor should hold the highest-level position possible: CEO, general manager or, at minimum, VP of the business line where the ExO Sprint will be conducted.

- The ExO Sprint Sponsor should be excited about the ExO Sprint and convinced of its value. He or she should also be prepared to allocate sufficient time to follow its progress, including spending quality time listening to and supporting each group.

- Set goals and expectations with the ExO Head Coach and communicate those goals and expectations to the ExO Sprint participants.

- Bear in mind that the ExO Sprint may frustrate and overwhelm ExO Sprint participants, especially during its first half. This is normal; they will be working in a different way and will need time to adapt.

- Take the time to find the right ExO Sprint participants and ensure they are able to allocate sufficient time to the initiative.

- Create one team made up of younger people who have limited experience of the company and the industry. They will bring a fresh perspective to the ExO initiatives ideation and development process.

- Participate directly in the ExO Sprint as an ExO Sprint participant. CEOs who have done this describe an amazing learning and team-building experience. Participation will also enable you to maximize the outcome of the ExO Sprint.

- Communicate to ExO Sprint participants that there are no losers or winners, and that it is most important to follow the process and do their best. This understanding will help them avoid frustration if, for example, their initiatives are eliminated following the ExO Disruption Session.

- Pick the right team to conduct the ExO Sprint. Choose exceptional ExO Speakers and ExO Trainers who are capable of blowing ExO Sprint participants' minds with the possibilities inherent in an ExO Sprint. Select ExO Coaches who are specifically trained in the ExO Sprint methodology.

- Ensure in advance that the budget allocated at the Launch Session of the ExO Sprint is enough to support the selected ExO initiatives. Manage the initiatives directly for a few months after the ExO Sprint is over to maintain momentum and gain the maximum benefit.

ExO Sprint Participant

- Be conscious that a lot of things are happening outside your company, many of them related to your business. Explore these developments and take advantage of them!

- Keep an open mind from the outset. It doesn't matter if the first ideas or experiments turn out to be completely crazy; by the end of the process, you'll have something great.

- Do not get attached to any one idea and be open to changing it. Remember that the best ideas come from iteration. No ego allowed!

- Get comfortable with the uncomfortable. Trust the process. Part of that process is learning how to use new management and innovation methodologies, so being unclear on how to do things is normal (especially during the first half of the ExO Sprint). Learning is an important part of your ExO Sprint path.

- Put the time in, as you will only get out of the ExO Sprint what you put into it. Assign at least two hours per day to meet with your team and work individually on the assignments. Set daily milestones and weekly priorities and tasks.

- Take advantage of the opportunity to work with people from other departments who bring different experiences. Building these connections and learning from them will only be a positive in your personal and professional development.

- Seek out those who can help with even small contributions (mockups, prototypes, surveys, etc.). Such assistance can make a difference in the success of your projects.

- Brainstorm with ExO practitioners and exponential technologies specialists about your ExO initiatives and carefully consider their input.

- The ExO Sprint is the perfect space to think big and have an impact within your organization and beyond. So be bold!

- The ExO Sprint process will transform not only your organization, but also you as a participant. Get ready to think exponentially in every aspect of your life. Enjoy!

ExO Head Coach

- Understand the project goals and expectations of the ExO Sprint Sponsor and aim to exceed them.
- Work with the ExO Sprint Sponsor(s) in advance of the ExO Sprint on optimal team member selection and team makeup.
- Have a weekly meeting with the ExO Sprint Sponsor(s) to make sure they are happy with the progress of the ExO Sprint and address any issues that may affect its success.
- Connect weekly with all ExO Coaches to catch up on the ExO Sprint progress, debrief about the previous week and align everyone for the coming week.
- Attend all weekly team meetings to review end-of-the-week assignments.

- Give the ExO Coaches their space. Avoid acting as a coach when it comes to guiding the teams; instead, support the coaches as they need it.
- Make sure ExO Sprint participants are engaged and excited about the ExO Sprint and that they have the necessary support from their ExO Sprint Sponsor(s).
- Support ExO Sprint participants and ExO Coaches emotionally and help them release tension by encouraging an atmosphere of fun and enjoyment around the learning process.
- Identify any immune system issues as quickly as possible and work with the ExO Sprint Sponsor(s) to counteract them.
- Ensure software tools that support the ExO Sprint are in place.

ExO Coach

- Check in to make sure your team isn't developing ExO initiatives that are clearly not in the interest of the company. Direct them as needed, following the scope communicated by the ExO Head Coach.
- Avoid guiding your team from a content point of view (e.g., by suggesting or evaluating ideas). Instead, guide it from a process point of view, driving members to complete assignments and run proper experiments to evaluate ideas.
- Connect the dots. Every week builds on the previous one. Make sure your team is building on what came before and incorporating already created materials.
- Keep your team in an exponential-thinking mindset.
- Push your team to experiment by having them operate in "search mode"; discourage them from operating in "execution mode."

- Check in weekly to see what they have learned, both from an ExO initiatives point of view and a personal point of view.
- Never deliver anything on behalf of your team. Your job is to guide them, not do the tasks for them.
- Ask your team for feedback so you can improve the way you coach and guide them.
- Always be available! Never disappear on your team. More than the actual amount of time you spend with them, it's about being available whenever they need you.
- Manage the human side. Remember, you are dealing with people and emotions, so keep on top of all internal dynamics in order to help your team solve any conflicts that may arise.

ExO Disruptor

• Learn about the company and its goals for the ExO Sprint prior to the Disruption Session, which will better enable you to provide context-based feedback.

• Educate yourself about other startups and disruptions in the industry before attending the Disruption Session. Such research will increase your ability to offer helpful insight.

• Write down all feedback for each ExO initiative presented by each team and share the key points verbally following the presentations. You can also send a more complete assessment after the Disruption Session and/or Launch Session.

• Start with positive feedback about the good things the teams have done to shape their initiatives. Follow up with honest and straightforward feedback on what they can do to improve.

• Provide process-oriented feedback and guidance, following the ExO framework—e.g., help them identify which initiatives are ExO Core Initiatives and which are ExO Edge Initiatives, as well as the implications of those designations.

• Provide content-oriented feedback and input based on your knowledge and experience as a specialist in a specific field. And remember, if you provide content-oriented input, you must make it clear that it's just a personal opinion, another hypothesis to be tested.

• Encourage teams to think using an exponential mindset.

• For ExO Edge Initiatives, evaluate whether they are "proper" ExO Edge Initiatives and whether they qualify as disruptive and scalable.

• For ExO Core Initiatives, evaluate whether they are "proper" ExO Core Initiatives and whether they improve the current business model (without changing it) and adapt the organization to external industry disruption.

• Advise teams on next steps (e.g., run a specific experiment, build a prototype) and what you expect from their projects by the end of the ExO Sprint process.

Recommended Reading

Abundance: The Future Is Better Than You Think, by Peter Diamandis and Steven Kotler

Blue Ocean Strategy: How to Create Uncontested Market Space and Make Competition Irrelevant, by W. Chan Kim and Renée Mauborgne

Bold: How to Go Big, Create Wealth and Impact the World, by Peter Diamandis and Steven Kotler

Business Model Generation: A Handbook for Visionaries, Game Changers, and Challengers, by Alex Osterwalder and Yves Pigneur

Crossing the Chasm: Marketing and Selling High-Tech Products to Mainstream Customers, by Geoffrey A. Moore

Exponential Organizations: Why New Organizations Are Ten Times Better, Faster, and Cheaper Than Yours (And What to Do About It), by Salim Ismail, Michael Malone and Yuri van Geest

Four Steps to the Epiphany: Successful Strategies for Products That Win, by Steve Blank

MVP: 21 Tips for Getting a Minimum Viable Product, Early Learning and Return on Investment With Scrum, by Paul Vii

Presentation Secrets of Steve Jobs: How to Be Insanely Great in Front of Any Audience, by Carmine Gallo

Presentation Zen: Simple Ideas on Presentation Design and Delivery, by Garr Reynolds

Reinventing Organizations: A Guide to Creating Organizations Inspired by the Next Stage of Human Consciousness, by Frederic Laloux

Sprint: How to Solve Big Problems and Test New Ideas in Just Five Days, by Jake Knapp

Talk Like Ted: The 9 Public-Speaking Secrets of the World's Top Minds, by Carmine Gallo

The Fourth Industrial Revolution, by Klaus Schwab

The Lean Startup: How Today's Entrepreneurs Use Continuous Innovation to Create Radically Successful Businesses, by Eric Ries